Cotton Was King

Morgan County Plantations

Alabama Plantation Series

Rickey Butch Walker

Cotton was King – Morgan County Plantation – Alabama Plantation Series
1st edition

Copyright 2022 © Bluewater Publications

BWPublications.com
Bluewater Publications
Florence, Alabama

Library of Congress Control Number: 2022937458

ISBN: 978-1-958273-03-6 Perfect

ISBN: 978-1-958273-04-3 eBook

All rights reserved under International and Pan-American Copyright Convention. No part of this publication may be reproduced or transmitted in any form or by any means, electronic or mechanical, including photocopying, recording, or by any information storage and retrieval system, without prior written permission from the Publisher.

Published in the United States by Bluewater Publications.
Printed in the United States of America.
BWPublications.com – Florence, Alabama

This work is based on the authors' personal interpretation of research.

Bluewater Publications
books by
Rickey Butch Walker

Cotton Was King – Franklin – Colbert County – Alabama Plantation Series, ISBN 978-1-949711-08-0, $24.95

Cotton Was King - Lauderdale County – Alabama Plantation Series, ISBN 978-1-934610-99-2, $24.95

Cotton Was King - Lawrence County – Alabama Plantation Series, ISBN 978-1-949711-14-1, $24.95

Cotton Was King - Limestone County – Alabama Plantation Series, ISBN 978-1-949711-35-6, $24.95

Appalachian Indians of the Warrior Mountains: History and Culture, ISBN 978-1-934610-72-5, $24.95

Appalachian Indian Trails of the Chickamauga: Lower Cherokee Settlements, ISBN 978-1-934610-91-6, $24.95

Celtic Indian Boy of Appalachia: A Scots Irish Cherokee Childhood, ISBN 978-1-934610-75-6, $24.95

Chickasaw Chief George Colbert: His Family and His Country, ISBN 978-1-934610-71-8, $24.95

Doublehead: Last Chickamauga Cherokee Chief, ISBN 978-1-934610-67-1, $24.95

Hiking Sipsey: A Family's Fight for Eastern Wilderness, ISBN 978-1-934610-93-0, $24.95

Soldier's Wife: Cotton Fields to Berlin and Tripoli, ISBN-978-1-9582730-09-08, $19.95

Warrior Mountains Folklore: American Indian and Celtic History in the Southeast, ISBN 978-1-934610-65-7, $29.95

Warrior Mountains Indian Heritage-Teacher's Edition, ISBN 978-1-934610-27-5, $39.95

Warrior Mountains Indian Heritage-Student Edition, ISBN 978-1-934610-66-4, $24.95

Black Folk Tales of the Shoals, ISBN 978-1-958273-07-04, $24.95

Cotton Was King,

Volume 5,

Morgan County, Alabama

Acknowledgements

Yolanda Morgan Smith, a local historian from Morgan County, Alabama, was very helpful in the completion of "Cotton Was King, Volume 5, Morgan County." She provided family information on many of the cotton planters of the county. I greatly appreciate her valuable assistance in census and agricultural information used in this book. Without her help, the quality of the book would have been greatly diminished.

I also wish to thank Claude Neal Hudson, Historian for the Rising Sun Masonic Lodge of Decatur, for editing the manuscript of Cotton Was King, Volume 5, Morgan County. He also wrote the review for this book, and I greatly appreciate his help.

Contents

Introduction 1
Fox's Creek 4
Mouse Town 6
    Burleson Trace 9
Fields-Cherokee 13
    George Fields 14
    Richard Fields Jr. 18
Cotaco (Morgan) County 19
Somerville 29
    Early Roads 29
    Early Ferries 31
    County Court 35
Decatur 36
    Rhodes Ferry 37
    Establishment of Decatur 38
    Decatur Railroad 40
    Indian Removal through Decatur 43
Planters and Slaves 48
Bibb, John D. 64
Blackwell, Samuel Jr. 67
    William Richard Blackwell 69
    Augustine S. Blackwell 71

Blackwell Family Cemetery 72

Blackwell, William Henry 73

Bouldin, Captain Green 75

    Captain James Massey Bouldin 79

    Green Bouldin Jr. 81

Brooks, Milton 82

Bryant, Cornelius 82

    Daniel Bryant 84

Burleson, Jonathan 84

    Burleson Cemetery 96

    Burleson Conclusion 97

Burnett, Greenville 98

    Bolling Clark Burnett 100

Colbert, Rhoda 100

Collier, Bouldin Carter 101

Crockett, John 107

Dallas (Dallis), Dennis 111

Dancy, Fancis 113

    Captain William Dancy 113

    Colonel William Francis Dancy 116

    Sarah "Sallie" Winfield Dancy Sykes 121

    Martha Mason Dancy Rhodes 124

Davis, Riley S. 128

Evans, Nathaniel 129

Fennel, Wiley 131

- James Fennell-Walnut Grove 135
  - Colonel Henry (Harry) W. Fennel 143
- Freeman, Reverend Fleming Fontaine 145
- Garner, Lawson William 148
- Garth, Jesse Winston 151
  - Garth, William Willis 159
- Humphreys, Dr. Carlisle 162
  - David Campbell Humphreys 163
- Johnson, Benjamin 165
- Kimbell, Edmond and James 166
  - Edmond Kimbell 166
  - Kimbell Cemetery 168
- Kolb, James 171
  - Joseph Kolb 172
- Lacy, John 176
  - Thomas Henderson Lacy 177
- Lane, Joseph 178
  - Joseph Lane Jr. 181
  - Delia Lane Burt 181
  - Isaac Lane 183
- Lewis, Owen 186
  - Nicholas Lewis 186
  - Harding P. Lewis 188
- Lile, Samuel 190
  - Lile, Peyton 191

Thomas Lile	193
McClanahan, Sarah	196
McClanahan, John	197
Menefee, Thomas	198
Moseley, William Sr.	199
William Moseley Jr.	200
Other Moseleys	202
Murphey, George	203
Dr. William E. Murphey	204
Smith Murphey	207
Orr, Christopher	207
John Orr	209
Jonathan Orr	211
Watkins Orr	214
Patterson, Andrew "Andy" McDonald	215
Perry, Aaron	219
Aaron Perry Jr.	220
Peyton, Thomas	222
Rather, Captain John Taylor	223
Rather, General John D.	227
Reed, William	233
Russell, Captain William Jr.	234
Smith, James L.	237
Stanback, Dixon	239
Stephenson, Arthur	240

- Stovall, Drury 242
    - Drury Stovall, Jr. 243
    - Major Peter G. Stovall 244
- Sykes, Benjamin Sr. 246
    - Benjamin Sykes, Jr. 247
    - Dr. William Sykes 247
- Terry, William Price 257
- Thomas, Joseph G. 258
- Thompson, Edward and Margaret 259
- Thompson, William 262
    - Elbert Hartwell Thompson 263
    - Thompson, Robert Asa 265
- Thompson, James 268
- Thurmon, John 268
    - Eliza Ann Thurman 269
- Troup, John 271
    - Colonel John Troup 272
- Wiggins, James 274
- Wilson, Greenberry Sr. 276
    - William Bradshaw Wilson 278
    - Greenberry Wilson Jr 279
- Wood, Aaron 283
- References 284
- Index 286

Morgan County

Introduction

As the other counties in northwest Alabama, Morgan County was originally the land of American Indian people for some 14,000 years or more. The area of Morgan County along the Tennessee River in the vicinity of Fox's Creek, Flint Creek, and Cotaco Creek appears to have been heavily occupied by the earliest inhabitants known as paleo Indian people.

The paleo period in the North Alabama area appears to have lasted from some 14,000 years ago to around 10,000 years ago. Based on paleo artifacts, Morgan County probably has more paleo Indian sites than any county in Alabama.

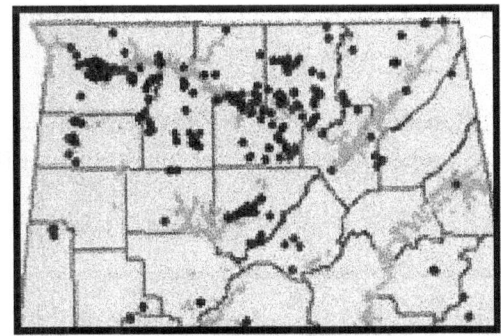

**Paleo Indian Sites
North Alabama**

After the paleo period, the Archaic Indian people lived in the area that became Morgan County along the Tennessee River from about 8,000 BC to 1,000 BC. Then the period of Woodland people lasted from about 1,000 BC to AD 1,000. The Mississippian people were the last of the prehistoric inhabitants who lived along the Tennessee River from AD 1,000 to AD 1540. The various periods of prehistoric people were based on the lifestyles, cultural changes, and various projectile point configurations over thousands of years.

In 1540, Spanish chroniclers recorded the historic journey of Desoto and his conquistadores through North Alabama. From the 1540s through the early 1800s, the Cherokee dominated the historical landscape of present-day Morgan County even though from time to time various tribes utilized the area for short term occupation and as hunting grounds. These tribes included the Yuchi,

Shawnee, Chickasaw, and Creek Indians, but none of these would be more dominate than the Cherokee.

In 1769 after the altercation with the Cherokee at Battle of the Chickasaw Old Fields near the northeastern corner of present-day Morgan County, the Chickasaw migrated to the extreme northwestern corner of Alabama and northeast Mississippi. The Chickamauga Cherokees quickly filled the void left by the retreating Chickasaws.

By 1770, the Chickamauga Cherokee under the leadership of Doublehead were occupying areas along the Tennessee River in Morgan County of North Alabama. From the 1770 through 1816, the Chickamauga faction of Lower Cherokees established settlements in the area. They lived, farmed, and controlled the area of Morgan County along the Great Bend of the Tennessee River until the Turkey Town Treaty of September 1816.

On January 10, 1786, the Chickasaw signed the Hopewell Treaty with the United States government for ownership of the area that became Morgan County. However, when the 1786 treaty was ratified, the Lower Cherokee Indians of the Chickamauga faction were actually occupying the land.

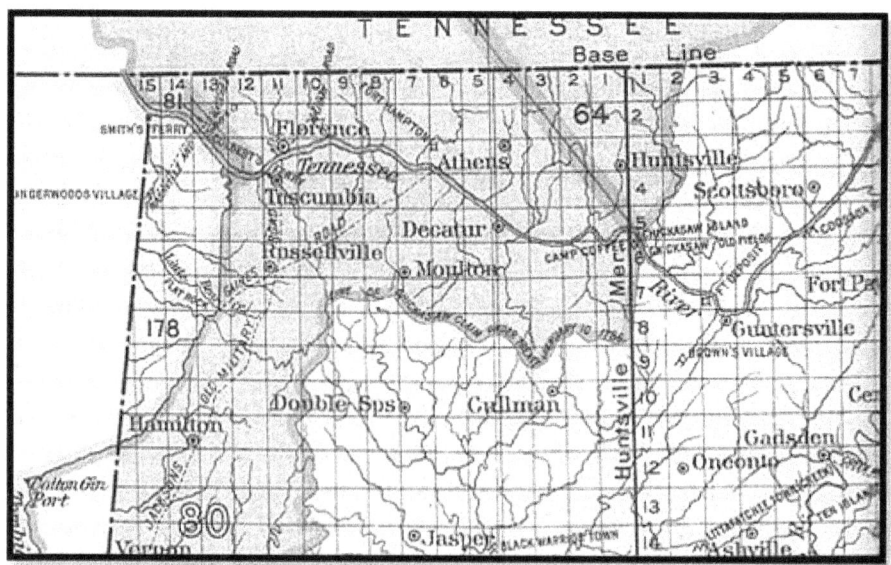

High Town Path-Chickasaw Boundary 1/10/1786
18th Annual Report, Bureau of American Ethnology

The 1786 treaty between the United States and the Chickasaws was designed to encouraged conflicts between the Chickasaws and the Cherokees by awarding the land in Morgan County and the rest of northwest Alabama to the Chickasaws. At the time of the treaty with the Chickasaws, the Chickamauga faction of Lower Cherokees were at war with United States government; therefore, the government refused to recognize the rightful claim of the Cherokee to the land that they occupied in what was to become Morgan County, Alabama.

Until 1802, the fierce Chickamauga warrior Doublehead had his stronghold just west of Fox's Creek at Doublehead's Town. The Cherokee village was on the south bank of the Tennessee River at river miles 293 and 294 at the crossing of old Brown's Ferry Road. The town was a few miles west Mouse Town which was located at the mouth of Fox's Creek in Morgan County.

Even though there were previous conflicts among the Indian tribes that occupied this area of the Tennessee River, Doublehead worked with the tribes of Chickasaw, Creek, and Shawnee to form alliances in order to organize the strongest historic Indian confederacy to ever occupy the Great Bend of the Tennessee River Valley. Doublehead would rule the area of present-day Morgan County with an iron fist, and under his leadership, the confederacy would protect the Great Bend of the Tennessee River from White encroachment until the early 1800s.

On January 7, 1806, Doublehead and other Chickamauga Cherokees signed the Cotton Gin Treaty which placed a cotton gin at Melton's Bluff on the Tennessee River some 10 miles west of present-day Morgan County. After the treaty, the Cherokees, following the leadership of Doublehead, began leasing lands along the river to White farmers including the lands of Morgan County.

The Cherokees were the first to bring Black slaves into the area of Morgan County of northwest Alabama. By time of his death on August 9, 1807, Doublehead and his brother-in-law John Melton had accumulated and owned some 100 Black slaves. The Cherokees were raising beef cattle, horses, hogs, and other farm animals; they were farming cotton, corn, and other crops with their black slaves.

Fox's Creek

Fox's Creek on the northwest corner of Morgan County was the namesake of Black Fox (Inali, Enoli, or Eunolee), who was the Principal Chief of the Cherokee Nation from 1801 to his death in 1811. Fox's Creek, named in honor of Chief Black Fox, is a small tributary to the Tennessee River near the north borders of Lawrence and Morgan Counties.

Fox's Creek flows into the Tennessee River near the northwest border of Morgan County at the Chickamauga Cherokee Indian village site of Mouse Town. The Indian town was a few miles upstream from Doublehead's Town at the Brown's Ferry crossing of the Tennessee River in present-day Lawrence County, Alabama.

Prior to his death in 1811, Black Fox lived at Mouse Town near the mouth of Fox's Creek in present-day Morgan County. "Alexander Gilbreath, then living in Huntsville, visited Black Fox's grave and nearby Chalybeate Springs…"(Elliott, 1972). Chalybeate Springs was within a few miles to the south of Fox's Stand in Lawrence County, Alabama.

After the death of Cherokee Chief Black Fox in 1811, Black Fox II, also known as John Looney, operated Fox's Stand on the old Brown's Ferry Road at its junction with the River Road from the east and the Black Warriors' Path from the south; Black Fox II was probably the son of the old Chief Black Fox. The Stand of Black Fox II was some two miles west of Doublehead's Town and was located on the Brown's Ferry Road which ran from present-day Courtland, Alabama, to present-day Huntsville, Alabama.

During the time that General John Coffee was surveying the Indian boundary lines for the Turkey Town Treaty of September 1816, Black Fox II operated his stand/trading post in Lawrence County, Alabama. General John Coffee noted the following in his diary, "26th July, 1816. Went to the river – crossed at Brown's Ferry – paid ferriage & c $1.25…This night went to Black Foxe's and lay all night; bought _ bushels of corn to carry with me. Hired ____ Lancaster to carry six bushels to Major Russell's, for which I am to pay three and half dollars - bought some salt from Fox, hired him and (Samuel B.) McClure to carry the corn to the wagon road about two miles - paid bill at Fox's $6.75." Coffee's notes continue, "1st August 1816-This morning we start in towards Madison County....2nd August 1816-This morning ...Come to the Black Fox'es - bought 2½ bushels corn - paid the bill $1.75 - Same day came on - crossed the Tennessee River at Brown's Ferry and came to Wilders where we lay all night."

After the Turkey Town Treaty of September 1816 took the Cherokee lands of Morgan County and northwest Alabama, Black Fox II, who also had the English name of John Looney, moved east and lived in the Cherokee Nation near Gunter's Landing. Chief John Looney was noted in historical records as living near present-day Guntersville, Alabama, which remained in the Cherokee Nation until 1838. During Indian removal, Chief John Looney, aka Black Fox II or Enoli, was removed to western Arkansas and eastern Oklahoma from the Guntersville area.

At the time of the 1838 Cherokee Removal from North Alabama, William (Bill) Bauck Looney of Looney's Tavern fame would have been about 11 years old. In 1827, Bill Looney was born in the southeastern corner of Lawrence County, Alabama, near the county lines of Morgan, Cullman, and Winston County Counties. Bill was the eleventh child of Moses and Mary Guest Looney; Mary Guest was a Cherokee Indian.

Bill Looney, a staunch Unionist during the Civil War, became known as Black Fox which was a name probably given him because of his kinship with the Cherokee Chief John Looney. Bill, aka Black Fox, led and directed several hundred Confederate deserters and pro-Union sympathizers to the Union Army at Decatur and other places during the Civil War between 1862 and 1865. On an occasion around 1863, five local men who were Union sympathizers were captured by the Confederate Home Guard and put in jail at Jasper, Alabama. They were given five days to make up their minds to join the Confederate Army or be killed before a firing squad. Bill Looney went to the Union commander at Decatur and got him to provide 26 Union soldiers to rescue the imprisoned men; they freed the men, burned the jail, and killed the jailer. After that Civil War episode, William (Bill) Walker, who was among those rescued and the great, great, grandfather of the author, joined the First Alabama Calvary of the Union Army on December 14, 1863, at Camp Davis, Mississippi. The author, Rickey

Butch Walker, was born at Hartselle in Morgan County, Alabama, on November 12, 1949.

Mouse Town

At the northwestern corner of present-day Morgan County was the Chickamauga Cherokee village known as Mouse Town which was located some three to four miles east of the head of Elk River Shoals. The Indian village was located at a strategic crossing of the Tennessee River from Mouse Town on the south side of the river to Cow Ford Landing on the north side.

The Chickamauga Cherokee town was located on the east side of Fox's Creek at its junction with Tennessee River. On December 18, 2003, Mr. Paul Ausbon and Mr. Bill Sams, whose ancestors lived in the area, said that Mouse Town was on the Tennessee River some two miles north of Highway 20. Mr. Ausbon said that he was born in the area in 1925, and that he had been told all his life about the Indian town called Mouse Town by his grandparents. They told the story an Indian and White settler fight that occurred at the old town site many years ago.

In August 1816 near Mouse Town, there was an altercation between four members of the Burleson family and the Cherokee Indians. The Burlesons along with four other White settlers were accused of murdering two to three Cherokees. The fight confirms that White settlers were leasing farm lands from the Cherokee Indians; other White settler farmers living in the area signed two petitions in 1816.

On August 12, 1816, White settlers sent the following letter from Mississippi Territory to the chiefs of the Cherokees in order for the innocent White farmers to avoid retaliation and punishment: "To any of the Chiefs or hed men of the Chirokee Nation. Wee feel it our Duty to let you know who commited that offence against your subjects so that the inesant may not suffer. The offence was committed on the twelveth Inst by these under named: James Burleson, John Burleson, Robt. Thrasher, Martin Tailer, Charle Tailer, John Bird, Edward Burleson, and Joseph Burleson. These are all wee have any knowledg of they have left the settlement and gone in to Madison County where they will be delt with acording to law as soon as it can be put in force against them and as for old fox he has went of with those men that committed this offene therfore wee subscribe our names on the other side." Signed by: Thomas Lovell, David Davolt, William Fears, David White, Lemuel Lovell, William Cosby, Rudolph McDaniel, George Cosby, Sam Cosby, Robert W. Woods, Sam B. McClure.

In a letter of August 15, 1816, the Cherokee Indians gave an account of two of their fellow Cherokee Indians killed at Mouse Town east of Elk River Shoals. "James Burleson and seven other white men killed two Cherokees. Hope you will cause whites to give up Negro Fox as he is considered one of our people and we wish to try him by our law." Signed by: Gourd (X), Charles Melton (X), William Rains, Isaac Wade, Breton Wider, Joseph Slaughter, John Lambe, Nelson Bonds, Walter Evans, Elick Melton, and William Phillips (Microcopy 208, roll 7, and number 3533).

On August 25, 1816, White settlers living and farming in the Mouse Town area identify to White authorities the people who killed the two Cherokees. The information was given in a letter from Mississippi Territory to Colonel Louis Winston (1784-1824), native of Virginia, who was appointed the district attorney general in 1809 for Madison County, Mississippi Territory. The letter was as follows: "Requesting him (Colonel Louis Winston) to have apprehended certain men who murdered two Cherokees. Two Indians were killed August 12, a few miles above Melton's (Bluff) at head of Shoals by white men having with them Negro Black Fox who belonged to Cherokee Nation. The Indians were killed by Edward Burleson, James Burleson, John Burleson, Joseph Burleson, Robert Thrasher, Martin Tailer (Taylor), Charles Tailer (Taylor), and John Bird were of the number who committed the deed and there were others in party whose names we do not know. They have left and gone to Madison County" (Microcopy 208, roll 7, and number 3544).

On September 5, 1816, the National Intelligenser, Washington, D.C., gave editorially the substance of a letter, dated August 13, 1816, to Colonel Winston from James Burleson. It states that Burleson, and others "who had settled near Mouse Town, on the south side of the Tennessee River to the number of eight men were attacked by a party of Cherokees armed with guns and war clubs, the number not known, on the night of the 11th inst. The whites resisted and three Indians were killed and one wounded. The fear of the Indians caused consternation among the White settlers, and many moved away leaving promising crops."

On September 10, 1816, from information at Huntsville dated August 17, 1816, the National Intelligenser gave further details concerning the disturbance. "It seems that a Mr. Taylor had rented a field from some Cherokees. In his absence they offered some insult to Mrs. Taylor, who escaped to the home of her father, James Burleson. Burleson, Taylor and others went to the Indian settlement (Mouse Town), where they found a number collected. They demanded an explanation. The Indians raised a yell and said fight. An attempt was made by the whites to cut them off from their arms. This produced a conflict."

On May 9, 1882, according to a letter from Waco, Texas, and printed in The Moulton Advertiser on May 25, 1882, page 2, column 4, "I noticed John Wheat, Maj. W. D. Thomason, William Crittenden, and Aaron Burleson. The latter will be remembered by the old people who lived between Courtland and Decatur in the year 1817, if any such are now living. He was a brother of General Ed Burleson of Texas Revolutionary fame. He was engaged in the killing of some Indians at Mouse Town on Foxe's Creek, east of Courtland in 1817, for which he fled the country, went to Missouri, thence to Texas. He has made many greasers as well as red skin bite the dust…He now lives Bastrop, Bastrop County (Texas)."

In the 1899 book Early Settlers of Alabama, James E. Saunders, writing many years later from oral tradition, said that the last recorded fight between whites and Indians in the area occurred on Foxes Creek near the Cherokee Indian village that he called Moneetown (Mouse Town). Saunders stated that "James Burleson and family killed three Cherokees and fled to Missouri."

In another account, "James Burleson settled with his family on the north side of the mountain on Fox Creek…, the family became involved in a feud following an altercation between a son-in-law, Martin, and the Cherokees. After three of the Indians were slain, James Burleson and his son Edward fled to Missouri" (Gentry, 1962).

Burleson Trace

According to local tradition, the Burleson family operated an early Tennessee River ferry from Cow Ford Landing in Limestone County to Mouse Town in Morgan County, Alabama. On a May 29, 1809, list of documented intruders, James Burleson, John Burleson, and Joseph Burleson were shown living in present-day Limestone County, Alabama. On September 5, 1810, the Burleson brothers signed the petition to President James Madison to stay on Indian land in Limestone County. Stories passed down through the Burleson line tell that members of their family were in present-day Morgan County, Alabama, by 1811.

In October 1813, James, John, Joseph, and other Burlesons from Mississippi Territory of present-day North Alabama served with General Andrew Jackson. During the Creek Indian War, the Burleson brothers fought the Creeks until the final Battle of Horseshoe Bend on March 27, 1814. The war officially ended on August 9, 1814, with the signing of the Treaty of Fort Jackson.

Several 1816 historical records show that the Burleson brothers were involved in a fight with the Cherokees at Mouse Town in Morgan County. By 1816, the Burleson brothers were farming lands in Morgan County that they probably leased from the Cherokees as did other early White settlers in the area.

Before 1818, the Burleson Ferry supposedly connected the roads from Athens in Limestone County by way of Cow Ford Landing to Mouse Town in Morgan County, and then by way of Burleson Trace to Moulton in Lawrence County, Alabama. Through Morgan and Lawrence Counties, Burleson Trace ran concurrent with portions of the present-day Old Moulton Road from Moulton to Decatur; some portions of the original old Burleson Trace can still be seen as deeply worn areas in the red clay ground.

From 1818 through 1827, Joseph Burleson was a trustee in the Town of Moulton; he entered two tracts of land near Moulton. On September 11, 1818, Joseph entered 82.54 acres, and on October 10, 1818, he entered 156.88 acres (Cowart, 1991). In addition to a land speculator, Joseph was a hotel operator and road builder. Joseph was interviewed by Anne Royall in 1818 and written about in her book "Letters from Alabama, 1817-1822."

According to Alabama legislation, Joseph Burleson and Associates were identified as a road building organization. As a road builder, Joseph Burleson upgraded game trails and old Indian paths to wagon roads. One of his first major roads ran from the ferry at Mouse Town at the mouth of Fox's Creek near Peck's Landing site to Moulton, then to Byler's Old Turnpike which connected to Tuscaloosa, and then to Jackson's Military Road at Pikeville in Marion County which connected to New Orleans.

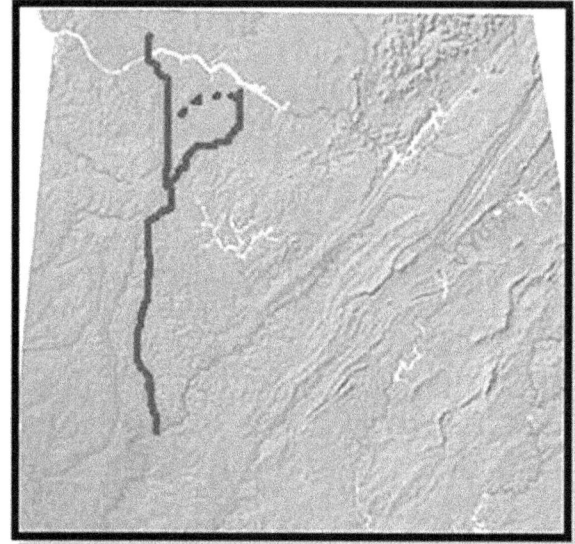

Byler Road-Shoals Creek to Tuscaloosa
Burleson Trace-Mouse Town to Moulton

On July 11, 1818, George Peck, who operated the Peck's Landing on the Tennessee River in the vicinity of the ferry, entered 80.24 acres in the East ½ of Northwest ¼ of Section 29 in Township 5 South and Range 4 West in Morgan County, Alabama, with assignee listed as J. (Joseph) Burleson (Cowart, 1981). George was married to Celia Fennel; therefore, George was a son-in-law to Wylie Fennel and a brother-in-law to James Fennel of the Walnut Grove Plantation of Morgan County.

On March 2, 1819, in <u>Letters from Alabama 1817-1822</u>, Anne Royall wrote the first of a few of her letters about Joseph Burleson while she was staying in Moulton, Alabama; she was probably renting a boarding room from Joseph. In her letters, Royall states that the Burleson family was "native of New Jersey, and moved from thence to North Carolina, and finally to Wataga." She wrote that the father of Joseph was the first White man to make a permanent settlement on the waters of Wataga Creek in 1774 or 1775. The creek empties into the Holston River in Tennessee, and the area became known as the Wataga Settlement. She also states that Joseph was a stout man about 50 years old, and he lost his father at 12 years of age. Royall stated that Joseph Burleson "at this time possessed of an independent fortune, and yet this man, with the manners of a courtier, cannot write his own name! though he reads very well."

On November 29, 1822, Joseph Burleson entered 240 acres of land in Township 11 South and Ranges 11-12 West in Marion County, Alabama. Joseph was acquiring land in the Pikeville area prior to being approved by the Alabama Legislature to complete Burleson Trace to Pikeville, Alabama.

On December 26, 1822, Joseph Burleson was approved authorization by the State of Alabama Legislature to complete the Burleson Trace to the Military Road (Nashville to New Orleans) at Pikeville in Marion County, Alabama. Joseph Burleson and Associates, whom were probably family members, were the legal organization listed in the legislation to construct the wagon road. On October 1, 1823, the Senate and House of Representatives of the State of Alabama convened in General Assembly specified that the turnpike road of Joseph Burleson and Associates be 16 feet wide clear of stumps and grubs and put the same in complete repair.

The Burleson Trace passed through Lawrence County from Mouse Town on the Tennessee River in Morgan County through Moulton and joined the Byler Road at Ebenezer Martin Gap south of Mt. Hope. From the Martin Gap, Burleson Trace followed concurrent with Byler's Old Turnpike Road to the Town of Haleyville. At the southwest edge of Haleyville, Burleson Trace turned west toward Pikeville. According to the legislation, the trace run "thence the nearest and most direct way, so as to intersect the Military Road, leading from Nashville to New Orleans, at Pikeville." Burleson Trace terminated at its junction with Jackson's Military Road at Pikeville in Marion County, Alabama.

Cotton and other farm products coming down the Tennessee River from the east could be offloaded on the south side of the river in Morgan County to wagons in order to avoid the water hazards of the treacherous Muscle Shoals. Farm products from Limestone County north of the river could be transported to Cow Ford Landing, then across the Tennessee River to Burleson Trace. Those goods could be shipped via Burleson Trace from the Tennessee River near the east end of the Elk River Shoals to either the Old Byler Turnpike leading to Mobile or to Jackson's Military Road leading to New Orleans.

Joseph Burleson and Associates were also authorized by the Alabama Legislature to establish turnpike gates to collect tolls as follows: "For each wagon and team, one dollar; two wheeled carriage, fifty cents; for each man and horse, twelve and a half cents; for each head of stock, three cents; and the penalty for avoiding tolls was ten dollars." By state law where Burleson Trace ran concurrent with the Byler Road portion starting at Ebenezer Martin Gap to just south of Haleyville, Joseph Burleson and Associates were not allowed to collect a toll; in that section of the road, those tolls were for Byler and Associates.

Sometimes around 1827, Joseph Burleson moved from Moulton to Pikeville where he lived at the forks of the Buttahatchee River for several years prior to migrating to Texas. After Joseph moved from Moulton, his trace became known as the Byler Fork, and later just the Byler Road; however, Burleson Trace was the true historic name. Today, a road sign over Highway 33 in Moulton, Alabama, misidentifies the route of Burleson Trace as the Byler Road.

While at Pikeville, Joseph Burleson encouraged family members to migrate and settle in Marion County, Alabama. Many members of the Burleson family took him up and became residents of the area with many still living in Marion County, today.

Around 1833, Joseph Burleson moved to Texas to join his brother James and other family members. The Burleson families in Texas were involved in the revolution that established the Republic of Texas. Today, the family bible of Joseph Burleson is in the Alamo Museum in San Antonia, Texas.

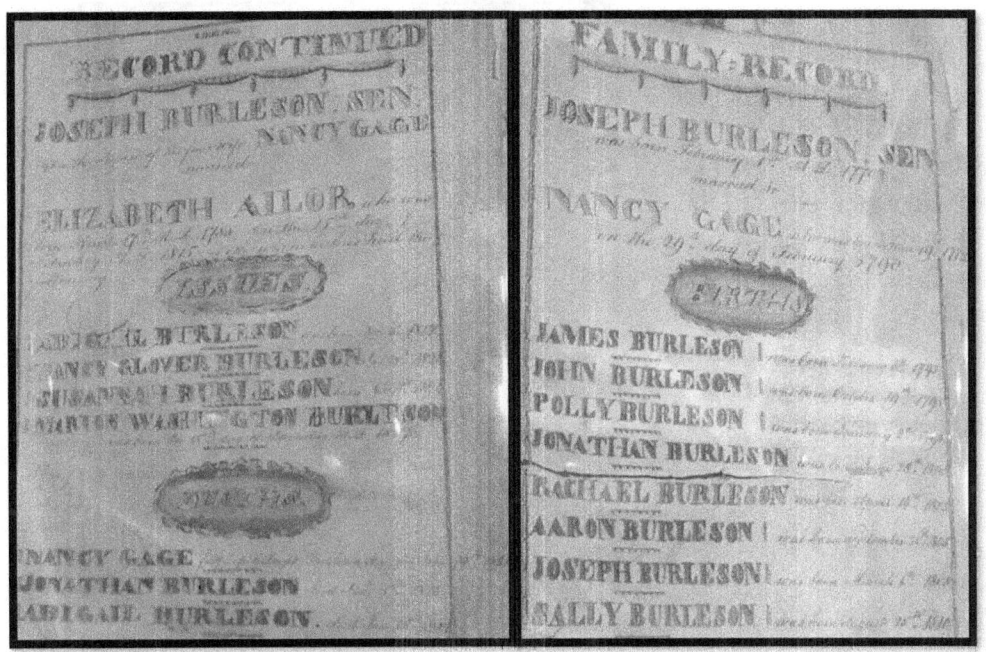

In 1839, George Daniel Russell, the grandson of Major William Russell, presented Rufus Burleson his grandfather's rifle (Some say it was given to Joseph Burleson of Texas). Therefore, the family of Joseph Burleson owned the rifle of Major William Russell of Franklin County, Alabama, which was use by Major Russell during the Creek Indian War and at the Battle of Horseshoe Bend. The Russell-Burleson Rifle was a 52 caliber Pennsylvania long rifle with an octagon barrel; today, the rifle is in the Alamo Museum in San Antonia, Texas.

Fields-Cherokee

Richard Fields (1744-1780) was a White man who married a quarter blood Cherokee Susannah Emory (1749-??). They had several children that were one-eighth mixed blood Cherokee. Susannah's parents were a White Englishman by the name of William Emory (1726-1770) and Mary Grant (1729-1766), a half blood Cherokee daughter of Ludovic Grant (1688-1756). Scotsman Ludovic Grant, an Indian trader, and his full blood Cherokee wife, Elizabeth Eughioote Coody Corntassel (1705-1727), were the grandparents of Susannah Emory.

The sons of Richard and Susannah Emory Fields were John Fox Fields (1770-?), Richard Fields Jr. (1771-1827), George Fields (1774-1849), and Turtle Fields (1776-1844). During the early 1800, some of the Fields mixed blood Cherokee family was living in the area that would become Morgan County, Alabama.

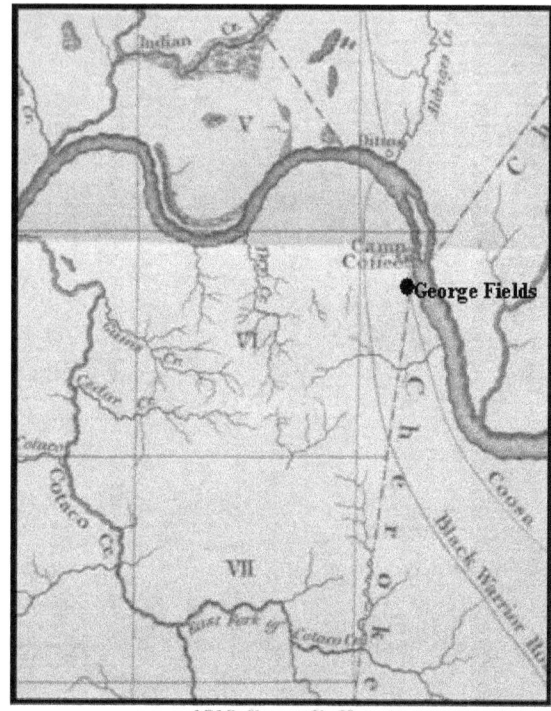

1818-Camp Coffee

George Fields

George Fields Plantation was located near the northeast corner of Morgan County, Alabama, near the Tennessee River just north of present-day Lacey's Spring Community. In the 1809 census of Cherokee Indians as reported by Return Jonathan Meigs, there were eight Cherokee males and three Cherokee females living on George Fields Plantation in Morgan County, Alabama. Even though the Fields were mixed blood people, they were listed in the 1809 census as Cherokee even though they were more White than Indian.

George Fields

Sarah Coody

George Fields was married three times. His first marriage was to Mary about 1792; Mary was born about 1776. His second marriage was to Jennie Brown about 1796, and she was born about 1780. Jennie was the daughter of Robert Brown, and she died after 1836.

The third marriage of George Fields was to Sarah Coody about 1806. She was the daughter of Joseph Coody and Elis Tassel. Sarah was born about 1783, and she died after 1860. Pictured adjacent to each other are George Fields and his third wife Sarah Coody.

By his three wives, George Fields fathered 12 children. He had Annie by his first wife Mary Fields. By his second wife Jennie Brown, the children of George included Archibald, Robert, Johnson, Susan, and Rachel. George was the father of John, Dempsey,

Annie Fields Ballard

Richard, Nannie, Rider, and Martha by his third wife Sarah Coody.

During the Creek War, George Fields was a captain of a group of Cherokees in the army of General Andrew Jackson. He served from October 7, 1813, until April 11, 1814. On November 9, 1813, George Fields was wounded at the Battle of Talladega fighting the Creek Indians.

George was shot through the right side of his chest and had to set upright in order to breathe. He was transported with the help of young John Brown, a half blood, in a setting position to Fort Talladega; John was the son of Captain John Brown of Browns Ferry. About two weeks after the Battle of Talladega, George Fields was brought to Fort Deposit in the Cherokee Nation a few miles east of his home.

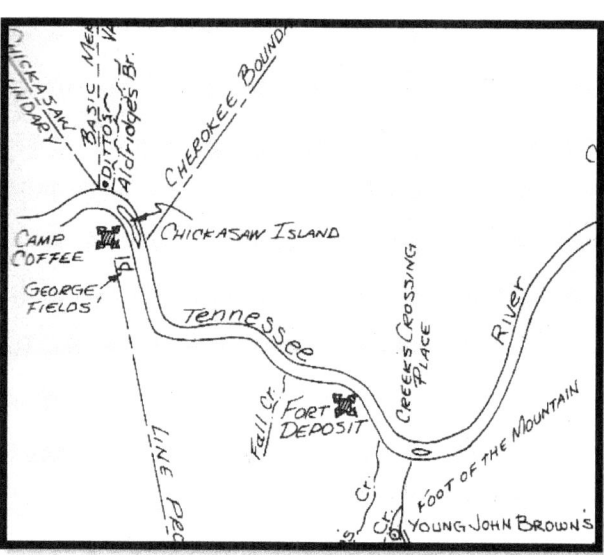

George Fields finally recovered from his wound suffered during the Creek Indian War. He moved from Alabama to Indian Territory between 1836 and 1837. At the age of 75, George Fields died on April 14, 1849, in Indian Territory west of the Mississippi River.

Judge Richard Fields, son of George Fields

George Fields had two of his sons, Richard (1808-1873) and Rider Fields, that owned and operated a ferry in the northeastern corner of Morgan County, Alabama. On November 1, 1831, Richard Fields and his brother Rider Fields were granted permission from the Cherokee Committee and Council to open a road and establish a ferry on the Tennessee River at or near the mouth of Caney

Creek opposite the mouth of the Flint River. The road was to intersect the road leading from Ditto's Landing to Blountsville at or near where Mr. George Hale lived on the mountain and known as a public stand.

On September 12, 1838, Richard Fields made a statement to the Commissioners that he and his brother Rider had hired and placed Simpson Black at the ferry to make improvements. The Fields had received permission on November 18, 1830, to employ Black; the permit from the proper authorities of the Cherokee Nation was obtained by Rider Fields. After the State of Alabama extended their laws over the Cherokee lands, Black refused to return the ferry to Richard and Rider Fields.

Richard Fields alleged that he paid for improvements to his ferry on the Tennessee River opposite the mouth of Flint River in Morgan County, Alabama, prior to December 29, 1835. Richard also claimed that Simpson Black had since the extended the laws of Alabama over the Cherokee Nation, and that he refused to surrender the possession of the ferry to Rider Fields.

Judge Richard Fields

Richard Fields claim was based on the fact that he was dispossessed of the ferry, but that he paid for the improvements on the ferry. The information proved that the ferry on the Original Survey identified as Blacks Ferry was the same one that had been the Fields Ferry some five miles northwest of Gunter's Landing. Reverend William Potter, Napoleon B. Clark, and Absalom Black confirmed the claim of Richard Fields, and they verified his possession of the ferry.

Richard Fields contested the right to the ferry, and he obtained a certificate from a Mr. Montgomery that was provided to Cherokee Indian agent Return J. Meigs. The improvements to the ferry were valued by Mr. Montgomery, and he listed the Richard Fields Ferry on Tennessee River opposite the mouth of Flint River in Morgan County, Alabama, with a value of $2,000.00. Richard Fields claimed that net income per year was $200.00 to $2,000.00; Richard was eventually paid the value of the ferry.

In the Register of Payments, Account for Richard Fields, there was an entry for him being paid $2,000.00 for his ferry on the south bank of the Tennessee River plus $1,000 for rent. After leaving Morgan County, Alabama, Richard Fields became a judge in the Cherokee Nation.

Richard Fields Jr.

In 1809, Richard (Dick) Fields Jr. also had a plantation that was enumerated by Return Jonathan Meigs, Cherokee Indian Agent. According to the 1809 Cherokee census by Meigs, Dick Fields Plantation had 18 people living on his farm. The folks enumerated included five Cherokee males, five Cherokee females, and eight White people.

In 1814, Richard, who was the son of Richard and Susannah Emory Fields, also fought with General Andrew Jackson during the Creek Indian War. He served as a captain of the Cherokee Auxiliaries like his brother George.

After the September 1816 Turkey Town Treaty ceded Morgan County and the other northwest Alabama counties, some mixed blood Cherokees entered land and/or were enumerated in the 1820 census in those counties. Thomas Glass, Merida Melton, Thomas Melton, and Richard Fields are just a few mixed bloods that were recorded in the area after the treaty.

On July 29, 1818, Richard Fields entered 81.21 acres in the East ½ of the Northeast ¼ of Section 32 of Township 7 South and Range 3 West in Morgan County, Alabama. His land entry was basically south to southeast of Falkville in the Flint Creek drainage.

By 1822, Richard Fields moved to Texas, and he became a diplomatic representative of the Western Cherokees in Texas. At that time, Duwali (Bowle), who was half Cherokee from a Scots father, served as chief of the Texas Cherokees.

Cherokee Chief Duwali (Bowle) and Richard Fields disagreed on loyalty to the existing powers in Texas. Bowle threw his allegiance to the Mexicans, and Richard Fields favored the Texans. Because of his political dispute with Duwali, Richard Fields was assassinated by his people in 1827.

Cotaco (Morgan) County

From 1770 and prior to the Turkey Town Treaty of 1816, the Chickamauga faction of Cherokees were occupying the area that became Cotaco (present-day Morgan) County, Alabama. Cotaco was considered to be a word of Cherokee origin that was corrupted by White translation. Some say that Cotaco was a Cherokee village chief who lived near the creek that was named in his honor; Fox's Creek in Morgan County was named in honor of Cherokee Chief Black Fox.

Living among the Chickamauga faction of Cherokee Indians were white settlers who were either leasing farm lands from the Cherokee or intermarried with the Indians. By the spring of 1806, White settlers were paying the Cherokee for farming rights to their lands in and around the Cotaco County area. In addition, some White settlers were squatters on Indian lands and were not intermarried or leasing lands from the Cherokee Indians.

By the 1809 census of the Cherokee by Indian agent Return Jonathan Meigs, nearly all the Chickamauga Cherokee towns along Big Bend of the Tennessee (Hogohegee) River had White folks enumerated. For example, just up river at Gunter's Landing, Meigs enumerated 554 inhabitants with 509 being Cherokee and 45 being White folks. A large percentage of the White people living among the Cherokees were attached to the tribe by marriage or related to those intermarried with the Cherokee.

About 1812, according to family tradition, Greenberry Wilson and his family were living near the area of Somerville. Greenberry remained in the area, and he was buried in Morgan County, Alabama.

During 1814, family members of Joseph Burleson and his nephew Jonathan Burleson were living in the area of present-day Morgan County, Alabama. Jonathan remained in the Flint Creek area south of Decatur. Today, some of his descendants still call Morgan County home.

In 1815, based on an early map showing Cotaco Creek, Thomas Sharp had established his home and farm in the Morgan County area. His place was shown west of Cotaco Creek and south of the Hogohegee River which was also known as the River of the Cherokee or Tennessee River.

Beginning with the Turkey Town Treaty of 1816, most Cherokee inhabitants moved from the area of Cotaco to lands identified as the Cherokee Nation east of present-day Morgan County, Alabama. In 1816, by treaty with the United States government, both the Cherokees and Chickasaws agreed to give up their land claims to the area of present-day Morgan, Madison, Lawrence, Limestone, Lauderdale, Colbert, and Franklin Counties of northwest Alabama; however, some mixed bloods remained in the area claiming their White ancestry.

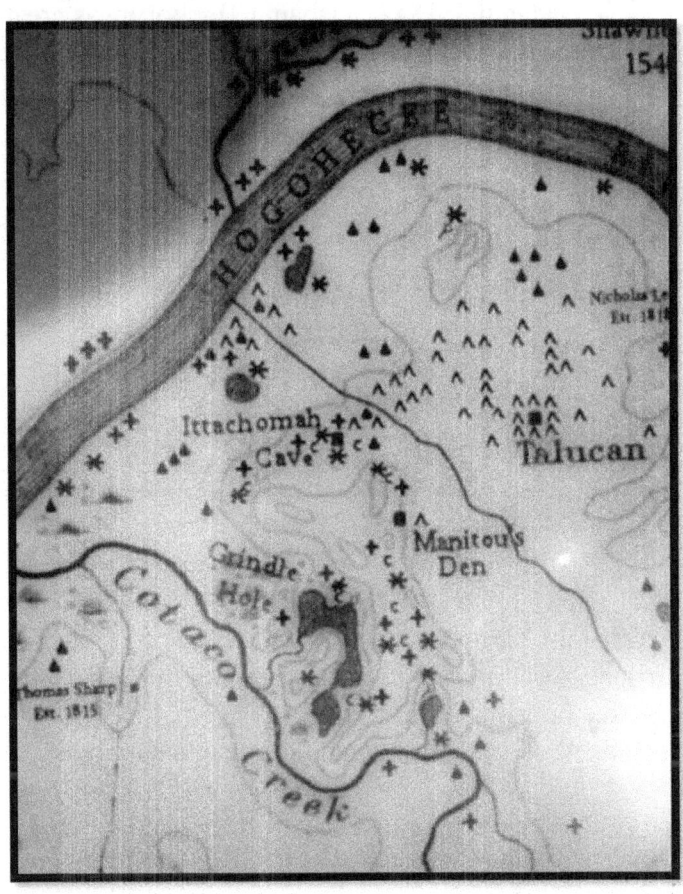

During 1816, General John Coffee surveyed the tribal boundaries of the Chickasaws, Cherokees, and Creeks to bring about their removal from that portion of Mississippi Territory (present-day northwest Alabama) taken by the Turkey Town Treaty of 1816. Also, General Coffee surveyed the Cherokee Nation tribal boundary that would make up the eastern side of Cotaco County. On that eastern edge of the county was Camp Coffee that was utilized during the Creek Indian War and named in honor of General John Coffee.

On December 4, 1816, Charles Lockhart was listed on the land records in the area that would become Morgan County; he was the earliest officially recorded land owner. Lockhart entered 160.28 acres in Section 6 of Township 8 South and Range 4 West in Morgan County, Alabama (Cowart, 1981).

On March 3, 1817, Alabama Territory was created from the eastern portion of Mississippi Territory. The Indian lands that eventually became Cotaco (Morgan) County were originally part of Blount County of Alabama Territory. Blount County was south of the Tennessee River, and Elk County was on the north side of the river.

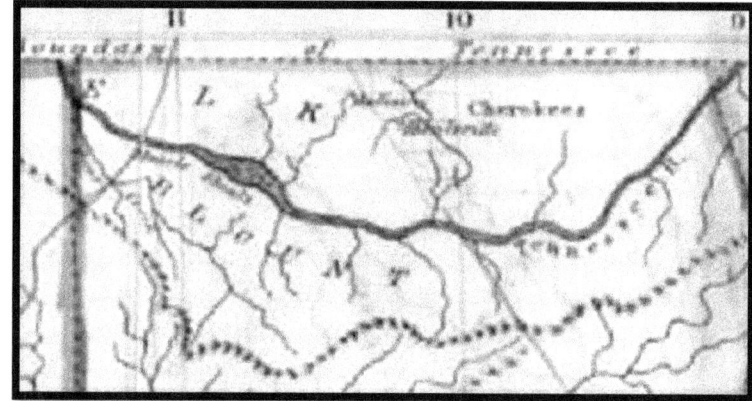

On March 6, 1817, United States President James Monroe appointed General John Coffee as the Surveyor General of the north district of Alabama Territory. A portion of that district south of the Tennessee River and west of the Cherokee boundary would eventually become Cotaco County. One of Coffee's first jobs was to establish a land office and survey the Town of Huntsville.

On February 2, 1818, Berry Robertson entered a tract of land in Cotaco County before the county was created by territorial law. Robertson had certificate number 657 for 72.5 acres of land in Section 19 of Township 7 South and Range 1 East in the area that would become Cotaco County two days later (Cowart, 1981). February of 1818 was the first widespread official land entries for Cotaco County.

On February 4, 1818, Cotaco (Morgan) County was created by Alabama Territorial Legislature. The tract of land lying west of the Cherokee boundary, south of the Tennessee River, and east of the western boundary of Range 5 West, and north of the southern boundary of Township 8 South was established as Cotaco County in Alabama Territory. Therefore, Cotaco County was created before Alabama was officially recognized as a state.

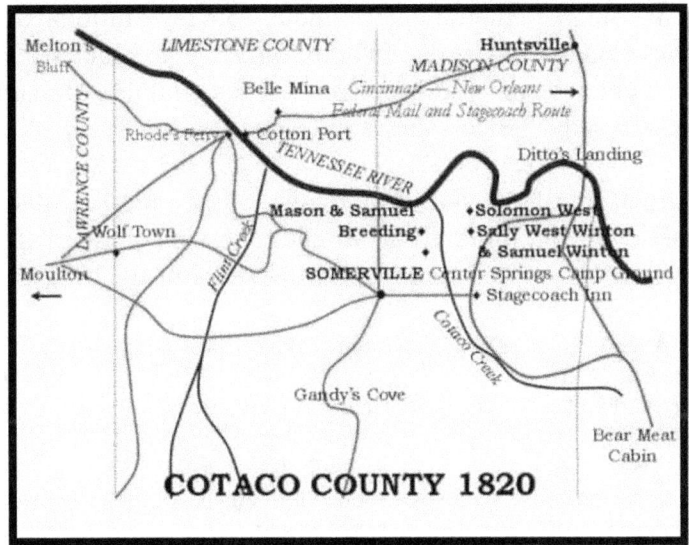

On February 4, 1818, John McKnitt Alexander Wallis (Wallace) and Richard Purden were listed on the official records as entering the first land on the date Cotaco County was created by territorial law. On that date, John McK. A. Wallis entered 79.9 acres in Section 1 of Township 7 South and Range 2 West with certificate number 2334; in 1830, John owned 18 Black slaves. On February 4, 1818, Richard entered 110 acres of land in Section 6 of Township 6 South and Range 2 West with certificate number 1570 in what would become Morgan County, Alabama (Cowart, 1981).

On February 5, 1818, David Hubbard entered 80.46 acres in Section 13 of Township 8 South and Range 5 West in Cotaco County, Alabama. From July 8, 1818, through July 15, 1818, David Hubbard entered some 400 additional acres in Cotaco (Morgan) County, Alabama (Cowart, 1981). In addition, a Hubbard and Black entered an additional 400 acres in the county.

On February 7, 1818, prior to the first public auction of land in Cotaco County, Alabama, Malcolm Gilchrist, a land speculator, entered 160.12 acres of land in Section 35 of Township 5 South and Range 2 West in Cotaco (Morgan) County, Alabama (Cowart, 1981). From July 6, 1818, through July 15, 1818, Malcolm Gilchrist entered approximately 3,424 additional acres in Cotaco (Morgan) County, Alabama. In addition, Daniel Gilchrist, the brother of Malcolm Gilchrist, entered some 900 acres in Morgan County, Alabama; in 1850, Daniel Gilchrist owned 87 Black slaves in Lawrence County.

In March 1818, the first Monday of the month, Cotaco County held its first public auction for land sales. The following are land speculators and Cotaco County residents who entered land in 1818 (Cowart, 1981):

William Abbott,
John Adams,
Littleberry Adams,
Henry Adkins,
James Alford,
Charles Anderson,
John Anderson,
Elisha Bagley,
Elizabeth C. Bagley,
Isaiah F. Bagley,
James Bagley,
Joab Bagley,
Nathan Bagley,
Daniel L. Bayless,
Reuben Bayless,
Augustine G. Beacham,
William Bean,
Abram Beedle,
George Benard,
John D. Bibb,
Thomas Bibb,
John Bird (Byrd),
William Bird,
Joseph Bishop,
John Black,
Isaac Blanton,
Elizabeth Blevins,
John Blevins,
John Bolton,
Alexander Boteler,
Green Boulding,
Joseph Bower,

Samuel Boyes,
Charles Boyles,
Henry Bracken,
John Brahan,
Fredrick Braugher,
Samuel Breeding,
James Bright,
James Brogen,
John Brown,
Stewart Brown,
Thomas Brown,
William Burgess,
Jonathan Burleson,
Greenville Burnett,
Henry Burns,
Hardy Burt,
John Burt,
Jabez G. Calloway,
Jeremiah S. Calvert,
Solomon Castleberry,
Jesse C. Childers,
James Childress,
William Childress,
Launcelot Chunn,
George Clarke,
Joseph Cobb (Kolb),
John Coffee,
Rhoda Colbert,
Bolling Collier,
Albert Cook,
Charles Cooper,
Noah Cooper,

John Condron,
John Couch,
Peter Couch,
James H. Cowan,
John Cowan,
Thomas D. Crabb,
Archie Craft,
Rhoda Crawford,
Robert K. Crockett,
Francis Crow,
Thomas Crow,
John Curren,
Matthew Cyrus,
Thomas Dallas,
William Dancy,
Nathan W. Dandridge,
Joshua Davidson,
John Davis,
Nicholas Davis,
Samuel Davis,
William Davis,
Enoch Dickson,
William Dickson,
James Dinsmore,
John Donaldson
(Donelson),
Bartholomew Donohoe,
Henry Donohoo,
William G. Dossey
(Dorsey),
Absalom Doughit,
Daniel L. Downs,

James Dunsmore,
Allen Dupree,
David Duvall,
Joseph Easley,
James Echols,
Samuel Echols,
John Eckford,
William F. Ecles,
Richard Elliott,
William Elliott,
Henry Evans,
Matthew Evans,
Nathaniel Evans,
Owen Evans,
William Farmer,
William (Willie) Fennel,
Richard Fields,
Alvah Finley,
Honore Fournier,
Claiborn D. Freeman,
John Gandy,
Brice M. Garner,
Jesse Winston Garth,
Roland Gatewood,
David Gibson,
Malcolm Gilchrist,
William F. Gillespie,
Alexander Givens,
John Glaze,
James Green (Greer),
Robert W. Green,
Samuel Greenlee,
William (Willis) Griffin,
John Guest,
Isaac Guest,
Adam Hall,
James Hamlin (Hamblin),
John Hamlin,
G. P. Harrell,
William Harris,
Thomas Hart,
William Harvey,
John Harvie,
John Hawkins,
Jacob Hayes,

Robert C. Hendley,
Samuel Henry,
John W. Hewlett,
Thomas Hodges,
McKinney Holderness,
Dennis Holmes,
Thomas Howlet,
David Hubbard,
Thomas Hubbard,
John Hudson,
Anderson Hutchison,
Joseph Inman,
John Jackson,
Thomas Jenkins,
Felix Jernigan,
Benjamin Johnson,
Daniel Johnson,
Henry Johnson (Johnston),
Robert M. Johnson,
Hesekiah Johnston,
William Johnston,
Felix Kennedy,
Pleasant Key,
Gaines Kibbe,
Edmond Kimbell,
William King,
Daniel Kirkland,
John Kyle,
Marvin Kyle,
Hopkins Lacy,
John Lacy,
Thomas Lacy,
James Lane,
Joseph Lane,
Isaac Lane,
Isom Lassiter,
Sarah Lauderdale,
George W. Lee,
Anthony Livingston,
James Livingston,
Samuel Livingston,
William Livingston,
Charles Lockhart,
Samuel Logan,
John W. Loony (Looney),

Stephen Lovelady,
James Lynn,
Burwell Marchbanks,
David A. Martin,
Francis F. Martin,
Robert Matthews,
Samuel McAdams,
Daniel McAllester,
David McCarley,
Robert McCarley,
Hugh McCarnes,
Roderick McCauley,
William B. McClellan,
William McClure,
John McCutchen,
Moses McDaniel,
Randolph McDaniel,
Archibald McDonnell,
David McGlathery,
Francis McKay,
John McKinley,
George McLeod,
Martin McMahon,
William McMillan,
Ormond Means,
Jarrat (Jonat) Menefee,
John Menefee,
Jonathan Medford,
Jacob Miller,
William Millikin
(Millican),
Josiah Minter (Winter),
William Mitchell,
James Montgomery,
Robert Moore,
Joseph Morrow,
Robert Morrow,
Samuel Morrow,
Thomas Morrow,
William Mosley,
George Murphree,
Thomas B. Murphy,
Smith Murphy,
John A. L. Murray,
Davis Neal,

James Nelson,
John Nesmith,
William Nunn,
Thomas Oden,
Jacob Orr,
Jonathan Orr,
John Owen,
Larkin Owen,
Jonathan L. Owens,
Robert Page,
Jeremiah Pate,
Edmund Patrick,
James Patterson,
Malcolm Patterson,
Andrew Patton,
Robert Patton,
Banyan Payne,
George Peck,
James Perrine,
Horatio Philpot,
Ethelred Pope,
Richard Purden,
William Rainey,
Adam Ramer,
John T. Rather,
Hezekiah G. Ratliff,
James Ratliff,
Samuel Ray,
Henry W. Rhodes,
Edward Richardson,
Berry Robertson,
Francis M. Roby,
James Rogers,
Eldred Rollings,
Robert Rowland,
Charles Royer,
Christopher Russell,
Thomas Russell,
John Ryan,
Thomas Ryan,
Nicholas Sandlin,
James Simpson,
Samuel Simpson,
Abraham Idmore,
Bur Slade, Skidmore,
Thomas Sk
Andrew Smith,
James L. Smith,
William Smith,
Hiram Smyth,
Skelton Standifer,
Arthur Stephenson,
Benjamin Stewart,
Jedediah Stinson,
Abram Stout,
Drury Stovall,
Peter Stovall,
Daniel Summers,
Jacob Surrat,
Benjamin Sykes,
James T. Sykes,
Joseph Sykes,
William Sykes,
Martin Taylor,
Gideon Terry,
Henry Thomas,
Edward Thompson,
Elbert H. Thompson,
James Thompson,
William Thompson,
John Thurman,
Hartwell Tucker,
George W. Turner,
William Turley,
Daniel Turney,
Joseph Turney,
John Vanpelt,
Milkijah Vaughn,
James Vest,
Obadiah Vest,
Featherstone Walden,
Charles Walker,
Joel Wallace,
James Wallis,
John M. A. Wallis (Wallace),
Joseph Wallis,
James Wardlow,
John Webster,
Benjamin Weeks,
James Welch,
Solomon West,
James Wheat,
James White,
Jesse White,
William H. Whittaker,
C. R. Wilburne,
Elijah Wiley,
Alexander Wilson,
Greenberry Wilson,
William Wilson,
John J. Winston,
David Wolf,
Bennett Wood,
Jonas C. Wood, and
Hiram Wright.

From July 9, 1818, through July 15, 1818, General John Coffee entered 1,210 acres of land in Cotaco County of Alabama Territory (Cowart, 1981). John Coffee was not only the Surveyor General of the area, but he was also a war hero, merchant, land speculator, slave owner, cotton planter, and an organizer of the Cypress Land Company. Until his death on July 7, 1833, Coffee was owner of the 1,280 acre Hickory Hills Plantation and 83 black slaves in Lauderdale County, Alabama. It is not known if General Coffee used his slaves to farm cotton on the some 1,200 acres that he owned in Morgan County or if he purchased the land for resale.

According to the 1818 census of Alabama Territory, there were 2,101 White people and 152 Black slaves in the area of Cotaco County. However, prior to 1818, White settlers, Black slaves, and mixed bloods intermingled with the Cherokee inhabitants of the area and many remained.

On March 2, 1819, the United States government authorized the occupants of Alabama Territory to form a state. The process of officially changing from Alabama Territory to becoming the State of Alabama took nearly 10 months.

Finally, on December 14, 1819, Alabama Territory was admitted into the union and became the State of Alabama; on this date, Cotaco County became a county in the State of Alabama. However, by the time the territory was admitted into the union as a state, most the counties of northwest Alabama had already been established except for Colbert County which was formed after the Civil War from the north part of Franklin County and the northwestern portion of Lawrence County.

On June 14, 1821, the original name of Cotaco County was change to Morgan County. The county was renamed in honor of the American Revolutionary war hero General Daniel Morgan of Virginia. Since the majority of the early cotton planters of the area were originally from Virginia, the name represented their home state and their home hero.

Somerville

On December 3, 1819, the Town of Somerville was incorporated as the first county seat of Cotaco County. Later in 1821, Somerville served as the county seat of Morgan County, Alabama. The town was named in honor of Lieutenant Robert M. Summerville who served under General Andrew Jackson during the Creek Indian War. Robert was the son of Joseph and Eliza Somerville of Clarksburg, Virginia. Lieutenant Summerville was killed at the Battle of Horseshoe Bend on March 27, 1814. The body Lieutenant Robert M. Summerville was weighted and sunk in the Tallapoosa River at Horseshoe Bend in Tallapoosa County, Alabama, to avoid scalping and desecration after the army retreated to Fort Williams (Find A Grave Memorial Number 42197441).

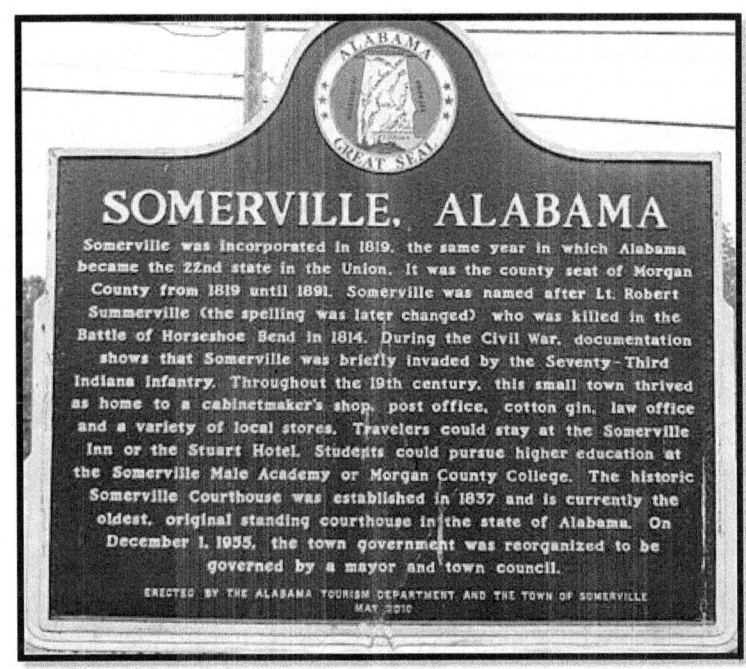

Early Roads

Prior to white settlement of the area, Somerville was a cross roads of Indian paths and trails. These early Indian roads facilitated the settlement of Morgan County by cotton farmers mainly from Virginia. The early aboriginal routes passing through Somerville included three major Indian roads:

1. Coosa Path was described by Captain Edmund Pendleton Gaines in December 1806. In October 1813, the trail was referred to as the Muscle Shoals Path by Cherokee Chief Path Killer. The route through Morgan County ran from Lacey's Spring to Somerville, and then Danville and basically circumvented the dangerous Muscle Shoals from Dittos to Tuscumbia Landing. The route at Lacey's Spring passed south toward the Coosa River crossing at Ten Islands. Along the Coosa Path through Morgan County, several early towns and communities flourished and included Lacey Springs, Valhermoso Springs, Cotaco, Somerville, Hartselle, and Danville.
2. South River Road was known across northwest Alabama as the River Road. In many cases, the route included an upper river road and lower river road along the south bank of the Tennessee River. The route of the river road basically paralleled the south bank of the Tennessee River across North Alabama and connected Indian villages from Gunter's Landing to Colbert's Ferry.
3. Creek Path was a north to south route which included forks that passed to the west through Somerville, Talcuh, and Dittos and crossed the Tennessee River. The Christian Cherokee lady Catherine Brown helped established the Creek Path Mission School some six miles south of present-day Guntersville. On July 18, 1823, she died at the home of Dr. Campbell near Triana; her body was returned to Creek Path where she was buried beside her brother who was the young John Brown.

1839 Mitchell Map

Somerville

After the Cherokee gave up their claims to the land and moved beyond the eastern boundary of Morgan County, Somerville became the hub of roads of the Cotton Kingdom of the county. Several prominent slave owning cotton planters traveled these early roads, paths, and trails to settle in the Somerville area; some represented Morgan County in the Alabama Legislature. Many of the earliest settlers were formerly Virginia cotton planters who moved along primitive roads initially to Nashville, then south to Huntsville. From Madison County, they crossed the Tennessee River on numerous ferries to claim the Indian lands of Morgan County after the Turkey Town Treaty took the area from the Cherokee in September 1816.

Early Ferries

Starting around the 1770s during which the Chickamauga Cherokees occupied the area of Morgan County and North Alabama, the Indians controlled and operated all major ferry crossings of the Tennessee River. Some of these Native crossings of primary routes of early travel included Gunter's Landing at present-day Guntersville, Fields Ferry south of Huntsville, Browns Ferry northeast of Courtland, Lambs Ferry south of Rogersville, Bluewater Ferry south of Elgin, Bainbridge Ferry west of Ford City, and Colberts Ferry at the Natchez Trace crossing.

There were four major ferry crossings of the Tennessee River into Morgan County which included overland routes to Somerville. These major ferries were:
1. Rhodes Ferry located at the Decatur crossing of the Tennessee River was owned by Dr. Henry W. Rhodes. Details on Rhodes Ferry were listed under the Decatur portion of the book.
2. Crabb Ferry was located at Monroe or Bluff City in Morgan County; the road was across the Tennessee River from the present-day County Line Road between Limestone and Madison Counties. On July 8, 1818, Thomas D. Crabb entered 110.04 acres along the Tennessee River in the middle part of Section 6 of Township 6 South and Range 2 West in Morgan County, Alabama. In addition, on July 9, 1818, Thomas D. Crabb entered two additional tracts along the river totaling 175.7 acres adjacent and west of his first tract in Section 1 of Township 6 South and Range 3 West in Morgan County, Alabama (Cowart, 1981). From July 9, 1818, through July 25, 1818, Thomas also entered approximately 560 additional acres south of his river properties.
3. Lewis Ferry appears to have been in two locations with one crossing at the river junction with the Louis Bluff Road in Morgan County; it probably crossed the river to Blueberry Road in Madison County. The ferry near Louis Bluff Road was halfway between Lacey's Spring and Triana. Nicholas Lewis started operation of one ferry in May 1820, after he received his ferry license. In May 1828, Nicholas Lewis got a government grant for his cotton gin, large warehouse, and other river improvements on his 160 acres at Talucah Landing. The Lewis Ferry at Talucah crossed the Tennessee River south of Triana in Madison County, Alabama. It also appears that the ferry was also known as Sunnyside Ferry or Talucah Ferry.

4. Ditto Ferry south of Huntsville began operation in 1807. According to historical records, James "John" Ditto (1743-10/30/1828) arrived in the area about 1802, and he was the first owner and operator of his ferry and riverside trading post. James was the son of William Ditto (1713-1744) and Jane Quine (1713-1747). James Ditto had landings on both sides of the Tennessee River in Morgan and Madison Counties. During the Creek Indian War, the ferry was very instrumental in getting the army of General Andrew Jackson across the Tennessee River. James Ditto was buried in the Ditto Homestead Cemetery south of Huntsville in Madison County, Alabama (Find A Grave Memorial Number 187423761). The Ditto Ferry, later known as Whitesburg Ferry, was the approximate location of the River Tennessee crossing of present-day Highway 231.

Other Morgan County ferries include:
1. Blacks Ferry, also known as Fields Ferry, was located on the Tennessee River opposite the mouth of Flint River in Morgan County, Alabama;
2. Burleson Ferry crossed Flint Creek between Priceville and Decatur;
3. Cain Landing was at the north end of Cain Road in Morgan County east of Bluff City;

4. Cotaco Ferry was near the mouth of Cotaco Creek in Morgan County;
5. Draper Ferry was at the end of Plymouth Rock Road in Morgan County and northeast of Valhermoso Springs;
6. Johnson Landing was at the end of Johnson Landing Road in Morgan County north of Valhermoso Springs;
7. Leman Ferry was north of Lacey's Spring and west of Whitesburg and appeared to connect to the north to Raiford Road in Madison County;
8. McKee Ferry was east of Bluff City in Morgan County and southeast of Jolley B. Road in Madison County very close to Stringfield Ferry;
9. McMahan Ferry was located east of Lacey's Spring at Hobbs Island;
10. Slaughter Landing or Ferry was at the Slaughter Road junction with the Tennessee River east of Triana a few miles;
11. Stringfield Ferry was just south and close to Blackwell Swamp, and it was to the west of Triana and Cotaco Creek which probably connected to the Jolley B. Road.

Today, ferries do not exist on the river in Morgan County with much of the waterfront lands along the Tennessee River including portions of Flint Creek and Cotaco Creek making up the Wheeler National Wildlife Refuge. The refuge consists of 35,000 acres along the river from Decatur to Huntsville; it extends along the south side of the river from Decatur to near Lacey's Spring in Morgan County, Alabama. The refuge was established to provide wintering habitat for waterfowl migrating south during the colder months of the year. Wheeler National Wildlife Refuge headquarters is located between Priceville and Decatur in Morgan County; the area is primarily a winter resting and feeding site for waterfowl in the Southeastern United States.

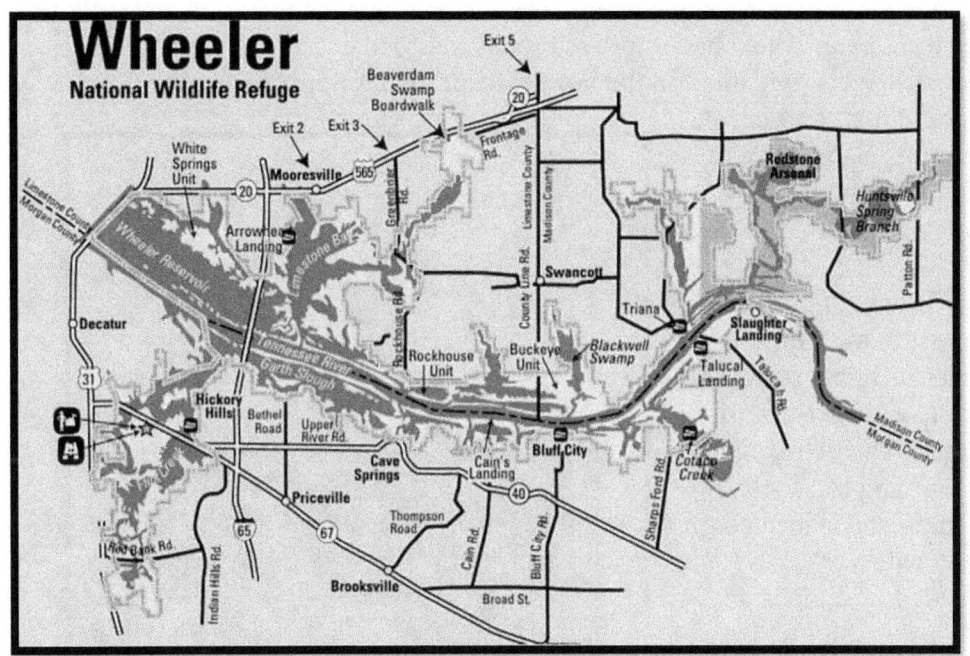

County Court

The first county court for Cotaco County met at the White House in Cotaco. Around 1819, the county seat was moved to Somerville. The Old Cotaco White House was built around 1818, and it was added to the Alabama Register of Landmarks and Heritage on March 8, 1994.

In 1825, the first courthouse built in Somerville was wooden structure. The original courthouse was eventually replaced with a brick building.

In 1837, the Somerville Courthouse located in the Town of Somerville was built with special taxes levied by the Alabama Legislature in 1836. The building replaced the wooden courthouse. For some 72 years, the courthouse at Somerville was used as the seat of government for Morgan County, Alabama.

In 1891, the Somerville county seat of Morgan County, Alabama, was moved to Decatur which had improved roads, railroad access, as well as the Tennessee River navigation on the north side of town. Supposedly, the courthouse records were moved from Somerville to Decatur at night under armed guard.

Somerville Courthouse

Today, the Somerville Courthouse is the oldest original standing courthouse in the State of Alabama. The two-story brick building has a stone foundation and is located on a grassy courtyard surrounded by a low stone wall. The courthouse is an outstanding landmark in Alabama, and follows the federal style of buildings found in the Virginia colony during the late 1700s and early 1800s.

Decatur

Before Decatur came into existence, an old north-south Indian trail ran through the middle of the area. The route was utilized for thousands of years by aboriginal inhabitants to the south who were hunting buffalo, elk, bear, deer, and other game to the north in the Duck, Cumberland, and Ohio River Valleys. Besides hunting, the Indian trail led north from the Tennessee River to the Big Lick or French Lick (Nashville) which was an ancient rendezvous point for trade and barter.

From 1770 through September 1816, the Chickamauga faction of Lower Cherokees lived and controlled the area of Decatur and Morgan County through which the old Indian trail passed. During these historic times, the trail was used by both the Creek and Cherokee as a trade and hunting route to the Big Lick or French Lick on the Cumberland River.

On September 16-18, 1816, the area that became Decatur was relinquished from claims of the Chickasaw and Cherokee by the treaty at Turkey Town. The Cherokee inhabitants of the area agreed to move beyond their new eastern boundary which was the east side of present-day Morgan County. The Chickasaw were not occupying the Decatur area but still had treaty claims; they were settled beyond Caney Creek of present-day Colbert County.

Rhodes Ferry

On July 11, 1818, Dr. Henry W. Rhodes first entered land in the area and established his ferry at the Tennessee River crossing of an old Indian trail. Rhodes Ferry Landing was the name for the early settlement located at the Tennessee River ferry crossing before it became known as Decatur. Prior to Dr. Rhodes, a McDaniel supposedly operated the ferry crossing of the Tennessee River.

The ancient Indian trail through Decatur became known by early settlers as the Old Jasper Road and utilized Rhodes Ferry for folks traveling north and south. The road became a very important north-south route across North Alabama, and it was one of several Mobile to Nashville Traces that was once used by occupying tribes of native people.

From Rhodes Ferry, the Old Jasper Road ran south to Jasper, to the Falls of the Black Warrior or Tuscaloosa River at Northport, Alabama, then on to Mobile or Pensacola. To the north, the old route eventually connected to Athens, Alabama, then to Columbia where it followed the Great South Trail (Old Huntsville Road) to Nashville, Tennessee. Later, portions of the original Indian path through Morgan County and Decatur became known as the Danville Road and eventually Highway 41.

The Rhodes Ferry community was also on an east-west stage coach route known in early records as the Tuscumbia Road. Edmund Kimbell, an early plantation owner, operated an inn on the old stage coach line to the west of

Decatur. The Tuscumbia Road ran concurrent with the former Indian trail of the South River Road or River Road. The road ran east and west from Tuscumbia, Courtland, and Decatur with the ferry crossing leading to Huntsville, Alabama.

The old River Road route from Tuscumbia, Alabama, by-passed the ferry crossing of the Tennessee River at Rhodes Ferry to the south. The River Road continued east of Decatur through Priceville, Alabama. Today, in Morgan and Colbert Counties, the old Indian path is still known as the River Road.

Establishment of Decatur

On January 13, 1820, President James Monroe (4/28/1758-7/4/1831), the fifth president of the United States, in a letter to General John Coffee, the Surveyor-General, reserved a site for the Town of Decatur, Alabama. During that year, the Town of Decatur was also recognized by the State of Alabama. The town was named in honor of Commodore Stephen Decatur Jr. (1/51779-3/22/1820), a distinguished United States Naval officer.

Commodore Stephen Decatur

The location of Decatur was east of the upstream end of the Elk River Shoals which was the eastern most rapids of the great Muscle Shoals of the Big Bend of the Tennessee River. West of Elk River Shoals was Big Muscle Shoals, Little Muscle Shoals, Colbert Shoals, Bee Tree Shoals, and Waterloo Shoals.

The shoals were a barrier to western water navigation of the Tennessee River from Decatur. From Elk River Shoals to Little Muscle Shoals, the river dropped 134 feet vertically in elevation in some 30 miles. That stretch of rapids created very treacherous and dangerous conditions for water navigation. These very hazardous shoals made water passage down the Tennessee River from Decatur impracticable and near impossible without high water.

The original Town of Decatur ran along the Tennessee River for approximately three miles and was some eight miles east of the first upstream shoals. The area chosen for Decatur was relatively flat land that was high enough in elevation that it was above the flood plain of the river.

To the west of town, large cotton plantations took up the flat fertile lands adjacent to the river. The rich alluvial soils to the west of town were ideal for cotton plantations and farming activities. To the south of the town was another old Indian path that became known as the River Road which ran from Chickasaw Island to Tuscumbia Landing. To the east of town, Flint Creek created a barrier for the expansion of Decatur eastward. To the north, the Tennessee River was the boundary of the town.

On June 5, 1820, General Jesse Winston Garth, Dr. Henry W. Rhodes, Isaac Lane, McKinney Holderness, and George Peck entered 1,085 acres of land in Morgan County, Alabama (Cowart, 1981). They purchased the land for the Decatur Land Company which lay in Sections 7, 16, 17, and 18 of Township 5 South and Range 4 West. The streets of Decatur were laid out on the land of the Decatur Land Company and became part of present-day old portion of the town.

Garth, Rhodes, Lane, Holderness, and Peck were the directors of Decatur Land Company, and they were considered the founders of the Town of Decatur. These men were wealthy owners of Black slaves, land speculators, and cotton planters originating from Virginia and North Carolina families. They moved to the Morgan County area to increase their wealth with the free labor of their Black slaves on newly established cotton plantations on the lands taken from the Cherokee and Chickasaw Indians.

On July 9, 1821, the Decatur Land Company made its first deed to a portion of their land. The company sold the first lot to Amos Hardin for $51.00. The parcel was Lot 36 which was adjacent to the river; it was on the corner of Water and Canal Streets.

Jesse Winston Garth was the only slave holder and cotton planter among the first directors of the Decatur Land Company to remain in Decatur. Isaac Lane, McKinney Holderness, and Dr. Henry Rhodes were wealthy cotton planters who left the area for lands opening up farther west, and George Peck died in 1826.

In addition to the five directors of the Decatur Land Company, the following families owned 40 or more Black slaves in the Decatur and Morgan County area: Bibb, Blackwell, Burleson, Collier, Dancy, Davis, Evans, Fennel, Fletcher, Freeman, Garner, Gibbs, High, Johnson, Kelly, Kolb, Lewis, Lile (Lyle), McClaran, Moseley, Murphy, Orr, Price, Rather, Stephenson, Sykes, Thompson, and Troup. These early settlers of large slave owning families played an important and significant role in the early development of the area around Decatur and Morgan County.

From 1819 through 1891, Somerville served as the county seat of government of Morgan County, Alabama. In 1892, the first county seat of Morgan County was changed from Somerville to Decatur. The larger population size, political control, major crossroads, railroad hub, and river access were probably some of the major reasons that the county seat of government was moved from Somerville to Decatur.

Decatur Railroad

On February 11, 1832, at Courtland, Alabama, under the leadership of Colonel Benjamin Sherrod, the Board of Directors accepted the charter of the Tuscumbia and Courtland Railroad. Colonel Sherrod was selected as the first president of the railroad. David Deshler of Tuscumbia was selected as chief engineer, and Dr. Jack Shackelford of Courtland was elected treasurer.

By December 14, 1834, the first rail line south and west of the Appalachians was extended some twenty miles from Courtland to Decatur. The corporation became known as the Tuscumbia, Courtland, and Decatur Railway Company. The purpose of the railroad promoters was to avoid the Muscle Shoals of the Tennessee River which was practically impassible most of the year. From Decatur towards the west to Tuscumbia, the Elk River Shoals, Big Muscle Shoals, and Little Muscle Shoals prevented the safe transportation of cotton down the Tennessee River.

This first railroad system in North Alabama was built primarily for the transportation of the cotton harvested from the vast plantations in the Tennessee Valley; the railroad avoided the dangers posed by the Muscle Shoals. The numerous wealthy cotton planters could utilize the river to get their cotton to Decatur where the cotton was offloaded on to rail cars for transport to Tuscumbia Landing. From Tuscumbia Landing, cotton could be loaded on to river steamers that would transport the cotton to New Orleans then to markets around the world.

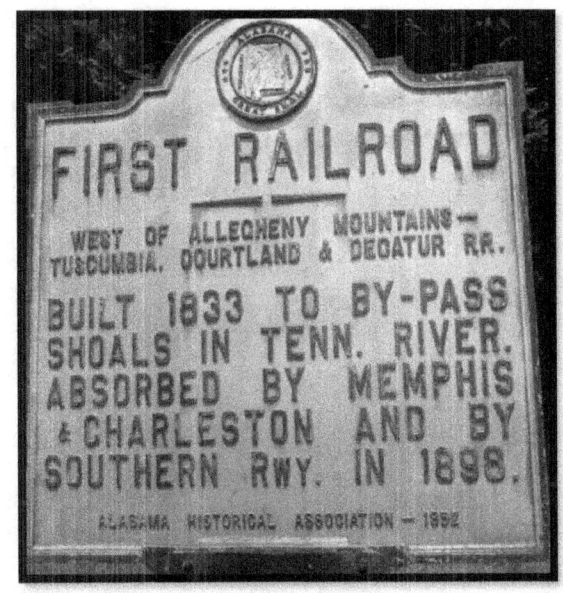

When the railroad ran into financial trouble, Colonel Benjamin Sherrod, whose family operated several cotton plantations in North Alabama, had to pay the entire indebtedness of $300,000.00 to the State of Alabama. The payment was promptly paid by Colonel Sherrod, and the monetary obligation was the largest debt ever made by any individual to the State of Alabama.

This first railroad utilized the power provided by a pair of horses or mules. The rail cars were short and flat, and they were about the size of the old mule pulled wagons. The rail line consisted of cross ties that were laid about every four feet. On top of the ties, wooden stringers with flat strips of iron were nailed in place which created the rails. When the iron rails on top of the stringers would bend up at the end, they were called snake heads and would cause a car to derail. The passengers would be called out by the conductor to nail down the snake head and put the car back on the track. The work fixing the rails and replacing the cars on the track would sometimes take a half a day.

In 1838, the Tuscumbia, Courtland, and Decatur Railway Company purchased the first locomotive engine brought to America by ocean steamer. The engine was delivered to Baltimore, and then by ocean steamer to New Orleans. The

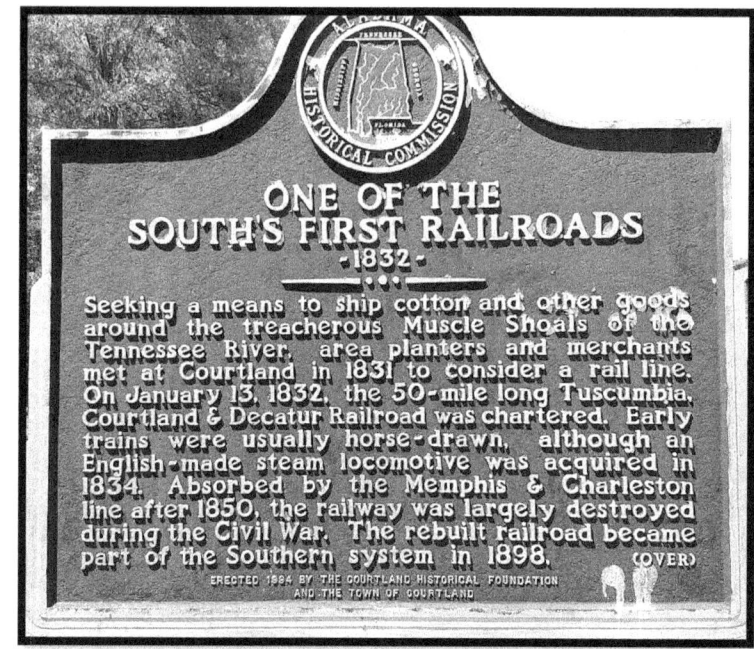

locomotive was transported up the Mississippi River to Paducah, Kentucky, and then transferred to a river steamer to Tuscumbia Landing where it was placed on the railroad tracks.

Prior to the 1838 purchase of the railroad locomotive, a Captain Lawson was the engineer who operated locomotives on the Baltimore Road. When the engine was purchased by the Tuscumbia, Courtland and Decatur Railway Company, Captain Lawson was paid to bring the locomotive to Tuscumbia. Captain Lawson ran the locomotive from Tuscumbia to Decatur until the start of the Civil War.

The old Tuscumbia, Courtland and Decatur Railroad was extended to Stevenson, Alabama, to the east and to Memphis, Tennessee, to the west. The old North Alabama rail line became the third railroad system in the United States; it eventually became a part of the Memphis and Charleston Railroad.

1830's Fulton Train Engine

Indian Removal through Decatur

On May 28, 1830, the Indian Removal Act was passed and provided for the consolidation of Indian lands, the enrollment of the Cherokee for removal, and for the appraisal of Indian owned property. On December 29, 1835, the Treaty of New Echota allowed the forced removal of Cherokee Indians from the southeastern United States. General Winfield Scott and his troops erected stockade forts throughout the Cherokee country to hold Indians detained for removal. Some 17,000 Cherokees were rounded up and held as prisoners until the removal process could begin.

During the 1837-1838 Indian removal, Decatur became the primary offloading point for railroad transportation around the Muscle Shoals for Cherokee Indian people being transported by water west of the Mississippi River to Indian Territory. The great mussel shoals was a barrier to transportation and was the major reason for constructing the Tuscumbia, Courtland, and Decatur Railroad system. Even though the primary purpose was for the transport of cotton and other farm goods around the Muscle Shoals, the railroad became a mechanism for Cherokee Removal during 1837 and 1838.

After completion of the railroad to Decatur, many of the Cherokee contingents removed west were transported in train cars around the shoals from Decatur to Tuscumbia. These Cherokees passed through Hillsboro, Courtland, Town Creek, and Leighton on their way to the Tuscumbia Landing. At the landing, they would board boats for removal to Indian Territory west of the Mississippi River.

Tuscumbia, Courtland, Decatur Railroad

March 7, 1837

On March 7, 1837, a Cherokee contingent was moved by railroad from Decatur through present-day Morgan, Lawrence, and Colbert Counties to Tuscumbia Landing. The first party of Cherokees to be transported from Decatur by railroad consisted of 466 Cherokees, half of whom were children. The following excerpt from page 224 and 225 of Indian Removal by Grant Foreman described the event.

"The boats reached Gunter's Landing on the sixth and were tied up to the island to prevent the Indians from going ashore and getting drunk...The steamer Knoxville was waiting for them here, and when the eleven flatboats were made fast to her, the flotilla set off at nine o'clock on the seventh..."

"On their arrival at Decatur, the Indians were placed on board open cars and compelled to sit in the cold from three-o'clock until dark awaiting the engine that did not arrive. The bewildered Indians who had never before seen a railroad train were left to find a place to sleep. The train of cars from the west was momentarily expected, and the Indians were afraid to lie down for fear of being run over. No lights were furnished them, and they were grouping in the dark, in a pitiful manner, but their humane physician succeeded in having a warehouse opened for them in which they made their beds on the floor for the night. In the morning the emigrants were again placed on the cars that delivered them in Tuscumbia by night. Here they camped awaiting the arrival of the boats that were to take them down the river. While in camp it rained hard and long, the weather was cold and windy, and the Indians were wet, cold, and miserable."

"About ten o'clock on the thirteenth, the steamboat Newark and two keel-boats arrived and moored to the landing near which the Indians encamped; immediately the whole posse of them were in motion bringing their effects to the boats…." (Foreman, 1932).

The rail trip by horse and mule power from Decatur to Tuscumbia took all day. The train probably stopped at each station or had several snake heads to nail down. From Tuscumbia, the group Cherokees traveled on keel boats which were attached to the steamboat Newark; they were then taken to Little Rock and from there to Fort Coffee.

June 9, 1838

On June 9, 1838, another removal contingent of Cherokee Indians arrived in Decatur, Alabama, to be transported around the Muscle Shoals by railroad. The following excerpt from pages 292 and 293 of the book <u>Indian Removal</u> by Grant Foreman described event.

"The boats succeeded without incident in passing through the remainder of the rapids and into smooth water by noon the next day. They ran all that day and night; passed Gunter's Landing at nine o'clock, stopped once to wood and at night landed six miles above Decatur, and such of the people as choose have gone ashore to sleep and cook. Starting early on the morning of the ninth, they reached Decatur at six o'clock to take the train to Tuscumbia but were compelled to remain until the next day. Then, the Indians and their baggage were transferred from the boats to the rail road cars. About 32 cars were necessary to transport the party, and no locomotive engines."

"As the Indians were much crowded on the train the twenty-three soldiers were discharged. The first detachment reached Tuscumbia at three o'clock and boarded the steamboat Smelter which immediately set off for Waterloo at the foot of the rapids without waiting for the second train of cars with the remainder of the party. When the second party reached Tuscumbia, they went into camp awhile awaiting transportation by water. As the guard had been discharged, whisky was introduced among them, much drunkenness resulting, and over one hundred of the emigrants escaped. The remainder was carried by water aboard a keel boat and a small steamer about thirty miles to Waterloo."

June 20, 1838

On June 20, 1838, a third removal contingent of Cherokees arrived in Decatur, Alabama. The following event was found on pages 294 and 295 of Indian Removal by Grant Foreman.

"On June 13, the second party of 875 captive Cherokee Indians departed from Chattanooga in charge of Lieut. R. H. K. Whitley, with five assistant conductors, two physicians, three interpreters, and a hospital attendant. After the preceding day had been spent in organizing the party and reuniting separated families as far as possible, they were placed on six flatboats and dropped down the Tennessee river to Brown's Ferry where more prisoners joined them. For two days, they remained there while clothing was purchased and offered to the Indians who refused to receive it neither would they be mustered, as all attempts to obtain their names were without success."

"When they left there, the flotilla was increased to eight flatboats tied together in pairs these safely negotiated the dangerous rapids and arrived at Kelly's Ferry in the evening. On the morning of the eighteenth with four flatboats moored on each side, the steamboat George Guess continued the descent of the river...."

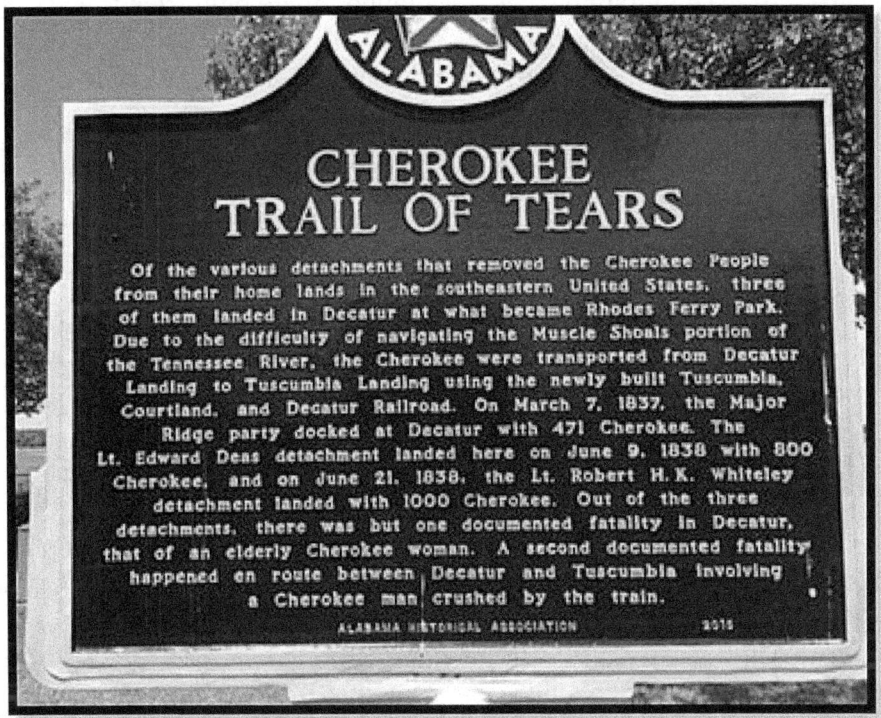

"On the twentieth they arrived at Decatur, and the next morning departed on two trains, arriving at the boat landing below Tuscumbia in the evening. One old woman died at Decatur and a man was killed by the cars when he attempted to rescue his hat. Before reaching Decatur twenty-five Indians had escaped from the party. The emigrants were required to remain at Tuscumbia several days before boats could be secured to carry them over Colbert Shoals, and during their stay two children died. They passed the shoals on the twenty-eighth and encamped opposite Waterloo, Alabama, while awaiting the arrival of the steamboat Smelter. During the stay here, three children died, there was one birth, and 118 Indians escaped."

Removal Conclusion

Even though most of the Cherokees had been forced from the area of Morgan County by 1817, many Indian people being removed had to pass through their former homelands. Since many mixed white settlers were of Cherokee ancestry, escapees of the emigrating Cherokees found refuge with friends and relatives located in the North Alabama area. Many Cherokee mixed-bloods and their descendants assimilated into the general population and avoided removal; today, their descendants remain in North Alabama.

Planters and Slaves

For several years after Indian removal, a mass influx of wealthy white cotton planters with their Black slaves arrived in Morgan County, Alabama, of the Tennessee Valley; the mass migration of White settlers was known as Alabama Fever. The vast majority of the planters originated in Virginia and North Carolina, and they were seeking better land to grow their cotton. The 1816 Indian land cessions by the Chickasaws and Cherokees open vast tracts of land in northwest Alabama, and many of the colonial cotton planters sought the rich farmlands along the Tennessee River, Fox's Creek, Cotaco Creek, and Flint Creek of present-day Morgan County.

The 1820 census was not available for Morgan County; therefore included in the book is information from the 1830, 1840, 1850, and 1860 censuses of Morgan County, Alabama. The census records included many individual slave owners and Black slaves that lived in Morgan County that are not included in this book; only those with 8 or more slaves are listed.

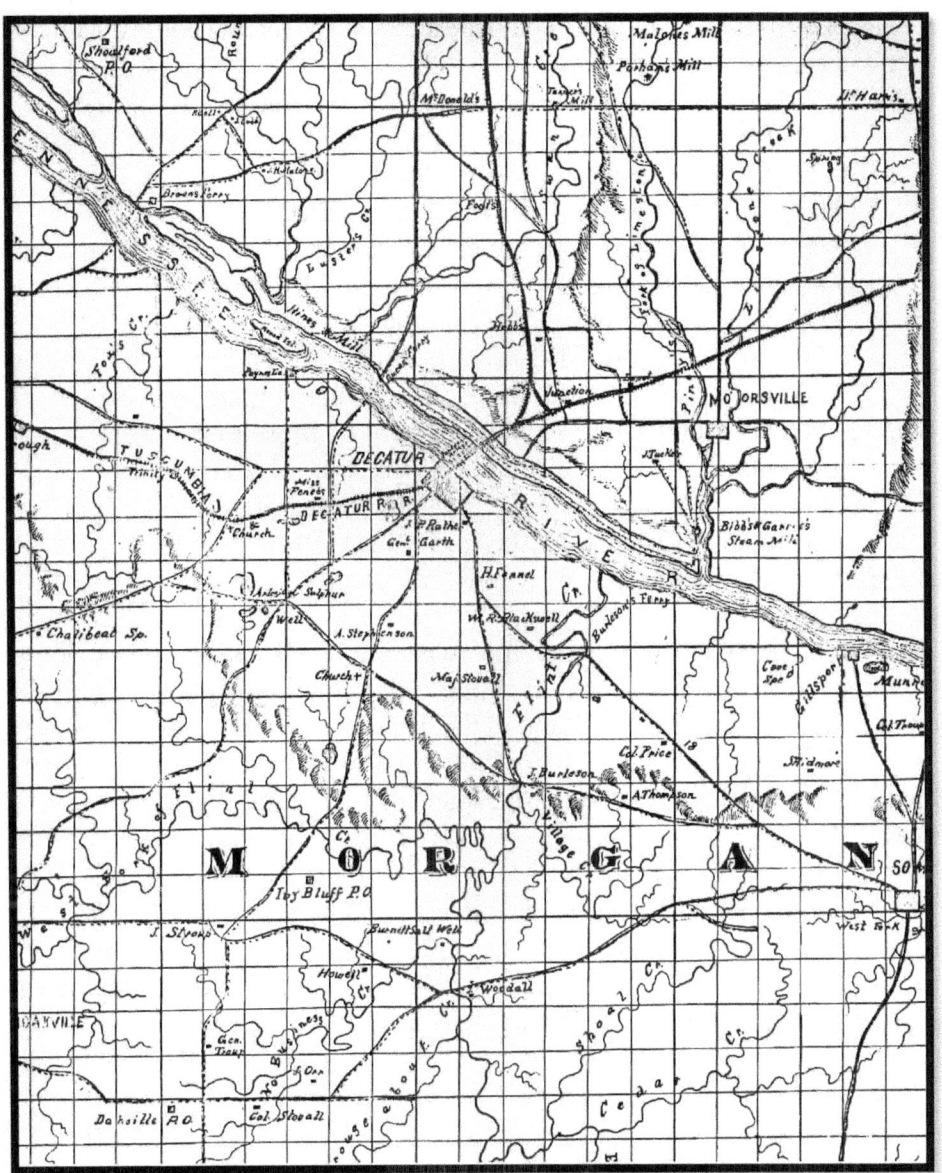

The 1860 Morgan County, Alabama, Agricultural Census identified the wealthiest cotton planters during that year based on their real estate value. The land barons of Morgan County with $20,000.00 or more in property were listed in order of land values and include the number of slaves listed in the 1860 Morgan

County, Alabama, Slave Schedules. The list includes two female cotton planters and slave owners:
1. $35,000.00, 9,700 acres, 182 slaves, Jesse W. Garth;
2. $30,000.00, 980 acres, 50 slaves, Thomas Gibbs;
3. $30,000.00, 1,360 acres, 45 slaves, Thomas Lile;
4. $30,000.00, 2,400 acres, 27 slaves, John W. Peck;
5. $24,000.00, 2,030 acres, 43 slaves, Charles W. Price;
6. $22,000.00, 1,108 acres, 94 slaves, William Moseley;
7. $20,000.00, 1,200 acres, 50 slaves, John A. Lile;
8. $20,000.00, 1,000 acres, 14 slaves, William M. Lundy;
9. $20,000.00, 1,048 acres, 11 slaves, Sarah Fennel Lane Morris;
10. $20,000.00, 1,000 acres, 31 slaves, Drury V. Moseley;
11. $20,000.00, 1,520 acres, 52 slaves, William E. Murphy;
12. $20,000.00, 1,100 acres, 52 slaves, John D. Rather;
13. $20,000.00, 1,150 acres, 20 slaves, Oscar A. Rolfe;
14. $20,000.00, 1,500 acres, 52 slaves, Margaret Thompson.

After 1860, the Civil War ended the ownership of slaves, and many of the Morgan County cotton planters lost everything. However, some planter families managed to hold on to vast tracts of land in the Tennessee River Valley. Today, those prior slave owning families that hold hundreds of acres of land still benefit economically from the land by renting to farmers or by farming the land themselves.

The following tables list the slave owners in alphabetical order by last name and cover the 1830 through 1860 census records for Morgan County, Alabama. Some years of slave ownership, numbers of slaves were missing or not recorded, and very few planters owned slaves over the span of 40 years of reporting.

Morgan County Slave Owners	1830	1840	1850	1860
Acock. John S.			9	
Adair, John T.			8	
Allen, John F.		16	23	
Anderson, James		10		
Arlaugh, Francis	11			
Axton, William		14		
Baker, William E.			8	27
Banks, Sarah	17			
Barnes, Sansea?	9			
Bean, B. F.				18
Bean, John W.				9
Bean, Susan			24	30
Bean, William		8		
Beauchamp, N. H.		17		
Bell, Elisha			12	
Bell, Elizabeth	18	26		
Benson, J. M. J.		9		
Benson, James		22		
Benson, Seaborn			19	
Bibb, Asenith			11	
Bibb, Henry		15		
Bibb, John D.	63			
Bibb, John H.		12		
Binding, Samuel		13		
Blackwell, Augustine S.				39
Blackwell, Martha				11
Blackwell, William Richard			56	
Blair, James H.			15	
Blake, John		8		
Bledsoe, Henry			7	
Bledsoe, Winneford			8	9

51

Morgan County Slave Owners	1830	1840	1850	1860
Boldas, Alexander	10			
Bolling, William T.			7	
Boteler, (Boteles) Alex		12		
Boteler, (Boteles) Alex Jr.		8		
Boteler, Benjamin			6	
Boteler, Nancy			10	
Bouldin, Green Jr.	4			
Bouldin, Green Sr.	16			
Bouldin, James M.		20		
Bouldin (Boling), Richard M.	8	17	33	30
Bouldin, Wiley F.				33
Breeding, James				8
Breeding, Samuel			33	
Breeding, Tabitha				12
Brooks, Milton	21	10		
Brown, Mary				8
Brown, Stewart			9	
Burleson, Aaron A.			7	17
Burleson, Dabney				8
Burleson, Jonathan	20	43	64	49
Burleson, William B.			11	15
Burnett, Greenwell	25			
Burt (Buck), David	10			
Burt, Ann G.		11	15	22
Burt, Henry A.	19		10	13
Burt, James	12			
John Burt, Captain	15	22		
Burt, John L.			11	11
Burt, Joseph J.			7	
Burt, William H.		14	9	8
Bush, David M.			6	9

Morgan County Slave Owners	1830	1840	1850	1860
Bush, Emaline			9	
Calloway, (Galloway) Jabez G.	14	10		
Chapman, Turner		9		
Chunn, M. T.			21	
Clark, J. C.		13		
Collier, Mary J.				8
Collier, Bouldin Carter	41			
Compton, William S.			19	
Condron, John		10		
Cowley, J.		7		
Crayton, Robert		11		
Crockett, John	37			
Crockett, Robert K.			13	
Crow, Francis	6			
Dallas, Dennis	23			
Dancy, C. F. M.				15
Dancy, David M.		15		
Dancy, Jane E.				16
Dancy, William	63			
Darwin Estate			11	
Darwin, Cealy		19		
Davis, Allen				19
Davis, F. M.				19
Davis, Nicholas	57			
Davis, Riley S.		27	16	
Dean, Dudley				12
Delvach ?, A. B.		19		
Dent, Hutcheson		16		
Dillard, Samuel			9	
Dinsmore, James J.	11		8	7
Donaldson, Thomas				12

Morgan County Slave Owners	1830	1840	1850	1860
Dossey, James		16		
Downs, Daniel			8	
Draper, David		9	19	13
Draper, Lucinda				11
Dunn, Jackson				15
Dupree, Allen	16			
Elliott, William	16			
Ellison, Jesse	18			
Evans, Franklin			6	
Evans, Nathaniel		18	47	
Farley, Henry R.			8	
Fennel, Henry W.			35	55
Fennel, Mary C.			31	
Fennel, Sarah	30			
Ferguson, John Y.			6	9
Fields, Jackson			7	18
Fletcher, Nathan			30	
Fletcher, Susan R.				40
Ford, Jonathan			6	
Ford, Middleton			7	
Ford, Thomas		29		
Fowler, John			8	
Freeman, Fleming	51			
Freeman, Laban T.	13	17		
Friend, Sarah	30			
Garner, Lawson		25	68	69
Garner, Thomas				15
Garth, Jesse Winston	139	167	189	182
Gibbs, Thomas				50
Gilbert, T. R.		8		
Gilbert, Wyatt	10			

Morgan County Slave Owners	1830	1840	1850	1860
Gill, William G.-Phillip Gill, Agent			18	36
Ginn, W. R.				15
Gizzard, William			17	28
Goff, Martha F.	13			
Graham, Nancy T.			11	
Grantland, T. E.-Trust for minor heirs				16
Green (Greene), Heran	13	9	2	
Green (Greene), Wilson			6	
Grizzard, Henry			8	10
Hamilton, Degan	16			
Harper, Wm. D.-guardian minor heirs				16
Harris, Albert H.				8
Hart, Thomas		11		
Hartselle, George				8
Haslett, Samuel			8	11
Hawkins, William		8		
Henston, Matthew C.	9			
Herring, Joseph		11	17	22
Hewlett (Hulett), Augustine A.	8		4	10
High, Henry A.	18	18	42	
Hill, Henry			11	
Hobbs, James R.				9
Holderness, McKinney	30			
Holladay (Holliday), Edward			21	
Hubbard, Thomas	13			
Hudson, Robert			7	12
Humphreys (Humphries), Samuel B.				16
Humphreys, Carlish	14	22		
Hunter, Edward			8	
Jackson, Isaac			11	
Jackson, J. M.				14

Morgan County Slave Owners	1830	1840	1850	1860
Jackson, Sarah				15
Jesse, H. David		11		
Johnson, Benjamin	8	23	18	
Johnson, David		13		
Johnson, Henry				12
Johnson, Hy	19			
Johnson, Mary		8		
Johnson, Robert Jr.				7
Johnson, Robert M.		16	52	25
Johnson, Roland T.			5	
Johnson, Washington			7	
Johnson, Weneford			12	
Johnson, William		9	12	
Johnson, Williamson		28		
Johnston, J. D.				8
Jones, Signal ?,		14		
Jones, William		11		
Kaizer, Andrew		8	17	
Kelly, Gains	44			
Kennon, A. W.			9	
Key, J.		16		
Key, Pleasant R.	13		20	
Key, William				8
Kimble (Kimbell), Edmond	23	21	28	
Kimble (Kimbell), Nancy			28	
Kimble, E. N. S.				22
Kimble, James	27	36		
Kimble, Nathan	13			
King, John			27	
Kirkland, Daniel		8	9	9
Kolb, David G.-J. McDowell-Agent				41

Morgan County Slave Owners	1830	1840	1850	1860
Kolb, James			20	
Kolb, Joseph	17	49	13	
Lacy, Thomas H.			33	
Lane, Isaac	28			
Lane, Jesse A.	12			
Lane, Jonathan		12	9	
Lane, Joseph	18			
Lanier, Thomas L. or S.		10		
Lewis, John O. and Z. R.				96
Lewis, Nicholas		66	100	
Lile (Lyle), Byler	21			
Lile (Lyle), John Allison				50
Lile (Lyle), Peyton		34		
Lile (Lyle), Thomas	19	30	52	45
Lindsay, Mark		18		
Lipscomb, Jason		8	7	
Long, Solomon S.			6	21
Lundy, Rachel A.		11		
Lundy, William M.			9	14
Lynn, Ausburn (Osborn)		10		
Marks, John S.				11
Martin, Dabney A.	19	17	22	
Matkin, Thomas Crow.	30			
Matthews, William Washington				18
McCarley, David			8	
McCartney, Alexander A.		8	8	12
McClanahan, John		42		
McClanahan, Sarah		23		
McClaron (McClaran), Charles		48		
McClellan, John J.			6	
McClellan, Matthew W.	5			

Morgan County Slave Owners	1830	1840	1850	1860
McClure, J. G.		11		
McCroskey, John			34	24
McCutcheon, Martha			6	9
McDaniel, John				16
McDaniel, Lucy J.				9
McDaniel, William		7	6	8
McDonald, William			9	
McGee, J.		18		
McKenzie (McKinsey), John	10	10		
McKinky, Francis	9			
Miller, John	9			
Minor, L. T.				15
Minor, Mrs. F. T.				23
Minor, William T.		10	23	
Minter, Josiah			9	
Mitchell, Drury			11	
Mitchell, Joseph				8
Morell, William		7	12	
Morris (Morriss), John J.			6	
Morris, Sarah A. Fennel Lane			13	11
Morrow, William			7	13
Moseley, Drury V.			15	31
Moseley, John P.		20	22	34
Moseley, Temperance		43		
Moseley, William	86			
Moseley, William Jr.			50	94
Murphy (Murphey), George	22	31		
Murphy (Murphey), James J.				21
Murphy (Murphey), Nathan K.			31	
Murphy (Murphey), Smith	24			
Murphy (Murphey), William E.		10	1	52

Morgan County Slave Owners	1830	1840	1850	1860
Murphy (Murphey), Williamson	9			
Neal, Davis		17		
Nelson, Greenberry	10			
Nevill (Nevell), James A.				9
Nevill (Nevell), Mary			7	
Nevill (Nevell), Osmond J.		14	17	
Nevill (Nevell), R. B.				12
Nevill (Nevell), Sterling M.				12
Neville (Nevell), H. S.				9
Newman, William	10			
Norton, A. M.		19		
Norwood, Theophilus		8	10	
Norwood, Thomas				8
Oden, John H.		13		
Odham, Henry	17			
Orr, Cynthia			14	36
Orr, Elizabeth		8		
Orr, Henrietta C.				5
Orr, John	28	37	32	
Orr, John C.			8	23
Orr, Jonathan		30	43	7
Orr, Nathan	8			
Orr, Phillip L.				17
Orr, Sarah A.				26
Orr, Watkins	8	27		
Orr, William W.				20
Orr, Willis F.			20	42
Ortnie ?, M.		8		
Owen, John	12			
Pate, Susannah	19			
Peck, John W.			18	27

Morgan County Slave Owners	1830	1840	1850	1860
Perry (Parry), Aaron	23			
Pettus, Elizabeth				8
Peyton, Thomas	23			
Philpot, Benjamin A.			8	
Philpot, Horatio			6	
Pope, A. E.		13		
Pope, Etheldred W.		9	1	
Potete, Hiram			6	
Price, Charles W.		14	36	43
Ragland, Samuel				18
Rather, John D.			15	52
Rather, John T.			11	
Ratliff, Hezekiah S.	22			
Ratliff, James			6	
Ratliff, Robert			12	
Reed, William	50	14		
Reeves (Reaves), Jehabed	9			
Reeves, Hickerson			6	
Rhodes, Henry W.	91			
Rice, George W.		13		
Rice, Green P.			8	
Roberts, J. F.				24
Robinson, John D.			10	9
Roby, William W.		32		
Rogers (Rodgers), Elizabeth			6	10
Rogers, George W. A.			10	
Rogers, William A. Sr.	13	18	7	
Rolfe, Oscar A.			20	20
Rolin, Robert			7	
Ross, Alexander		10		
Russell, Christopher			11	

Morgan County Slave Owners	1830	1840	1850	1860
Russell, John H.				9
Russell, Martha			7	
Russell, William		20		
Ryan, Thomas			10	
Ryan, William				12
Sacey ?, Polly	16			
Sanders (Sander), Thomas W.	10			
Sawyers, James		7	8	
Scruggs, Finch P.			10	
Scruggs, Henry F.			9	
Serney, Daniel	10			
Sewel, William			6	
Sharpley, Wallace L.				9
Simpson, James			7	
Simpson, Rubin			5	
Simpson, Stephen				16
Skidmore, Abraham	11			
Slaughter, William A.	10			
Smith, Catharine			20	23
Smith, James L.	16	36		
Socey?, Thomas	23			
Speaks, Wiley			10	
Stanback, Dixon	26			
Stanback, Edward B.		10		
Stephenson, Arthur	13	27	41	
Stephenson, E.				9
Stephenson, William				19
Stewart (Stuart), Jacob	8			
Stewart (Stuart), John			7	
Stewart (Stuart), Robert A.		8	10	17
Stone, T. B.		16		

Morgan County Slave Owners	1830	1840	1850	1860
Stovall (Storadle), Blis	28			
Stovall, Drury (Dewey)	8	20	22	
Stovall, Peter	26	5	6	
Stow, John	21			
Strain, Thomas A.		16	14	12
Sutherland, John	20			
Sykes, James S.		12		
Sykes, James T.	46			
Sykes, Joseph	38	45		
Sykes, L. B.		64		
Sykes, William A.		67		
Talifero, Porchy ?	16			
Tapscott, John T.			6	
Tate, James	30			
Taylor, Thomas	9			
Templeton, Archibald	10			
Terry, David		13		
Terry, Henry H.		8		
Terry, Matilda				11
Terry, William Price		23		
Thomas, J. G.		37		
Thompson, Edward and Margaret	30	21	37	52
Thompson, Edward N.			29	44
Thompson, Elbert H.	31			
Thompson, John A.		17	4	
Thompson, Robert A.		26	48	58
Thompson, William	27			
Thurman, John	53	17		
Todd, James M.				10
Troup (Troop), E. J. S.				33
Troup (Troop), John Jr.			36	

Morgan County Slave Owners	1830	1840	1850	1860
Troup (Troop), John Sr.	14	39		
Troup (Troop), Matthew W.			15	40
Troup (Troop), Walter	9			
Tucker, Charles		9	10	
Turner, Harry B.			8	
Turner, Nancy			10	
Turney, Daniel			15	
Turney, George B.				8
Turney, Joseph Sr.		12	18	10
Turney, William				13
Turrentine, James	16			
Walden, Rheasha (Racia) N.			7	
Wallis, John McKnitt A.	18			
Wallis, Joseph	9			
Watkins, William			10	
Watts, William T.				17
Welch, Catharine			16	
Wiggins, George			8	
Wiggins, Jacob L.				9
Wiggins, James	21	29		
Wiggins, Jessie			6	
Wiggins, Mary			11	
Wiggins, Susan			25	
Williams, John W.			15	10
Williams, Thomas R.			9	
Williams, William			35	
Wilson, Greenberry	10	20	23	25
Winton, Susan			10	
Wise, Edward			31	28
Wise, James			11	17
Wolf, David			11	

Morgan County Slave Owners	1830	1840	1850	1860
Wolf, Martha				20
Wood, Aaron		34		
Wood, Jonas C.	12	17		

Bibb, John D.

On March 10, 1788, John Dandridge Bibb was born in Prince Edward County, Virginia; he was the son of William Bibb and Sally Wyatt. He was a brother of William Wyatt Bibb and Thomas Bibb, the first two governors of Alabama.

On June 14, 1810, John Dandridge Bibb entered 160.66 acres of land in Section 26 of Township 3 South and Range 1 West in Madison County. On June 13, 1811, John entered another 160 acres of land in Section 6 of Township 3 South and Range 1 East in Madison County of Mississippi Territory (Cowart, 1979). Based on his land records, it appears that John D. Bibb was in Madison County of Mississippi Territory by the summer of 1810.

On May 6, 1812, John Dandridge Bibb married Mary Xenia Oliver at Petersburg in Elbert County, Georgia. Mary was born on September 18, 1799; the daughter of John Thompson and Frances Oliver, natives of Petersburg, Virginia.

John Dandridge Bibb and Mary Xenia Oliver Bibb had 14 children, but only six lived to adulthood (Saunders, 1899).
1. Charles Sydney Bibb was born in Petersburg, Georgia, on April 2, 1813, and he died on July 8, 1813.
2. Elvira Antoinette Bibb was born in Madison County on September 6, 1814; she married Dr. Samuel Booth Malone on April 2, 1833. They lived in Columbus, Mississippi, and had three children: Ellen Booth married William Gibson, and she died in Matagorda, Texas, about 1864; Selwyn B. Booth who was killed at the second battle of Manassas; and, Antoinette Booth married Alfred Glover of Alabama.

3. Sarah Frances Bibb was born in Madison County on September 26, 1816; she died at Sharon in Montgomery County, Alabama, on September 19, 1821.
4. Mary Dandridge Bibb was born in Montgomery County in Alabama Territory on March 17, 1818; she died on October 14, 1821.
5. William Crawford Bibb Sr. was born in Montgomery County, Alabama, on January 1, 1820. William first married Priscilla A. Sims of Tuscaloosa, Alabama, on May 11, 1842; their children were Cornelia D. Bibb, John Dandridge Bibb, and Mary Frances Bibb. In 1853, William married a second time to Rebecca Lanier Harris, daughter of General Jeptha Harris; their children were William Crawford Bibb Jr. and Sallie Hunt Bibb. William Crawford Bibb Sr. died in Montgomery on May 23, 1896.
6. Edwin Augustus Bibb was born on January 11, 1822; he died on September 28, 1835.
7. Lavinia Arabella Bibb was born on January 20, 1824; she died on October 28, 1825.
8. John Dandridge Bibb was born in Morgan County, Alabama, on November 14, 1826; he died on August 27, 1827.
9. Dandridge Asbury Bibb was born in Morgan County, Alabama November 10, 1827; he married Emma Taylor in 1849. Dandridge became a medical doctor; he died in 1861 leaving three children, Elizabeth Sophia Bibb, Laura E. Bibb and Dandridge A. Bibb.
10. Algernon Sidney Bibb was born in Morgan County on January 4, 1829; he married Mary E. Carraway in 1841, by whom he had two children; Mary Katharine who married Van Lyttle, and Charles C. Bibb. In 1876, Algernon Sidney Bibb married Miss Hoad of Murfreesboro, Tennessee, and they lived in Phillips County, Arkansas; they had four children.
11. Mary Cornelia Bibb was born in Columbus, Mississippi, on April 26, 1832; she was a twin to a still-born infant, and she died on September 5, 1832.
12. Laura Angerone Bibb was born at Columbus, Mississippi, on October 19, 1833; she married Henry L. Rogers in 1852. Laura died in Tuskegee, Alabama, in July 1866.

John Dandridge Bibb became a lawyer, legislator, judge, slave owner, and cotton planter. In 1818, he moved from Madison County to Montgomery County; by 1830, he was living in Morgan County, Alabama.

On February 2, 1818, John Dandridge Bibb entered 80.16 acres of land in Madison County of Alabama Territory. His land entry was in Section 30 of Township 4 South and Range 1 West (Cowart, 1979). Then on July 13, 1818, John Dandridge Bibb entered two tracts of land in Morgan County, Alabama, with Nathaniel W. Dandridge. One parcel was 157.59 acres and the other tract of land was 78.8 acres both of which were located in Section 12 of Township 6 South and Range 4 West in Morgan County (Cowart, 1981).

In 1818, John Dandridge Bibb moved to Montgomery, Alabama, where he was judge of the territorial court. John was also a member of the constitutional convention of 1819.

John Dandridge Bibb
3/10/1788-5/9/1848

In 1822, John Dandridge Bibb served as an Alabama State senator from Montgomery County, Alabama. After his time as a state senator from Montgomery, John moved back to Morgan County by 1826.

In the 1830 Morgan County, Alabama Census, John Dandridge Bibb was listed with two White males between 0 and five years old, one White male between five and 10 years old, one White male between 10 and 15 years old, one White male between 40 and 50 years old, one White female between 15 and 20 years old, and one White female between 30 and 40 years old.

In 1830 in Morgan County, Alabama Census, John D. Bibb owned 39 Black male slaves and 24 Black female slaves for a total of 63 slaves. He became a cotton planter in Morgan County, and he entered additional property adjacent to his land that he and Nathaniel W. Dandridge had entered in 1818.

On June 6, 1830, and June 21, 1831, John Dandridge Bibb entered two additional tracts of land in Section 12 of Township 6 South and Range 4 West in Morgan County, Alabama (Cowart, 1981). One parcel was 78.8 acres and the other was 157.59 acres, respectfully; both pieces of land were located in Section 12 of Morgan County.

In 1832, John Dandridge Bibb moved his family and slaves to his new cotton plantation on the Yazoo River in Carroll County, Mississippi. He became a very successful and wealthy cotton planter in Mississippi.

On October 13, 1846, Mary Xenia Oliver Bibb died in Carroll County, Mississippi. In less than two years, on May 9, 1848, John Dandridge Bibb died on his Mississippi cotton plantation. They were originally buried in Mississippi, but their son William Crawford Bibb had their remains reinterred in Montgomery, Alabama.

Blackwell, Samuel Jr.

In 1774, Samuel Blackwell Jr. (1774-1849) was born, in Fauquier County, Virginia, to Samuel Blackwell Sr. and Elizabeth Tyler Blackwell (1755-1828). In 1828, Elizabeth Tyler Blackwell died, and she was buried in the Blackwell Family Graveyard in Decatur, Alabama.

Samuel Blackwell Jr. came to Alabama with his younger brother William Henry Blackwell. Based on census records, it appears that the families of Samuel and William Henry Blackwell came from Fauquier County, Virginia, to South Carolina, Georgia, and then to the Tennessee River area of Limestone and Morgan Counties of North Alabama. The route of the two brothers was based on the birth children listed in census records.

On February 7, 1818, Samuel Blackwell Jr. entered 180 acres in Section 13 of Township 5 South and Range 3 West in Limestone County, Alabama. Samuel entered the Northwest ¼, and his brother, William Henry Blackwell, entered the Southwest ¼ in the southeast corner of Limestone County; the land they entered was adjacent to the west county line of southwest Madison County (Cowart, 1984).

Before 1821, Samuel Blackwell Jr. (1774-1849) married Sarah M. Dent (1798-1881); she was born in Maryland. Samuel was 24 years older than Sarah.

On April 28, 1828, Samuel Blackwell Jr. entered 158.59 acres of land in the Southwest ¼ of Section 31 of Township 5 South and Range 2 West in Madison County, Alabama.

On July 22, 1830, Samuel Blackwell Jr. entered 78.54 acres of land in the West ½ of the Southeast ¼ of Section 30 of Township 5 South and Range 2 West in Madison County, Alabama (Cowart, 1979).

According to the 1830 Limestone County, Alabama, United States Census, Samuel Blackwell Jr. owned 36 Black slaves. Also listed near Samuel Blackwell Jr. was his brother William H. Blackwell who owned 39 Black slaves.

On April 29, 1831, Samuel Blackwell Jr. entered 157.07 acres of land in the Southwest ¼ of Section 30 of Township 5 South and Range 2 West in Madison County, Alabama (Cowart, 1979).

In the 1840 Limestone County, Alabama, United States Census, Samuel Blackwell Jr. owned 42 slaves in Limestone County. In 1840, William H. Blackwell owned 60 black slaves. Together, the two Blackwell brothers owned 102 slaves in Limestone County.

In 1849, according to tombstone records, Samuel Blackwell Jr. died, and Sarah Dent Blackwell died in 1881. Samuel Blackwell Jr. and Sarah Dent Blackwell are buried at Blackwell Cemetery in Morgan County, Alabama.

William Richard Blackwell

On August 31, 1820, William Richard Blackwell was born to Samuel Blackwell Jr. and Sarah Dent Blackwell. Census records indicated that William Richard Blackwell was born in Georgia.

William Richard Blackwell married Martha W. Collier; she was born about 1825. Martha was the daughter of Dr. James Bouldin Collier who was born on June 16, 1795, in Lunenburg County, Virginia. James Bouldin Collier was the son of James Collier (1755-1832) and Elizabeth Bouldin (1763-1828) of Virginia.

By February 4, 1818, James Bouldin Collier, father-in-law of William Richard Blackwell, had migrated with his family to Madison County of Alabama Territory. James Collier, father James Bouldin Collier, had entered large tracts of land around Triana where he established his Myrtle Grove cotton plantation.

On June 3, 1819, James Bouldin Collier married Sarah Ladd; she was probably the mother of Martha W. Collier, wife of William Richard Blackwell. On June 5, 1828, James Bouldin Collier and Francis Slaughter were married in Morgan County, Alabama. James B. Collier was the brother-in-law to William Henry Blackwell who was the brother of Samuel Blackwell Jr., the father of William Richard Blackwell.

On March 21, 1833, James B. Collier entered 39.88 acres in the southeast ¼ of the northeast ¼ of Section 25 of Township 7 South and Range 4 West in Morgan County, Alabama (Cowart, 1981). On May 9, 1839, James Bouldin Collier died in Limestone County, Alabama.

William Richard Blackwell and Martha W. Collier Blackwell had the following children:
1. Reuben Blackwell
2. J. Stanton Blackwell 1845-1845
3. Eugenia Blackwell 1846-1846
4. Samuel Blackwell 1848-1918
5. William R. Blackwell 1850-1851
6. James W. Blackwell 1852-1852
7. James C. Blackwell 1855-1856.

According to the November 13, 1850, Division 10, Morgan County, Alabama Census, Household 105, William R. Blackwell was a 29 year old farmer born in Georgia. His farm was valued at $10,000. Also living in the household with William was his wife, Martha W. Collier a 25 year old female born in Alabama. William's mother, Sarah M. a 52 year old female born in Maryland, also lived in the household of her son. The census also identified Augustine S. a 16 year old male student born in Alabama, Reubin W. a six year old male born in Alabama, Samuel a two year old male born in Alabama, and John Allen a 26 year old male overseer born in Alabama.

Augustine S. Blackwell was probably the son of Samuel Blackwell Jr. and Sarah M. Dent Blackwell. Find A Grave says that Augustine was the son of William Richard Blackwell; however, if that was true when Augustine was born, William Richard Blackwell would have been 13 years old and Martha W. Collier Blackwell would have been nine years old which would be highly unlikely.

In the 1850 Morgan County, Alabama Slave Schedule, William R. Blackwell owned 56 slaves. His slaves included 53 being Black and three Mulatto slaves. Mulattos were usually the offspring of a White male slave owner and his Black female slave.

On January 4, 1855, William R. Blackwell entered 40 acres in Section 6 of Township 7 South and Range 1 East; this land was on the eastern edge of Morgan County near the old Cherokee boundary established in 1816. On January 4, 1855, William entered another 40 acres in Section 6 of Township 7 South and Range 1 West in Morgan County, Alabama (Cowart, 1981).

On October 7, 1857, at the age of 37 years old, William Richard Blackwell passed away in Morgan, Alabama. William was buried in the Blackwell Family Cemetery at Decatur in Morgan County, Alabama (Find A Grave Memorial Number 32409858).

In 1860, Martha W. Collier Blackwell, wife of William Richard Blackwell, was listed as owning 11 Black slaves.

Augustine S. Blackwell

About 1834, Augustine S. Blackwell was probably born in Limestone County, Alabama, since his father Samuel Blackwell Jr. was living in Limestone between 1830 and 1840. More than likely Augustine S. Blackwell was the son of Samuel Blackwell Jr. and Sarah M. Dent Blackwell.

According to the July 20 and 22, 1860, Morgan County, Alabama Census, Page 343A, P. O. Flint River/Decatur, Augustine S. Blackwell was a 25 year old male farmer. In 1860, the value of his real estate was $12,000 and his personal property was valued at $40,000.

In 1860, living in the household of Augustine S. Blackwell was Sarah M. Dent Blackwell (widow of Samuel Blackwell Jr.) a 62 year old female housekeeper born in Maryland. Augustine was more than likely the son of Sarah M. Dent Blackwell who was living in his household.

According to the 1860 Morgan County, Alabama Slave Schedule, Augustine S. Blackwell owned 39 slaves with 36 being Black and three Mulatto slaves of these 19 were female and 20 were male. Augustine was listed as having 10 slave houses at his plantation.

According to the 1860 Morgan County, Alabama, Agricultural Census, Augustine S. Blackwell owned 500 acres of improved land and 820 acres of unimproved land worth $12,000.00. He also owned $250.00 worth of farm equipment and $2,000.00 worth of livestock.

Blackwell Family Cemetery

The Blackwell Family Cemetery is located in Morgan County at 2401 Country Club Road Southeast, Decatur, Alabama, 35601. The cemetery is near the tennis courts located behind the Decatur Country Club. In a 1934 Tennessee Valley Authority (TVA) map, there were only three tombstones among some 20 graves. Even though most of the grave stones were removed or destroyed years ago, a large stone monument near the entrance contains on all four sides the names of those who are supposedly buried in the cemetery that do not have a tombstone. The cemetery is surrounded by a chain link fence.

Blackwell, William Henry

On November 27, 1792, William Henry Blackwell was born, in Fauquier County, Virginia. He was the son of Samuel Blackwell Sr. and Elizabeth Tyler Blackwell (1755-1828), and he was a brother of Samuel Blackwell Jr.

On December 14, 1817, William Henry Blackwell married Eliza Wyatt Collier who was born on May 21, 1797. Eliza was the daughter of James Collier and Elizabeth Bouldin of Virginia who were married on July 3, 1788. Elizabeth Bouldin Collier was born on February 13, 1763, and died in Madison County, Alabama, on February 23, 1828. Elizabeth was the daughter of James Bouldin and Sally Watkins of Charlotte County, Virginia.

William Henry Blackwell and Eliza Wyatt Collier Blackwell had the following children:
1. Bouldin C. Blackwell, 12/16/1818-10/13/1859, (Find A Grave Memorial Number 70347643)
2. Martha Wyatt Blackwell Pickett, 10/20/1833-1/24/1897, (Find A Grave Memorial Number 50983134)
3. William Henry Blackwell, 1835-1899, (Find A Grave Memorial Number 184346066)
4. Mary Ann Battle Blackwell Wiggs, 1/16/1838-2/28/1875, (Find A Grave Memorial Number 160002219)

On February 4, 1818, William Henry Blackwell entered 78.94 acres of land in the West ½ of the Southeast ¼ of Section 19 of Township 5 South and Range 2 West in Madison County of Alabama Territory (Cowart, 1979). On July 30, 1830, William Henry Blackwell entered 78.54 acres of land in the East ½ of the Southwest ¼ of Section 19 of Township 5 South and Range 2 West in Madison County, Alabama (Cowart, 1979).

On February 7, 1818, William Henry Blackwell entered 180 acres of land in the Southwest ¼ of Section 13 of Township 5 South and Range 3 West in Limestone County, Alabama. Samuel Jr., brother of William Henry Blackwell entered the Northwest ¼; the land the brothers entered was in the southeast corner of Limestone County and was adjacent to the west county line of southwest Madison County (Cowart, 1984).

On June 6, 1830, William Henry Blackwell entered 78.54 acres of land in Section 30 of Township 5 South and Range 2 West in Madison County, Alabama (Cowart, 1979). The land he entered was adjacent to land of his father-in-law, James Collier.

According to the 1830 Limestone County, Alabama, United States Census, William Henry Blackwell owned 39 Black slaves. Also listed near William was his brother Samuel Blackwell Jr. who owned 36 slaves in 1830. In 1830, James Collier, the father-in-law of William Henry Blackwell, owned 55 Black slaves in Madison County, Alabama; James Collier died on August 20, 1832.

On June 3, 1831, William Henry Blackwell entered 160 acres of land in the Northwest ¼ of Section 14 of Township 6 South and Range 2 West in Morgan County, Alabama. On November 28, 1832, William Henry Blackwell entered 40 acres of land in the Northeast ¼ of the Northeast ¼ of Section 14 of Township 6 South and Range 2 West in Morgan County, Alabama (Cowart, 1981).

On June 12, 1837, William Henry Blackwell entered 162.18 acres of land in Section 28 of Township 4 South and Range 2 West in Madison County, Alabama (Cowart, 1979). The same tract of land had been entered by his brother-in-law Charles Collier on July 6, 1830.

On November 26, 1846, William Henry Blackwell died in Morgan County, Alabama. He was buried in the Blackwell-Collier Cemetery in Limestone County, Alabama (Find A Grave Memorial Number 70347693).

On July 25, 1856, Eliza Wyatt Collier Blackwell died. She was the wife of William Henry Blackwell and daughter of James and Elizabeth Collier. Eliza Wyatt Collier Blackwell was buried in the Blackwell-Collier Cemetery in Limestone County, Alabama (Find A Grave Memorial Number 70347757).

Bouldin, Captain Green

On October 2, 1767, Green Bouldin was born at Drake's Branch in Charlotte County, Virginia. The parents of Green Bouldin were Thomas Bouldin and Martha Matilda Moseley Bouldin. On January 1, 1742, Martha was born in Charlotte County, Virginia; she was the daughter of Edward Moseley and Amey Green. Martha was a sister to Richard Moseley, Mary Moseley Goode, Amey Moseley Collier, Hillery Moseley, William Moseley, Elizabeth Moseley, Letitia Moseley Herndon, Arthur Moseley, Sally Moseley Patrick and Rebecca Moseley Johnston. Martha Matilda Moseley married Thomas Bouldin in 1758. Thomas and Martha Moseley Bouldin had the following children: Thomas Bouldin III,

Green Bouldin, William Bouldin, Mary Bouldin, Martha Patsy Bouldin Moseley, and Nancy Clark Bouldin Potter, and Mary Bouldin Rowland. Sometimes after 1808, Martha Moseley Bouldin died in Henry County, Virginia.

On April 28, 1791, Green Bouldin married Mary "Polly" Graves in Henry County, Virginia; she was born about 1773 in Pittsylvania County, Virginia. Mary was the daughter of William and Mary Graves of Henry County, Virginia. Mary was a descendant of Captain Thomas Graves, who served as a Representative of the First Assembly in Jamestown, Virginia, in 1619.

Green Bouldin and Mary Matilda Moseley Bouldin had the following children:
1. Colonel William Graves Bouldin was born on March 21, 1792, in Henry County, Virginia. He married Elizabeth Purnell Hammond on July 11, 1821, in Madison County, Alabama. William served as a Captain in the Alabama State Militia in the War of 1812, and rose to the rank of Colonel before the end of the war. William helped organize the Democratic Party in Alabama before moving to Texas in 1850. In 1855, Elizabeth Hammond Bouldin died and was buried near their home in Bouldin-Routt Cemetery. William died on September 30, 1857; he was buried beside his wife in Bouldin-Routt Cemetery at Chappell Hill in Washington County, Texas (Find A Grave Memorial Number 70839952).
2. Richard T. Bouldin was born in December 1793 in Henry County, Virginia.
3. Captain James Massey Bouldin was born on March 13, 1795; he died in Morgan County, Alabama, on October 21, 1844.
4. Green Bouldin Jr. was born in 1796; he died after 1883.
5. Thomas U. Bouldin was born about 1798 in Henry County, Virginia.
6. Mary Bouldin Majors was born February 8, 1799, in Henry County, Virginia. She married Noble L. Majors on May 18, 1820, in Bedford County, Tennessee; Mary died October 4, 1852.
7. Amey Green Bouldin was born about 1800; she married Thomas Payne on January 13, 1816, in Henry County, Virginia. Amey was buried in the Payne Cemetery in Henry County, Virginia.
8. Elizabeth Bouldin was born about 1802; she married Frederick Hood. According to the 1830 Lawrence County, Alabama Census, Frederick

Hood, husband of Elizabeth Bouldin, had eight Whites and four Black slaves

9. Massey Bouldin was born about 1804.

On land given to him by his father, Green Bouldin first farmed land in Henry County, Virginia. The tract consisted of 310 acres on Grassy Creek. Later, his father conveyed to Green Bouldin another 134 acres along the waters of Grassy Creek.

In 1818, Green Bouldin migrated with his family and slaves from Henry County, Virginia, to Morgan County, Alabama. Green was a very wealthy plantation owner with many slaves and large landholdings in Morgan County near the western edge of the City of Decatur along the Old Moulton Road.

On July 15, 1818, Green Bouldin entered 160 acres of land in the Northeast ¼ of Section 34 in Township 5 South and Range 5 West in Morgan County, Alabama (Cowart, 1981).

Prior to 1828, Mary "Polly" Graves Bouldin died and was buried in the Bouldin Family Cemetery in Decatur, Alabama. After the death of his wife Mary, Green married Elizabeth Jiggets Driver, a widow who had six children from her previous marriage.

On August 10, 1828, Epharaim Bouldin was born at Trinity in Morgan County, Alabama; he was the son of Green and Elizabeth Bouldin. Epharaim was married to Mariah Hobbs Bridgforth, Susie Boyd, and Elizabeth Baugh. Epharaim died about 1893 in Lincoln, Tennessee.

In 1829, Elizabeth Jiggets Driver Bouldin died. She was buried in the Bouldin Cemetery at Decatur in Morgan County, Alabama (Find A Grave Memorial Number 68961541).

On February 16, 1830, Green Bouldin entered 160 in the Southeast ¼ of Section 34 in Township 5 South and Range 5 West in Morgan County, Alabama (Cowart, 1981).

In the 1830 Morgan County, Alabama Census, Green Bouldin was listed with only five black slaves. Probably in 1820, Green owned several slaves.

On October 2, 1830, Green Bouldin died in Morgan County, Alabama. He was buried in the old Bouldin Cemetery in Decatur, Alabama (Find A Grave Memorial Number 67861388).

At his death, Green had a list of his slaves, their value, and how they were distributed to his family. Since he had no will, the estate of Green Bouldin was sold and all the proceeds were divided among his children as ordered by the Probate Court of Morgan County, Alabama. According to the court records, the following was the list of slaves of Green Bouldin and their monetary value:
1. Negro man Charles abt. 38 years old $425.00.
2. Negro man George abt 36 years old $425.00.
3. Negro man Gilbury? abt 37 years old ins? $50.00.
4. Negro Boy Norman abt 15 years old $375.00.
5. Negro boy Henry abt 10 years old $250.00.
6. Negro boy Soloman abt 3 years old $175.00.
7. Negro boy Anthony abt 2 years old $100.00.
8. Negro boy Martin abt 8 months old $75.00.
9. Negro boy Washington abt 8 months old $75.00.
10. Negro woman Dinah abt 39 years old $325.00.
11. Negro woman Priscilla abt 28 years old $325.00.
12. Negro woman Rhoda ?? $325.00.
13. Negro woman Becky abt 27 years old $325.00.
14. Negro girl ?Darniel? abt 12 years old $225.00.
15. Negro girl Mary abt 4 years old $130.00.
16. Negro girl Eliza abt 3 years old $110.00

The obituary for Green Bouldin was as follows: "Died on 2nd instant at his residence in Morgan County, AL in his 63rd year, Capt. Green Bouldin. He was a native of Henry County, VA. and for some years prior to his decease resided in this state."

On October 16, 1830, the Huntsville Advocate wrote the following: "Captain Green Bouldin: Died – On the 2d inst., at his residence in Morgan Co. this excellent citizen in the 63rd year of his age. He was a native of Henry County,

Va. and for some years prior to his decease, resided in this State. Having been favoured with a large family of descendants, and having raised them up in the light of his own honest and benevolent example, (with the exception of an infant son, the child of his latter days, who is left in the desolation of an early orphanage) – he departed, blessing them, and blessed by them. His was not the example of theory but that of a train of virtues which constantly declared him to society as one honest, benevolent, kind and true in all the domestic and social relations. His was a life not of profession, but of action – when such a man, whose worth we have long known and felt, is called to the sleep of his Fathers, we feel bereaved, and it is only left for us to cherish him in memory and emulate his virtues."

The Bouldin Cemetery was on his cotton plantation, and it was not maintained over the years. The cemetery is in a wooded area on Auburn Drive across the street from Julian Harris School in Decatur.

Captain James Massey Bouldin

On March 13, 1795, James Massey Bouldin was born in Henry County, Virginia. He was the son of Green Bouldin Sr. and Mary Graves of Virginia.

On August 18, 1824, James M. Bouldin married Margaret Bouldin, the daughter of Richard Bouldin and Elizabeth Moseley. Margaret was born on October 1, 1795, in Charlotte County, Virginia.

On December 2, 1829, James Massey Bouldin entered 120.55 acres of land in the Northwest ¼ of Section 34 in Township 5 South and Range 5 West in Morgan County, Alabama (Cowart, 1981).

According to the 1830 Morgan County, Alabama Census, James Massey Bouldin was between 30 and 40 years old. Listed in his household was four Whites and five Black slaves.

On October 5, 1832, James Massey Bouldin entered 40 acres of land in the Southwest ¼ of the Northwest ¼ of Section 33 in Township 5 South and Range 5 West in Morgan County, Alabama (Cowart, 1981).

In April 1831, Margaret Bouldin died in Morgan County, Alabama. She was buried in the Bouldin Cemetery at Decatur, Alabama.

On October 26, 1831, James Massey Bouldin married Mary Tabitha J. Hammond in Madison County, Alabama. Mary was born on December 3, 1809, in Madison County; she was the daughter of Eli Hammond and Mary Owen. On April 18, 1840, Mary Tabitha J. Hammond Bouldin died in Madison County, Alabama.

> **GRAVE IN A SWAMP**
>
> **Hunter Uncovers Last Resting Place of Man Long Since Dead.**
>
> NEW DECATUR, Ala., March 24.—(Special.)—Out about four miles from this city, in what is known as the "Black Bottom," a hunter the other day discovered a moss covered slab and after scraping away the moss he found this inscription carved on the rough stone: "In memory of James M. Bouldin, born March 13, 1795, died Oct. 21, 1844, aged 49 years, 7 months and 8 days."
>
> The oldest citizens here know nothing of such a man, neither had they ever heard of this grave before. The grave is in the heart of the swamp and is surrounded by giant forest trees.

According to the 1840 Morgan County, Alabama Census, James Massey Bouldin was between 40 and 50 years old. James was head of his household containing one White male between 0 and five years old, two White male between 10 and 15 years old, one White male between 40 and 50 years old, and one White female between 10 and 15 years old. In 1840, James Bolling owned 20 Black slaves with nine males and 11 female slaves.

On October 21, 1844, James Massey Bouldin died at the age of 49 years, seven months and eight days; he was buried in the Bouldin Cemetery at Decatur in Morgan County, Alabama (Find A Grave Memorial Number 68976250). James had a list of his slaves as part of his estate being settled. He had names and value of his slaves.

Green Bouldin Jr.

Around 1796, Green Bouldin Jr. was probably born in Henry County, Virginia. He was the fifth son of Green Bouldin Sr. and Mary "Polly Graves Bouldin.

Around 1818, he migrated with his family to Morgan County, Alabama. On July 15, 1818, his father entered land in Morgan County, Alabama.

On August 14, 1830, Green Bouldin Jr. entered 80 acres of land in East ½ of the Southeast ¼ of Section 17 in Township 5 South and Range 5 West in Morgan County, Alabama (Cowart, 1981).

According to the 1830 Morgan County, Alabama Census, Green Bouldin Jr. was between 20 and 30 years old. In his household, Green had four Whites and four Black slaves.

On July 26, 1831, Green Bouldin Jr. entered 160 acres of land in Section 23 in Township 5 South and Range 5 West in Morgan County, Alabama (Cowart, 1981).

Prior to 1837, Green Bouldin Jr. married Mary Ann Driver in Limestone County, Alabama. They had the following children:
1. Robert G. Bouldin (3/27/1837-7/23/1907) was buried in DeWitt County, Texas (Find A Grave Memorial Number 66141215).
2. Joseph E. Bouldin was born in 1840 in Mississippi.
3. Virginia Carolyn Bouldin was born in 1842 in Mississippi.
4. James Augusts "Gus" Bouldin (1845-1913) was born in Mississippi and buried at Waelder in Gonzales County, Texas (Find A Grave Memorial Number 10756125)
5. William Green Bouldin (3/21/1851-4/9/1917) was born in Mississippi and was buried at Hardwood in Gonzales County, Texas (Find A Grave Memorial Number 8151671).

In 1883, Green Bouldin Jr. died in Washington County, Texas. He was buried in the Bouldin-Routt Cemetery at Chappell Hill in Washington County, Texas (Find A Grave Memorial Number 70839761).

Brooks, Milton

In the 1830 Morgan County, Alabama Census, Milton Brooks was head of his household which had one White male between 10 and 15 years old, one White male between 15 and 20 years old, one White male between 30 and 40 years old, one White female between 10 and 15 years old, one White female between 15 and 20 years old, and one White female between 20 and 30 years old. In 1830, Milton Brooks owned 21 Black slaves with 10 males and 11 females.

On April 8, 1835, Milton H. Brooks married Mary A. Skidmore according to the 1835 marriage records of Morgan County, Alabama. The father of Mary A. Skidmore Brooks was John Skidmore who was born about 1783; he was the son of Thomas Skidmore and Charity Chapman.

According to the 1840 Morgan County, Alabama Census, Milton Brooks household had one White male between 30 and 40 years of age. No females were listed in the home in 1840. In 1840, Milton Brooks owned 10 Black slaves with five males and five females.

Bryant, Cornelius

On November 8, 1795, Cornelius Bryant of Morgan County, Alabama, was probably born in Virginia. He was a veteran of the War of 1812 and member of the West Tennessee Militia. Cornelius first married Mary Ann Rice (????-1838).

Cornelius and Mary Ann Rice Bryant had the following childen:
1. Martha Bryant (1825-1832).
2. Mary Bryant (1826-1897).
3. Jane Bryant (1828-1832).
4. Hannah Bryant (1829-?) married Jackson Boyer 29 March 1850.
5. Elizabeth A. Bryant (1831-1897).
6. Daniel Bryant (1833-1864) married Jane McCaig.

7. Margaret Bryant (1836-?) married Philip Higdon.
8. Mary Ann Bryant (1838-) married John Crockett.

According to the 1830 Morgan County, Alabama Census, the Cornelius Bryant household had one White male between 15 and 20 years old, one White male between 30 and 40 years old (Cornelius Bryant), three White female between zero and five years old, one White female between five and 10 years old, and one White female between 20 and 30 years old. In 1830, Cornelius owned 28 Black slaves with 11males and 17 females.

In 1838, Cornelius and Mary Ann Rice Bryant had a son, Daniel Bryan (1838-1864). Mary probably died during the birth of their son Daniel.

In the 1840 Franklin County, Alabama Census, the Cornelius Bryant household had one White male between five and 10 years old, one White male between 40 and 50 years old (Cornelius Bryant), two White females between zero and five years old, two White females between five and 10 years old, two White females between 10 and 15 years old, and one White female between 15 and 20 years old. According to the 1840 Franklin County, Alabama Census, Cornelius Bryant did not own any slaves.

On February 7, 1849, Cornelius Bryant married a second time to Kisseah Jane Robertson (1/15/1830-8/7/1888). They had the following children:
1. Frances Caroline Bryant (1850-1872) married V. C. Ramsey.
2. Sarah Tabitha Bryant (1851-1853).
3. Luisa Rebecca Bryant (1857-1939) married _____ Pounders on January 28, 1879; they had one daughter, Sarah.
4. James David Bryant (1855-1858).
5. Andrew Jackson Bryant (1860-1939) first married Martha A. McCaig; she died in 1897. His second marriage was to Arminty Emma Rutland; she died in Oct 1906.
6. Thomas Green Bryant (1864-1938).

On August 7, 1878, Cornelius Bryant died in Colbert County, Alabama. He was buried in the Old Newsom Springs Cemetery in Colbert County, Alabama (Find A Grave Memorial# 92512686).

Daniel Bryant

In 1838, Daniel Bryant was born in Morgan County, Alabama. He was the son of Cornelius Bryant and Mary Ann Rice Bryant.

On March 5, 1863, at age 25, Daniel joined Company E of the 64th Illinois, USA, at Glendale, Mississippi; he was enlisted by M. W. Manning for a period of three years. Daniel was mustered into service on July 10, 1863; he was listed as a veteran and resident of Glendale in Tishomingo County, Mississippi. Daniel was listed as 30 years old, but he was actually 25; his height was five feet 11 ½ inches with dark hair, hazel eyes, and fair complexion. Daniel's marital status was not applicable and occupation listed as farmer; his place of birth was given as Morgan County, Alabama.

On December 31, 1863, another service record indicates Daniel Bryant re-enlisted in Pulaski, Tennessee, by Lieutenant Knickerbocker. His time of service was given as a period of three years; he was mustered in on January 9, 1864, at Pulaski, Tennessee.

On August 14, 1864, Daniel Bryant died of disease at Rome, Georgia; he was a private in the United States Army during the Civil War. Daniel was buried in the Marietta National Cemetery at Marietta in Cobb County, Georgia, Plot: Section C, Site 1347 (Find A Grave Memorial# 38294178).

Burleson, Jonathan

On October 6, 1789, Jonathan Burleson was born in North Carolina. His father was John Burleson (1768-1824), who was born in Mecklenburg County, North Carolina. The mother of Jonathan was Abigail Moore who was born about 1770; at 26 years old, Abigail died about 1796 in North Carolina.

As a young boy, Jonathan Burleson moved from North Carolina with his family to Warren County, Kentucky. Later, Jonathan was with the Burleson Family when they migrated from Kentucky into Mississippi Territory of the Muscle Shoals region of the Tennessee River. In the early 1800s, three brothers,

James, John, Joseph Burleson (sons of Aaron Burleson (1712-1782) along with Jonathan the son of John, migrated to the Mississippi Territory of present-day North Alabama.

On January 7, 1806, Chickamauga Cherokee Chief Doublehead signed the Cotton Gin Treaty with the United States giving him a large tract of land from Elk River to Cypress Creek and 10 miles to the north of the Tennessee River from the mouth of those streams. The area north of Tennessee River at the Muscle Shoals given to Doublehead by treaty with the government became known as Doublehead's Reserve. In the treaty, the Cherokees gave up claims north of the Tennessee River in the northwest Alabama portion of Mississippi Territory except for Doublehead's Reserve. However, the Cherokees still controlled and lived in the area south of the Tennessee River at the Muscle Shoals including present-day Morgan County.

By the spring of 1806, Doublehead and other Cherokees were leasing lands in Doublehead's Reserve and areas under their control south of the Tennessee River to White settler farmers. Sometimes around the summer of 1806 to 1807, the Burleson brothers settled in the area of the Muscle Shoals of the Tennessee River while it was still under control of the Chickamauga Faction of Lower Cherokee Indians. The Burleson family members were documented as living in areas that would later become Limestone, Madison, Morgan, and Lawrence Counties of North Alabama.

On September 5, 1810, James Burleson, John Burleson, Joseph Burleson, and Jonathan Burleson signed the Sims Settlement petition to stay on Indian lands. In the petition, the Sims Settlement settlers stated to United States President James Madison that they were encouraged to move to the area in the winter of 1806 and spring of 1807. Since James Burleson, John Burleson, Joseph Burleson, and John's son Jonathan Burleson signed the petition, they acknowledged with their signatures that they were in agreement with the petition. Therefore, the Burleson brothers, James, John, and Joseph were probably in this area of Mississippi Territory by 1807.

By 1810 and 1812, both James and John had entered land in Madison County of Mississippi Territory. Prior to December 1810, James Burleson officially entered land in Madison County. A little over a year later in February

1812, John entered the land next to the property that had belonged to his brother James.

On December 22, 1810, Robert Martin Jr. was assigned 158.6 acres in the Northwest ¼ of Section 19 of Township 3 South and Range 1 West in Madison County of Mississippi Territory (Cowart, 1979). The property was originally entered by James Burleson prior to being owned by Robert Martin.

On February 24, 1812, John Burleson entered 158.6 acres in the Northeast ¼ of Section 19 of Township 3 South and Range 1 West in Madison County of Mississippi Territory (Cowart, 1979). The land of John Burleson was adjacent to property that his brother James Burleson originally entered prior to 1810.

On September 15, 1813, Jonathan Burleson married Elizabeth Caroline Byrd at Huntsville in Madison County of Mississippi Territory. Elizabeth was born on September 4, 1796, in Virginia; she was the daughter of Reverend Williams Byrd (1774-1856) and Lydia Adair. Lydia Adair Byrd was born on March 21, 1770; she died on October 9, 1838.

Jonathan Burleson

Jonathan Burleson and Elizabeth Byrd Burleson had the following children with all being born in Morgan County, Alabama, except Jane. The Jonathan Burleson family information was verified by David Burleson of Westview in January 2021:
1. Jane Burleson was born on February 25, 1815 in Madison County of Mississippi Territory (present-day Madison County, Alabama).
2. Dr. Aaron Adair Burleson was born on August 1, 1816, in Morgan County, Alabama. In 1850, Aaron Burleson bought the Burleson-

Hinds-McEntire house in Decatur; he sold the home in 1869. According to the 1860 Morgan County Agricultural Census, Aaron A. Burleson owned 800 acres of land. During the Civil War, he was a doctor for the Confederate States of America. At age 82, Aaron died on May 11, 1899, at Hartman in Johnson County, Arkansas, west of Memphis, Tennessee. Aaron was buried in Elmwood Cemetery at Memphis in Shelby County, Tennessee (Find A Grave Memorial Number 13422786).

3. William Byrd Burleson was born on February 23, 1818; he married Minerva Ann Stephenson (1822-1907). In 1850, William owned 11 slaves, and in 1860, he owned 400 acres of land and 15 slaves. William died on December 16, 1865, at age 47; he was buried in the Burleson-Stephenson Cemetery at Decatur in Morgan County, Alabama (Find A Grave Memorial Number 11303394).

4. Eliza Hodges Burleson was born on April 22, 1820, in Morgan County, Alabama; on February 9, 1841, she married Rawley Roland Sivley (1808-1887). Eliza died on December 18, 1893, in Anson County, North Carolina; she was buried in Raymond Cemetery in Hinds County, Mississippi (Find A Grave Memorial Number 122643329).

5. Reverend Richard Byrd Burleson was born on January 1, 1822; in 1847, he married Sarah Leigh Burleson (1829-1854). In 1856, Richard married his second wife Mary Frances Halbert (1827-1913). Richard died on December 21, 1879, at Waco in McLennan County, Texas, at age 57; he was buried in Oakwood Cemetery at Waco, Texas (Find A Grave Memorial Number 128897191).

6. Dr. Rufus Columbus Burleson was born on August 7, 1823; in 1853, he married Georgia Jenkins (1833-1924). Rufus was an early president of Baylor University. Rufus died on May 14, 1901, at Waco in McLennan County, Texas, at age 77 years (Find A Grave Memorial Number 9742530).

7. Elizabeth Burleson was born on December 30, 1825, and she died on September 2, 1837; she was buried in the Burleson family cemetery in Morgan County, Alabama.

8. Emily F. Burleson was born about 1828; she married William D. Williams, and they moved to Texas. Emily died in 1870 at Waco. Texas.

9. Edna F. Burleson was born on December 22, 1829; in 1845, she married Dr. William Madison Turney (1825-1894). Edna died on August 3, 1867; she was buried in Burleson Cemetery in Mogan County, Alabama (Find A Grave Memorial Number 49619414).
10. Isabella Burleson was born on July 5, 1831; she married S.B. Humphreys. Isabella died on May 31, 1906, at age 74.
11. Dabney Adair Burleson was born on February 15, 1835; he married Sallie Ann V. Orr (1839-1908). According to the 1860 Morgan County, Alabama, agricultural and population censuses, Dabney owned 1,335 acres of land and eight slaves. Dabney served in the Army of Confederate States of America with most of his service in the Tennessee Valley under General Phillip Dale Roddy. Dabney died on July 24, 1912, at Hartselle in Morgan, Alabama, at age 77; he was buried at Bethel Baptist Church Cemetery just north of Hartselle on Bethel Road in Morgan County, Alabama (Find A Grave Memorial Number 11787390).
12. Mary Ann Burleson, a twin of Dabney, was born on February 15, 1835; she was married three times and widowed three times. Mary Ann died before 1900 in El Paso, Texas.
13. Mattie H. Burleson was born on September 22, 1837; she married Jonathan Gibson Orr (1834-1905). Mattie died on April 20, 1923, at age 85 at Trinity in Morgan County; she was buried in the Orr Cemetery at Danville in Morgan County, Alabama (Find A Grave Memorial Number 31780977).

In October 1813, Jonathan Burleson enlisted for duty in the Creek Indian War with the army of General Andrew Jackson. During the war, Jonathan Burleson was an Ensign Lieutenant in the 7th Battalion of Perkins Regiment with the Mississippi Militia; at the time of the Creek War, Mississippi Territory included all of present-day North Alabama. On August 9, 1814, the Creek War officially ended with the signing of the Treaty of Fort Jackson at Wetumpka, Alabama.

Around 1814, some of the Cherokee farm lands in or near Morgan County were leased to members of the Burleson family. The Burlesons were living and farming in the vicinity of Mouse Town near the mouth of Fox's Creek in present-day Morgan County, Alabama, when an incident with the Cherokees was noted in several historical records.

By August 1816, John Burleson, James Burleson, Joseph Burleson, Edward Burleson (son of James), Martin Taylor (son-in-law of James) and three others were accused of killing two or three Cherokees at Mouse Town in the northwest corner of present-day Morgan County, Alabama. Jonathan Burleson was not mentioned as being involved in the fight with the Cherokees at Mouse Town; however, the Burleson family members were among the very first White settlers in Morgan County.

In September 1816, the Cherokees signed the Turkey Town Treaty giving up their land claims of northwest Alabama Territory including Morgan County. After the treaty, the Cherokees were removed from the areas west of Madison and Morgan Counties. The treaty effectively prevented any of the Burleson Family being prosecuted for the killing of the Cherokees, and it probably ended the pursuit and punishment to the members of the Burleson family involved in the killing of the Cherokees at Mouse Town.

According to the Turkey Town Treaty, the Cherokees agreed to move from the area beyond the eastern boundary of Morgan County; by 1838, they were forced to the west of the Mississippi River. After the Cherokees moved from Morgan County in 1816, Jonathan Burleson and his wife Elizabeth Byrd Burleson began officially acquiring lands that they were farming in the Flint Creek area south of present-day Decatur and north of present-day Hartselle in Morgan County, Alabama.

Around 1817, Jonathan Burleson built log cabin for his family near the east bank of Flint Creek in Morgan County, Alabama. With the help of his many Black slaves, the log cabin was later enlarged to a large two story log house to accommodate him, his wife, and their twelve children.

According to family history and an old Morgan County map, Jonathan established Burleson Ferry across Flint Creek about two miles south of the Tennessee River. The ferry provided passage across Flint Creek and access to Decatur as well as lands east and west of the creek. Probably some of the slaves of Jonathan Burleson were assigned operational duties of the ferry. The ferry was located were present-day Highway 67 crosses Flint Creek between Piceville and Decatur.

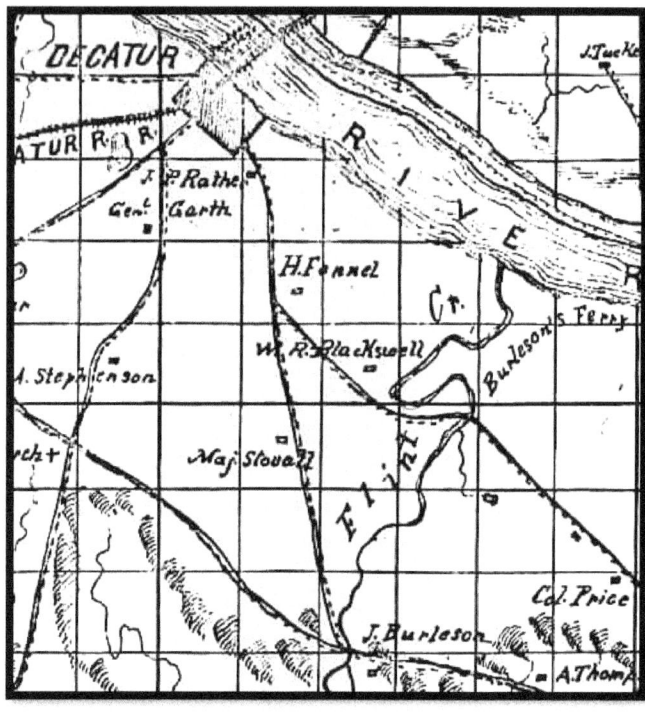

Jonathan Burleson probably had another ferry across Flint Creek about one half mile west of his log home at the base of Burleson Mountain; another early road passed just north of his two story log house and crossed Flint Creek a short distance to the west. The old map shows his original home place on the east side of Flint Creek some three miles south of his main ferry. It is not known if tolls were charged for using Burleson's Ferry, but most ferries collected tolls for transporting people, livestock, wagons, and other farm products across streams.

On July 13, 1818, Jonathan Burleson entered some 477 acres of land in Township 6 South and Range 4 West in Morgan County, Alabama. In the following years, he entered hundreds of acres in Morgan County including land in northern Mississippi.

Before 1820, Jonathan Burleson was elected secretary of a group known as the "First Legislature" which was made up of citizens organized to stop a gang of horse thieves that operated in the area. Jonathan also served as a county commissioner and justice of the peace in Morgan County, Alabama.

In 1824, John Burleson, father of Jonathan, died in Morgan County, Alabama. At the time of his death, John Burleson owned 160 acres near Wolf

Town which was near present-day Belleview Baptist Church on the Old Moulton Road just east of the Lawrence-Morgan County line.

In September 1824, Jonathan Burleson was listed as one of the deacons of Cedar Springs Baptist Church. The church is now known as Mount Pisgah Baptist Church in Morgan County, Alabama.

The 1830 Morgan County, Alabama Census identified the following in the household of Jonathan Burleson: White Males 0-5: 1; White Males 5-10: 1; White Males 10-15: 2; White Males 30-40: 1; White Males 40-50: 1; White Females 0-5: 2; White Females 10-15: 1; White Females 15-20: 1; White Females 50-60: 1. In 1830, Jonathan A. Burleson owned 20 Black slaves with nine being males and 11 being females.

On July 12, 1839, Elizabeth Byrd Burleson, wife of Jonathan, died at the age of 42 years. She was buried in Burleson Cemetery on the old home place at the base of Burleson Mountain in Morgan County, Alabama (Find A Grave Memorial number 11303320).

In 1840 after the death of his wife Elizabeth, Jonathan may have had an underlying reason to quickly start construction of his new Westview Plantation house on Burleson Mountain. In moving into a new house, Jonathan would be removed from the old home that held precious memories and had served him and his beloved wife Elizabeth so well.

The 1840 Morgan County, Alabama Census identified the following in the household of Jonathan Burleson: White Males 0-5: 2; White Males 5-10: 2; White Males 10-15: 1; White Males 40-50: 1; White Females 10-15: 2; White Females 15-20: 1, White Females 40-50: 1. According to the 1840 Morgan County, Alabama Census, Jonathan A. Burleson owned 43 Black slaves.

In 1841 with the help of his Black slaves, Jonathan Burleson completed his Westview Plantation house on the top western edge of Burleson Mountain about one mile east from his original home site. An October 6, 1841, date was engraved in a stone imbedded in the northeast chimney of his Westview home.

Westview was located some nine miles south of Decatur and four miles north of Hartselle in Morgan County, Alabama. The home overlooks the vast Flint Creek Valley to the west where Jonathan owned large tracts of land. Flint Creek flows into the Tennessee River near the present-day Point Mallard Park in Decatur, Alabama.

The eastern, northern, and western views from the Westview plantation home are unending and spectacular. Some six or more different counties can be seen from the roof of Westview which include Morgan, Madison, Limestone, Lauderdale, Lawrence, Winston, and possibly Colbert and Franklin of North Alabama. Except for Winston County, these are the counties that were opened to White settlers after the Cherokees and Chickasaws gave up their land claims in the Turkey Town Treaty of September 1816.

Westview was basically a square two storied clapboard plantation home with a central hallway downstairs and upstairs. There were two rooms on each side of a huge hallway downstairs. Upstairs consisted of one long room on the south side of the hallway and two rooms on the north side of the hall. The attic area appeared to be for storage with access to the top of the house. The chimneys were probably of slave made brick.

Westview

On April 23, 1843, Jonathan Burleson married Ann Roby Humphreys in Morgan County, Alabama; she was born about 1806 in Georgia. Ann had first married David Carlisle Humpherys; he was a doctor in Somerville who died in 1842. Jonathan and his second wife Ann Roby Burleson lived at Westview.

On July22, 1845, Jonathan and Ann Roby Humphreys Burleson had one child Roby A. Burleson. Roby was the only child born to Jonathan and Ann Burleson. At 24 years old, Roby died on January 5, 1870, in Morgan County, Alabama.

By 1850, the Westview Plantation of Jonathan Burleson consisted of some 7,000 acres in Morgan County. "By the 1850's, Westview Plantation resembled a small village. There were twenty to thirty slave cabins, an overseer's house, a blacksmith's shop, a mill, a carpenter's shop, a cotton gin, a tannery, several barns, smoke houses, and other farm related outbuildings" (Fulenwider, 1998).

According to the 1850 Morgan County, Alabama Slave Schedule, Jonathan Burleson owned 64 Black slaves that planted, cultivated and harvested his vast cotton fields. In the census, two of the sons of Jonathan were also slave owners: Aaron Adair Burleson owned seven Black slaves, and William Byrd Burleson owned 11 Black slaves. Together, Jonathan and his sons Aaron and William owned 82 slaves in Morgan County in 1850.

According to the 1860 Morgan County, Alabama Slave Schedule, Jonathan Burleson owned 49 slaves. Of those slaves, 43 were Black and six were Mulattos that were housed in 11 slave cabins. Of the 49 slaves, 19 were females and 30 were males. In addition, Jonathan Burleson had three sons that were owners of Black slaves:
1. Aaron Adair Burleson owned 17 slaves and 800 acres of land;
2. Dabney Adair Burleson owned eight slaves and 1,335 acres of land;
3. William Byrd Burleson owned 15 slaves and 400 acres of land.

In 1860, Jonathan and three of his sons owned a total of 89 slaves in Morgan County, Alabama. Jonathan accounted for at least 15 less slaves than he owned in 1850. Part of his slaves may have been utilized on a large tract of land that he had obtained in northern Mississippi, or he might have given his sons some of his slaves.

According to the 1860 Morgan County, Alabama, Agricultural Census, Jonathan Burleson owned 700 acres of improved land and 2000 acres of unimproved land worth $15,000.00. He also owned $500.00 worth of farm equipment and $5,000.00 worth of livestock. Jonathan had obviously converted a lot of his land to pasture his vast livestock herd.

Prior to the start of the Civil War, Jonathan had become a very successful cotton planter. He had some 7,500 acres of land which included 880 acres in North Mississippi and the rest in Morgan County, Alabama. He also had a substantial labor force of Black slaves to work and maintain his cotton plantations.

From 1862 to the end of the war in 1865, Jonathan Burleson witnessed firsthand the invasion of his home and surrounding farmlands by Union soldiers that were comprised of southern Union sympathizers and northern Yankee troops. During the war, five of his sons were serving as soldiers in the Rebel Army of the Confederate States of America (CSA).

It was very surprising that the Westview Plantation home was somehow spared from the northern fires that destroyed many beautiful antebellum homes of the southland. The invading Union army could have easily destroyed the plantation home as they did many other plantation homes in the South. It was speculated that Jonathan being an elderly gentleman probably prevented the destruction of his Westview home.

For the four long years of conflict and civil unrest, Westview Plantation began to fall to the ravages and deterioration of a state of war. During that time, Jonathan Burleson lost ownership of his black slaves that worked his cotton plantations. Without the slave labor force, the Westview Plantation experienced a severe economic blow. The loss of labor also led to a steady and rapid decline in the production of cotton and other products that kept the farm flourishing. Maintenance and upkeep of the home, outbuildings, barns, pastures, and croplands suffered and began to fall in a state of disrepair with time.

Jonathan never recovered from the loss of his farm labor and economic devastation caused by the Civil War. Like all other cotton planters in the area, Jonathan felt the results of the defeat of the South. After some 50 years of struggling to build his own cotton plantation and enterprise, Jonathan obviously became depressed at the demise of his beloved Westview Plantation, and his health began to decline quite rapidly.

On September 24, 1866, Jonathan Burleson died at his Westview home in Morgan County, Alabama. He was buried next to his beloved Elizabeth on his plantation in the family cemetery at the base of Burleson Mountain near Flint Creek in Morgan County, Alabama (Find A Grave Memorial Number 11303290). After Burleson's death in 1866, much of his land was sold.

In 1876, Ann Robey Humphreys Burleson died in Morgan County, Alabama. She was buried in the Burleson-Stephenson Cemetery at Decatur in Morgan County, Alabama (Find A Grave Memorial Number 142551440).

On October 19, 1979, Westview was listed on the Alabama Register of Landmarks and Heritage. On January 15, 1982, the Westview Plantation home of Jonathan Burleson was placed on the National Register of Historic Places.

Today, David and Anne Burleson maintain their historic Westview dwelling so well that it would be the envy of the best antebellum museums. It is very fitting that the Westview home and surround land remains in the Jonathan Burleson family under the care of David and Anne Burleson.

Rickey Butch Walker and David Burleson at the grave of Jonathan Burleson

Burleson Cemetery

There are two Burleson Cemeteries in Morgan County, Alabama. One Burleson Cemetery is just northeast of the junction of the Moadus Road and Danville Road. This Burleson Cemetery is on the east side of the Danville Road next to the Renasant Bank and is surrounded by a wrought iron fence.

The old Burleson Cemetery was where Jonathan Burleson was buried; nearby, Jonathan had built his first home around 1816. The cemetery at the old Burleson home place is at the northwestern base of Burleson Mountain. It is east of Highway 31 and just ¼ mile south of the Red Bank Road on the east side of Lyon Road. Burleson family members buried in the cemetery include:

1. Burleson, Jonathan, October 6, 1789-September 24, 1866.
2. Burleson, Elizabeth, September 4, 1796-July 12, 1839.
3. Burleson, Elizabeth, 1 year, 7 months, 3 days
4. Byrd, Lydia March 21, 1770-October 9, 1838.
5. Turney, Isabella A.E., June 2, 1856.
6. Humphreys, Eliza Dora, May 4, 1853-July 22, 1854.
7. Humphreys, Aaron Burleson, October 4, 1855-December 13, 1861.
8. Humphreys, Carlisle, November 4, 1861-January 20, 1863.
9. Humphreys, Mary Helen, December 23, 1851-June 21, 1864.
10. Turney, Edna F., March 1, 1858-March 3, 1858.
11. Turney, Emily L., December 5, 1846-January 15, 1848.
12. Turney, Eliza L., April 12, 1849-July 8, 1849.

Edna Burleson Turney, daughter of Jonathan Burleson, was the mother of the Turney children; her husband was Dr. William Turney. Isabella Burleson Humphreys, daughter of Jonathan Burleson, was the mother of the Humphrey children; her husband was S.B. Humphreys.

Burleson Conclusion

From the original construction in 1841, Westview Plantation home was occupied by six generations of the family of Jonathan Burleson. For 180 years, the Jonathan Burleson home survived the ravages of the Civil War, fire, violent storms, extremely cold winters, scorching hot summers, and deterioration due to time.

In 1997, David and Anne Burleson began restoration of Westview which took over one and a half years to complete. In order to compliment the historic home, they searched for years to find the appropriate antebellum furniture to match the time period of the construction of Westview. Some of the furnishing in the home and most of the materials used during the original construction over 180 years ago are still maintained. Ann Burleson pointed out a cradle that is believed to be an original piece of furniture of Jonathan Burleson. The cradle was supposedly used to rock at least six generations of Burleson children.

David and Anne Burleson, who now live in Westview, have maintained the original character of the historic house in one of the most majestic settings of North Alabama. One would be utterly amazed that the home on the very western edge of the top of Burleson Mountain was able to withstand all the forces that Mother Nature could throw at it and still be in immaculate condition. Credit for the pristine appearance of the home goes to the Burleson family and their love of Westview, especially David and Anne Burleson. The Jonathan Burleson farm, home sites, and cemetery in Morgan County, Alabama, have been a vital part of the Burleson family heritage, traditions, and history for over 200 years.

Burnett, Greenville

On November 21, 1793, Greenville Burnett was born in Chatham County, North Carolina, to Ellicksander Burnett (1770-1805) and Elizabeth Herndon(1776-1844). Greenville Burnett served in the war of 1812.

Greenville Burnett was the husband of Adelaide Elizabeth Gillespie Burnett, and they had six children.
1. William C. Burnett (1821-1875)
2. Caroline Burnett (1825-1911)
3. Willis Burnett (1829-1864) married Mary Elizabeth Walker
4. Fannie Burnett (1832-1889)
5. Greenville Burnett(1834-1868)
6. Edwin Burnett (1837-1920)

Greenville Burnett entered the following tracts of land in Morgan County, Alabama:

1. On July 11, 1818, Greenville Burnett entered 80.24 acres in the West ½ of Northeast ¼ of Section 29 in Township 5 South and Range 4 West in Morgan County, Alabama.

2. On July 26, 1830, Greenville Burnett entered 79 acres in the Southwest ¼ of Section 20 in Township 5 South and Range 4 West in Morgan County, Alabama.
3. On November 26, 1830, Greenville Burnett entered 80.24 acres in the West ½ of Northwest ¼ of Section 29 in Township 5 South and Range 4 West in Morgan County, Alabama.
4. On May 26, 1831, Greenville Burnett entered 80.24 acres in the East ½ of Northeast ¼ of Section 29 in Township 5 South and Range 4 West in Morgan County, Alabama.
5. On March 29, 1832, Greenville Burnett entered 79.38 ¾ acres in the East ½ of Southeast ¼ of Section 6 in Township 7 South and Range 4 West in Morgan County, Alabama.
6. On September 5, 1833, Greenville Burnett entered 79.38 ¾ acres in the West ½ of Southeast ¼ of Section 6 in Township 7 South and Range 4 West in Morgan County, Alabama (Cowart, 1981).

According to the 1830 Morgan County, Alabama Census, Greenville Burnett had the following in his household: White Males 0-5: 1, 5-10: 1, 10-15: 1, 40-50: 1; White Females 0-5: 2, 5-10: 1, 20-30: 1; Slaves: Males 13, Females 12, Total Slaves 25.

Between 1840 and 1850, Greenville moved near other Burnett family members in Monroe County, Mississippi. He had at least one brother and cousin who also moved to Monroe County.

The county was originally attached to Alabama until a survey of the boundary line in the winter of 1820 established the area as Mississippi. The county lay primarily on the east side of the Tombigbee River.

According to the 1850 Monroe County, Mississippi, Slave Census, Greenville Burnette owned 17 slaves. In the 1860 Monroe County, Mississippi Census, Greenville Burnett owned 42 Black slaves.

On May 7, 1861, Greenville Burnett died at West Point in Clay County, Mississippi. Clay County was formed from part of Monroe County and lies west of the Tombigbee River.

Bolling Clark Burnett

Bolling Clark Burnett was a cousin of Greenville Burnett of Morgan County, Alabama. He was born in 1797 in Dinwiddie, Virginia, to Taliaferro Burnett and Mary Baugh.

On September 27, 1837, Bolling Clark Burnett entered 80.04 acres of land in the West ½ of the Southeast ¼ of Section 26 in Township 6 South and Range 8 West in Lawrence County, Alabama (Cowart, 1991). Bolling Clark Burnett was the fourth sheriff of Lawrence County, Alabama.

Around the 1840s, Bolling moved to Mississippi, with other Burnett family members including Greenville Burnett. In Monroe County, Mississippi, Bolling Clark Burnett became a wealthy cotton planter with many slaves to work his plantation.

Bolling was closely associated with his cousin Daniel Burnett of the famous Cotton Gin Port and construction of the Ferry. Daniel Burnett (1795-1844) was born in Chatham, North Carolina, and married Phoebe Pruitt (1806-1870). Daniel was the brother of Greenville Burnett, Cornelius Burnett, and John F. Burnett.

On April 1, 1862, Bolling died in Monroe County, Mississippi. Bolling Clark Burnett was buried in the Whitfield-Burnett Cemetery at Aberdeen in Monroe County, Mississippi (Find A Grave Memorial Number 41976686).

Colbert, Rhoda

The birth date of Rhoda Colbert was between 1770 and 1780, according to the 1830 census records. Rhoda Colbert entered the following tracts of land in Morgan County, Alabama.
1. On July 9, 1818, Rhoda Colbert entered $80.54^{3/4}$ acres in the East½ of Southwest ¼ of Section 5 in Township 6 South and Range 3 West in Morgan County, Alabama. Rhoda was listed with certificate number

751 in the land records with John Coffee who had the same certificate number.
2. On July 9, 1818, Rhoda Colbert entered 80.54 ³/⁴ acres in the West½ of Southwest ¼ of Section 5 in Township 6 South and Range 3 West in Morgan County, Alabama. Rhoda was listed with certificate number 1078 in the land records with John Coffee who had the same certificate number.
3. On July 9, 1818, Rhoda Colbert entered 159.72½ acres in the Southeast ¼ of Section 6 in Township 6 South and Range 3 West in Morgan County, Alabama. Rhoda was listed with certificate number 1079 in the land records with John Coffee who had the same certificate number.
4. On July 20, 1830, Rhoda Colbert entered 156.84 acres in the Northeast ¼ of Section 7 in Township 6 South, and Range 3 West in Morgan County, Alabama.
5. On July 20, 1830, Rhoda Colbert entered 79.52 acres in the East ½ of Northwest ¼ of Section 8 in Township 6 South, and Range 3 West in Morgan County, Alabama (Cowart, 1981).

According to the 1830 Morgan County, Alabama Census, the Rhoda Colbert household had the following: White Males 20-30: 1; White Females 50-60: 1 (Rhoda); Slaves: Males 12, Females 13, Total Slaves 25.

In the 1840 Morgan County, Alabama Census, no Colbert was listed in Morgan County. Rhoda Colbert was probably associated with the Chickasaw Colberts, and he either moved or died prior to 1840.

Collier, Bouldin Carter

On July 3, 1788, after the death of his first wife Elizabeth Littlepage, Colonel James E. Collier married Elizabeth Bouldin, daughter of James Bouldin and Sally Watkins of Charlotte County, Virginia. James Bouldin was the oldest son of Colonel Thomas Bouldin of Pennsylvania, who settled in Lunenburg County, Virginia, in 1744.

On July 8, 1789, Bouldin Carter Collier became the first born child of James E. Collier and Elizabeth Bouldin. Bouldin Carter Collier was born in Lunenburg County, Virginia, and he had the following siblings:

1. Wyatt Collier was born on August 19, 1791, in Lunenburg County, Virginia. In 1828, he married Janet Jane Walker, who was born in Elect, Scotland, on May 17, 1805. She died on August 8, 1869, and is buried in the Florence Cemetery in Lauderdale County, Alabama (Find A Grave Memorial Number 38552126). Wyatt owned The Oaks Plantation, 64 black slaves, and 1,453 acres on the Tennessee River in West Lauderdale County, Alabama. He died on October 6, 1856, and is buried in the Florence Cemetery in Florence, Alabama. (Find A Grave Memorial Number 38552165).
2. Martha Watkins Collier was born on August 29, 1793, in Lunenburg County, Virginia; she died on February 4, 1867. On June 15, 1812, Martha married William Alexander Slaughter; he was born in 1792 in Culpeper County, Virginia. In 1879, William died and was buried in Neshoba County, Mississippi.
3. Dr. James Bouldin Collier was born on June 16, 1795; he married Sarah Ladd (Land) on June 03, 1819. On June 05, 1828, James married Frances Slaughter in Morgan County, Alabama. James Bouldin Collier died on May 09, 1839.
4. Eliza Wyatt Collier was born on May 1, 1797, in Lunenburg County, Virginia. On December 19, 1817, she married William Henry Blackwell in Madison County, Alabama; he was born on November 27, 1790, and died November 26, 1846. William Henry Blackwell owned 60 Black slaves in 1840, and he was buried in the Blackwell-Collier Cemetery in Limestone County, Alabama (Find A Grave Memorial Number 70347693). Eliza died on July 25, 1856, in Madison County, Alabama. She was buried in the Blackwell-Collier Cemetery in Limestone County, Alabama (Find A Grave Memorial Number 70347757).
5. William Edward Collier was born on August 10, 1799, in Lunenburg County, Virginia. He first married Emily Rosalie Stewart. On December 08, 1829, he married Jane Ophelia Stewart Slaughter (2/11/1805-12/11/1830); Jane was buried in the Blackwell-Collier Cemetery in Limestone County, Alabama (Find A Grave Memorial Number 81980136). On February 7, 1818,

William E. Collier entered 160.5 acres in Section 21 of Township 5 South and Range 2 West; and, on July 2, 1831, he entered 160.5 in Section 11 of Township 5 South and Range 2 West in Limestone County, Alabama (Cowart, 1984). On June 7, 1830, he entered 78.5 acres in Section 30 of Township 5 South and Range 2 West in Madison County, Alabama (Cowart, 1979). William died in 1833 in Madison County, Alabama.

6. Governor Henry Watkins Collier was born on January 17, 1801, in Charlotte County, Virginia. On April 26, 1826, he married Mary Ann Williams Battle in Tuscaloosa, Alabama. Mary was born on May 16, 1803, in Nash, North Carolina, and died on April 09, 1867, in Tuscaloosa, Alabama (Find A Grave Memorial Number 68719731). Henry Watkins Collier served as Chief Justice of the Alabama State Supreme Court from 1828 to 1849. From 1849-1853, Henry Watkins Collier was the 14th Governor of Alabama. Henry died on August 28, 1855, at Bailey Springs, Alabama. He is buried in Evergreen Cemetery in Tuscaloosa County, Alabama (Find A Grave Memorial Number 7365985).

Governor Henry Watkins Collier

7. Thomas Bouldin Collier was born on January 08, 1803, in Abbeville, South Carolina. In 1824, he married Mary Dent in Madison County, Alabama. In the 1840 Limestone County, Alabama Census, Thomas B. Collier owned 30 Black slaves. In the 1850 Limestone County, Alabama, Agricultural Census, Thomas B. Collier owned 81 Black slaves, 980 acres of improved land and 1,200 acres of unimproved land worth $32,715. He also had $600 worth of farming equipment and livestock valued at $3,524.

8. Charles Ephraim Collier was born on January 10, 1805, in Abbeville, South Carolina. On June 19, 1828, Charles married Elizabeth Goowyne Stewart of Madison County, Alabama. Elizabeth was born on December 6, 1812, and she died on May 21, 1878. She is buried in the Blackwell-Collier Cemetery in Limestone County, Alabama (Find A Grave Memorial Number 70347828). On December 25, 1830, Charles Ephraim Collier entered 75.5 acres in Section 20 of Township 5 South and Range 2 West. On July 12, 1837, he entered 162.18 acres in Section 28 of Township 4 South and Range 2 West in Madison County, Alabama (Cowart, 1979). He died on March 7, 1888, and is buried in the Blackwell-Collier Cemetery in Limestone County, Alabama (Find A Grave Memorial Number 70532090).
9. Alfred Alexander Collier was born on August 05, 1807, in Abbeville, South Carolina, and he died on July 10, 1808, in Charlotte County, Virginia.

Prior to 1802, the father of Bouldin Carter Collier, James E. Collier, was a large land owner in Lunenburg County, Virginia. James followed his father to South Carolina where he became a large cotton planter. In 1803, James and Elizabeth had a son, Thomas Bouldin Collier, who was born in Abbeville District, South Carolina. Therefore, Bouldin Carter Collier migrated with his family from Virginia to South Carolina.

On September 5, 1810, William and James Slaughter, sons of John Slaughter, signed the Sims Settlement petition to stay on the Indian lands. On March 3, 1811, John Slaughter, whose family members were related to the Collier family through marriage, entered 160.3 acres in the Southeast ¼ of Section 11 of Township 1 South and Range 3 West in Limestone County, Alabama (Cowart, 1984).

On March 11, 1811, Bouldin Carter Collier and Wyatt Collier, the two oldest sons of James and Elizabeth Bouldin Collier, entered 161.4 acres of land in Section 8 of Township 4 South and Range 1 West in Madison County of Mississippi Territory (Cowart, 1979). Therefore by 1811, Bouldin Carter Collier and Wyatt Collier had migrated to Madison County of Mississippi Territory.

On June 15, 1812, Martha Watkins Collier, the sister of Bouldin and Wyatt, married William Alexander Slaughter (1792-1879); probably the son of William Slaughter of the Sims Settlement. On December 6, 1813, William Slaughter entered 161.3 acres in the Northwest ¼ of Section 26 of Township 1 South and Range 3 West in Limestone County (Cowart, 1984); just two miles south of John Slaughter in the same township and range. This William may have been the husband or father-in-law of Martha W. Collier.

By February 4, 1818, James E. Collier, who followed his sons Bouldin and Wyatt to Mississippi Territory, entered some 1,308 acres of land in Sections 29 and 30 of Township 5 South and Range 2 West in Madison County (Cowart, 1979). One 150 acre tract was entered with his son Charles Ephraim Collier. On the land he entered, James built and settled on his Myrtle Grove Plantation near Triana in Madison County.

On February 7, 1818, Bouldin Carter Collier entered 240.8 acres in Townships 4, 5 South and Range 3 West in Limestone County, Alabama (Cowart, 1984).

On July 8, 1818, Bouldin Carter Collier entered 79.69 acres of land in the west ½ of the northwest ¼ of Section 6 of Township 7 South and Range 2 West in Morgan County, Alabama (Cowart, 1981).

On March 13, 1824, Sarah Slaughter (born 1778), the widow of John Slaughter, gave up her rights to the Limestone County estate of her late husband John who died in December 1812; she was the second wife of John Slaughter. Since Bouldin Carter Collier married a Sarah Slaughter from Limestone County, Alabama, he may have married a daughter of the widow Sarah Slaughter that had the same name. The 1830 census indicated that the wife of Bouldin was between 20 and 30 years old; at that time, widow Sarah Slaughter would have been 52 years old.

On February 23, 1828, Elizabeth Bouldin Collier, the mother of Bouldin Carter Collier, died at age 65. She was buried in the Collier Cemetery at Triana in Madison County, Alabama (Find A Grave Memorial Number 39774355). Elizabeth and her husband James are buried beside each other in the Collier Cemetery on their Myrtle Grove Plantation at Triana.

On June 5, 1828, James Boulding Collier, brother of Bouldin Carter Collier, married Frances Slaughter of Morgan County. William Edward Collier, brother of Bouldin Carter Collier, married Jane Ophelia Stewart Slaughter, widow of Lawrence Smith Slaughter (1798-1826). William and Ophelia were only married one year and three days before she died at the age of 25 years and 10 months. It is uncertain if the Slaughter family members married to the Collier family members were closely related.

According to the 1830 Madison County, Alabama Census, James E. Collier, the father of Bouldin Carter Collier, owned 55 Black slaves. In 1830, Bouldin Carter Collier owned 41 Black slaves in Morgan County with 19 being males and 22 females. In the 1830 Morgan County, Alabama Census, William A. Slaughter, husband of Martha Watkins Collier, owned 10 Black slaves in Morgan County, Alabama.

The 1830 Morgan County, Alabama Census listed the following in the household of Bouldin Carter Collier: White Males, 40-50: 2, White Females: 0-5: 2, White Females: 20-30: 1.

From June 1831 through November 1831, Bouldin Carter Collier entered some 802 acres of land in Morgan County, Alabama, as follows:
1. On June 20, 1831, he entered 159.38 acres of land in the southwest ¼ in Section 6 of Township 7 South and Range 2 West in Morgan County, Alabama (Cowart, 1981).
2. On June 20, 1831, Bouldin entered 160.56 acres in the southwest ¼ of Section 22 of Township 7 South and Range 3 West in Morgan County, Alabama (Cowart, 1981).
3. On June 20, 1831, he entered 160.96 acres in the southeast ¼ of Section 21 of Township 7 South and Range 3 West in Morgan County, Alabama (Cowart, 1981).
4. On July 4, 1831, Bouldin entered 160.18 acres in the northeast ¼ in Section 1 of Township 7 South and Range 3 West in Morgan County, Alabama (Cowart, 1981).
5. On July 25, 1831, he entered 80.44 acres in the west ½ of the northwest ¼ in Section 27 of Township 7 South and Range 3 West in Morgan County, Alabama (Cowart, 1981).

6. On November 9, 1831, Bouldin entered 80.48 acres in the east ½ of the southwest ¼ of Section 21 of Township 7 South and Range 3 West in Morgan County, Alabama (Cowart, 1981).

On August 20, 1832, James E. Collier died at age 74. He was buried in Collier Cemetery at Triana in Madison County, Alabama, on his Myrtle Grove Plantation near the Tennessee River about 20 miles southwest of Huntsville (Find A Grave Memorial Number 17954217). His obituary reads: "Died at his residence near the village, on Monday the 20th instant, after a severe illness of two weeks, Mr. James Collier, in the 77th year of his age. Mr. Collier was a native of Virginia, and at an early period of his life entered the Revolutionary Army."

On October 4, 1834, and on May 10, 1836, William A. Slaughter, husband of Martha Watkins Collier, entered approximately two 40 acre tracts of land in Sections 5 and 7 in Township 7 South and Range 2 West in Morgan County, Alabama (Cowart, 1981). Both of these tracts were near his brother-in-law Bouldin Carter Collier who had entered land in the adjacent Section 6 of the same township and range.

On November 20, 1834, Bouldin Carter Collier entered 40.22 acres in the northwest ¼ of the northeast ¼ of Section 27 of Township 7 South and Range 3 West in Morgan County, Alabama (Cowart, 1981).

On May 9, 1839, Bouldin Carter Collier died in Limestone County, Alabama. He was probably buried in the Collier Cemetery at Triana or in the Collier-Blackwell Cemetery in Limestone County.

Crockett, John

On February 28, 1785, John Crockett was born in Lancaster County, South Carolina. He was the son of Elijah Crockett (October 6, 1757-March 3, 1798) and Mary Davie (December 15, 1759-September 20, 1823). Elijah was born in Anson County, North Carolina, and Mary was born in Whitehaven, England; they died in Lancaster County, South Carolina, and were buried in the Waxhaw Presbyterian Church Cemetery (Find A Grave Memorial Numbers 10224732 and 10224731).

Elijah and Mary Davie Crockett had the following children that were born in Lancaster County, South Carolina:
1. Mary Crockett was born on February 24, 1784. On February 22, 1803, Mary married Robert McCorkle; she died on July 26, 1856.
2. John Crockett was born on February 28, 1785. In 1830, John Crockett owned 37 slaves in Morgan County, Alabama.
3. Archibald D. Crockett was born on May 22, 1786; he died on November 25, 1815.
4. Margaret McClanahan Crockett was born on October 2, 1787. In 1813, Margaret married John McKnitt Alexander Wallis in Mecklenburg County, North Carolina. In 1830, John M. K. A. Wallis owned 18 slaves in Morgan County, Alabama. Margaret died on September 10, 1853, at Memphis in Pickens County, Alabama (Find A Grave Memorial Number 59950880).
5. William Davie Crockett was born on March 22, 1789; he died on September 11, 1792.
6. Anne Crockett was born on January 11, 1791. In 1819, Anne married James Williamson Wallis; she died in December 1865.
7. Robert Karr Crockett was born on June 27, 1792. On December 19, 1822, Robert married Angerona Richardson in Morgan County, Alabama; she was the daughter of Edward Richardson(1758-1843) and Mary Locke (1765-1835). Angerona was born on October 6, 1800, and she died on May 30, 1883, at Flatonia in Fayette County, Texas (Find A Grave Memorial Number 147093460). In 1850, Robert Karr Crockett owned 13 slaves in Morgan County, Alabama. On November 22, 1852; he died and was buried in the Richardson Cemetery at Decatur in Morgan County, Alabama (Find A Grave Memorial Number 39869299).
8. Sarah Davie Crockett was born on April 3, 1794. Sarah married John McKenzie; she died on October 17, 1847, at Wetumka in Elmore County, Alabama. John McKenzie owned 10 slaves in Morgan County, Alabama, in 1830 and 1840.
9. Elizabeth Crockett was born on August 11, 1795. On April 10, 1823, Elizabeth married Joseph E. Wallis (3/9/1801-3/15/1865) of Mecklenburg County, North Carolina (Find A Grave Memorial Number 46595457). In 1830, Joseph Wallis owned nine slaves in

Morgan County, Alabama. On December 31, 1866, at age 71, Elizabeth Crockett Wallis died at Chappell Hill in Washington County, Texas; she was buried next to her husband in the Atkinson Cemetery (Find A Grave Memorial Number 46595376).

10. Elijah Crockett was born on January 23, 1797. On May 27, 1813, Elijah married Martha Durden. On May 24, 1831, Elijah Crockett entered 160.07 acres of land in the Southwest ¼ of Section 7 in Township 7 South and Range 1 West in Morgan County, Alabama (Cowart, 1981); in 1823, he died in Mobile, Alabama.

It appears that John McKnitt Alexander Wallis, James Williamson Wallis, and Joseph Edmund Wallis were brothers that married three Crockett sisters. John McKnitt Alexander Wallis married Margaret M. Crockett in1819. James Williamson Wallis married Anne Crockett in 1819. Joseph Edmund Wallis married Elizabeth Crockett in 1823. The three Wallis men were entering land in the same area of east Morgan County along with their Crockett brothers-in-laws John, Robert, and Elijah Crockett from 1818 through 1833.

Based on land records, it appears that John Crockett followed his brother Robert K. Crockett and his brothers-in-law John McKenzie, James W. Wallis, John McKnitt A. Wallis, and Joseph E. Wallis to Morgan County, Alabama. Robert first entered land in 1818; however, it was not until November 13, 1830, that John Crockett first entered 79 acres of land in West ½ of the Northwest ¼ of Section 13 of Township 7 South and Range 2 West in Morgan County, Alabama (Cowart, 1981).

On August 14, 1818, Robert Crockett and Joseph Wallis (Wallace) entered 79.97 acres of land in the east ½ of the northwest ¼ of Section 12 of Township 7 South and Range 2 West in Morgan County, Alabama (Cowart, 1981). Joseph Wallis, the brother-in-law of Robert and John Crockett, owned nine black slaves in 1830. In 1850, Robert Crockett owned 13 black slaves.

On July 28, 1821, John McKenzie, another brother-in-law of John and Robert Crockett, entered 160.04 acres of land in the Northwest ¼ of Section 11 of Township 7 South and Range 2 West in Morgan County, Alabama (Cowart, 1981). According to the 1830 and 1840 Morgan County, Alabama Census, John McKenzie owned 10 black slaves during both census periods.

On October 17, 1823, Robert K. Crockett, John McKnitt A. Wallis, and Joseph Wallis entered 79.72 acres of land in the east ½ of the northwest ¼ of Section 2 of Township 7 South and Range 2 West in Morgan County, Alabama (Cowart, 1981). John McKnitt Alexander Wallis and Joseph Edmund Wallis were brothers who were the brothers-in-law of John Crockett and Robert Crockett.

On February 17, 1825, John Crockett married Mary Haynes Davies in Morgan County, Alabama. Mary was born on June 25, 1790, in Halifax County, North Carolina.

John and Mary Haynes Davies Crockett had the following children:
1. Sarah Crockett was born on June 26, 1826.
2. Mary Davie Crockett was born on June 12, 1828.
3. William Davie Crockett was born on September 25, 1830, in Morgan County, Alabama.
4. William Richardson Crockett was born on September 25, 1830, in Morgan County, Alabama.
5. John Elijah Crockett was born on July 6, 1832, in Morgan County, Alabama.

According to the 1830 Morgan County, Alabama Census, the John Crockett household had the following: White Males 40-50: 1; White Females 0-5: 2, White Females 40-50: 1. In 1830, John Crockett owned a total of 31 Black slaves which included 12 males and 19 females; some records indicate that he owned 37 slaves.

On May 24, 1831, John Crockett entered 159.92 acres of land in the Northeast ¼ of Section 13 of Township 7 South and Range 2 West in Morgan County, Alabama; on the same date, he entered 159.95 acres in the Southeast ¼ of Section 12 of Township 7 South and Range 2 West in Morgan County, Alabama. On August 2, 1831, John Crockett entered 80.11 acres of land in the East ½ of the Northeast ¼ of Section 14 of Township 7 South and Range 2 West in Morgan County, Alabama (Cowart, 1981). On November 4, 1833, James Wallis, the brother-in-law of John Crockett, entered 39.98 acres in the same section.

On November 29, 1832, John Crockett entered 40.01 acres of land in the Southeast ¼ of the Southeast ¼ of Section 11 of Township 7 South and Range 2 West in Morgan County, Alabama (Cowart, 1981). Also in the same section, John McKenzie, brother-in-law of John Crockett, owned 160.04 acres in the Northwest ¼ that he entered on July 28, 1821.

From January 1836 through February 1837, John Crockett was included in a partial list of customers of Troup's General Store located at Somerville, Alabama. The list identified John Crockett as being in the area during that time period.

Probably prior to 1840, John Crockett and his family migrated west and eventually wound up in Texas. On November 24, 1849, Mary Haynes Davies Crockett died in Texas. On May 15, 1853, John Crockett died in Texas.

Dallas (Dallis), Dennis

In 1795, Dennis Dallas of Morgan County, Alabama, was born in Kentucky. His father was Joshua Dallas Sr. (1760-1848), and his mother was Nancy Keith (1772-1835). Joshua and Nancy Keith Dallas had the following children:
1. Dennis Dallas (1795-1849)
2. Agnes Dallas (1799-1866)
3. Joshua Dallas (1802-1879)
4. Marmaduke Dallas (1806)
5. Robert David Dallas (1815-1850)
6. John Dallas

In the War of 1812, Dennis Dallas served and fought in the Battle of Horsehoe Bend with his brother John. Dennis was with the Copeland Regiment of Tennessee Volunteers.

According to the 1820 Franklin County, Tennessee Census, Dennis Dallis was a resident of the area. By 1830, Dennis Dallas was living in Morgan County, Alabama.

About 1825, Dennis Dallas married Agnes Dougan. They had the following children:
1. John Newton Dallas (1826-1907) married Martha Jane Owen (1829-?).
2. Sarah M. Dallas (1835-?)

In the 1830 Morgan County, Alabama Census, the Dennis Dallis household had the following: White Males 0-5: 1, 5-10: 1, 30-40: 1 (Dennis Dallas); White Females 0-5: 2, 5-10: 1, 30-40: 1; Slaves: Males 12, Females 11, Total Slaves 23.

According to the 1840 Morgan County, Alabama Census, Regiment 39, the Dennis Dallas household had the following: White Males10-15: 1, 15-20: 1, 40-50: 1 (Dennis Dallas); White Females 0-5: 1, 5-10: 1, 10-15: 2. The number of slaves of Dennis Dallas was not listed in 1840 census of Morgan County, Alabama.

In the Franklin County, Tennessee, Court Minute book, 1832-1837, is the following: "Be known that at the July term of the Circuit Court holden for the County aforesaid, at the Courthouse in the town of Winchester on the 26th day of July 1837, personally appeared in open Court, Mary Noe of Franklin, Tennessee, and Travis Barbee of Lawrence County, Alabama, and Satisfactorily proved to the Court that Mary, who intermarried with Peter Noe, Margaret who intermarried with Travis Barbee of Lawrence County, Alabama, Agness who intermarried with Dennis Dallis of Morgan County, Alabama, Jane Doudan of Lawrence County Alabama. Robert C.J. Dougan of Fayette County, Tennessee, and Sharp Dougan of Marshall County, Alabama, dec'd, who died on the 10th day of February 1837 leaving at the time of his death no widow and that at the United States under the Act if Congress of the 7th day of June 1832 and was the identical James Dougan mentioned in as original pension certificate in his possession on the day of his death and which is here shown to the Court and of which the following is a true copy, viz: War Department, Revolutionary Claim-I certify that in conformity with the law of the United States of the 7th day of June, 1832. James Dougan of the State of Tennessee who was an Ensign Lieutenant and Major in the Army of the Revolution is entitled to receive Two Hundred and One dollars and Sixty Six cents per annum during his natural life; commencing on the 4th day of March 1836, and payable semi-annually on the 4th day of March and the 4th day of September in every year. Given at War office of the United States this 19th day of March, One Thousand Eight Hundred and thirty four. Lew. Cass, Secretary of War, Examined and Countersigned, J.L. Edwards, Commissioner of Pensions."

About 1849, Dennis Dallas died in Lincoln County, Tennessee. After 1850, Agnes Dougan Dallas, the widow of Dennis Dallas, and John C. Dickey, the widower of Agnes Dallas Dickey, married each other. It appears that Dennis Dallas and his sister Agnes Dallas Dickey both died before 1850, and that their widowed spouses married each other.

In the 1850 Lincoln County, Tennessee Census, Agnes Dougan Dallas Dickey and the children listed were the children of John and first wife Agnes Dallas. Accordingly, Agnes Dougan Dallas Dickey was the aunt and the step-mother of the children listed in the census.

After 1850, John C. Dickey went to Texas to get a land grant of 320 acres in Ellis County, Texas. John left his family in Lincoln County, Tennessee, and he lived in one room at the Fanthorp Inn in Anderson, Texas, until his death in 1852. Agnes Dougan Dallas Dickey passed away in 1866.

Dancy, Fancis

Francis Dancy and Mary Winfield Mason Dancy had the following children: William Dancy, Sarah "Sallie" Winfield Dancy Sykes, William Francis Dancy, and Martha Mason Dancy Rhodes. Through their mother, the Dancy children were the cousins of General Winfield Scott who removed the Cherokees from Alabama, Georgia, North Carolina, and Tennessee during the Indian removal of 1838.

Captain William Dancy

On July 2, 1780, Captain William Dancy was born in Greensville County, Virginia. His parents were Francis Dancy and Mary Winfield Mason Dancy.

On December 13, 1802, Captain William Dancy married Priscilla Turner. Priscilla Turner was born on March 18, 1784, to Simon Turner and Elizabeth

Person. Her sister was Burchett Lundy Turner; Burchett married Dr. William Sykes. The sons of Burchett and William Sykes were slave owners and cotton planters in Morgan County.

Captain William Dancy and Priscilla Turner Dancy had the following children:
1. Louisa T. Dancy married Joseph Sykes; Joseph owned 38 slaves in 1830 and 45 slaves in 1840 in Morgan County, Alabama. Joseph Sykes and Louisa T. Dancy moved to Mississippi after 1840. Louisa died on March 31, 1887; she was buried in Friendship Cemetery at Columbus in Lowndes County, Mississippi (Find A Grave Memorial Number 13259893).
2. David Mason Dancy, Sr., Methodist preacher, married Jane E. Mason. On June 1, 1836, David Mason Dancy entered 40.12 acres in Section 29 of Township 5 South and Range 5 West in Morgan County, Alabama (Cowart, 1981). In 1840, David owned 15 slaves in Morgan County, Alabama.
3. John Winfield Scott Dancy (9/3/1810-2/13/1866) first married Sarah Evalina Rhodes (1820-1836) in 1835, the daughter of Dr. Henry W. Rhodes. After her death, John moved to Texas; he married Lucy Ann Nowlin (1828-1902). John Winfield Scott Dancy was one of the leaders of the Republic of Texas, and later a Texas State Senator. John was buried in at Old LaGrange City Cemetery in Fayette County, Texas (Find A Grave Memorial Number 68887998).
4. A. G. Dancy, nothing is known of him.
5. Dr. Charles Francis Mason Dancy (9/7/1814-9/7/1875) married Sarah Dandridge Garth. In 1850, Charles owned 15 slaves in Morgan County, Alabama. Dr. Charles Francis Mason Dancy was buried in the Garth Cemetery at Decatur in Morgan County, Alabama (Find A Grave Memorial Number 21589916).
6. William Joseph Dancy (12/8/1817-6/2/1820) was buried in Gunn Cemetery at Trinity in Morgan County, Alabama (Find A Grave Memorial Number 32462453).

On September 13, 1813, Captain William Dancy took oaths of office of the Greenville County, Virginia Militia. He was in the Company of Light

Infantry attached to the 1st Battalion of the 50th Regiment and 15th Brigade. He fought for Colonel James Byrne and General William Chamberlayne.

On July 15, 1818, William Dancy entered 159.88 acres of land in the Southeast ¼ of Section 13 of Township 5 South and Range 5 West in Morgan County, Alabama (Cowart, 1981). On the same day, William Dancy entered 159.78 acres of land in the Southeast ¼ of Section 20 of Township 5 South and Range 5 West in Morgan County, Alabama (Cowart, 1981). On that same date, William Dancy entered 160.9 acres of land in the Southwest ¼ of Section 21 of Township 5 South and Range 5 West in Morgan County, Alabama (Cowart, 1981). Based on his land entries, it appears that William Dancy moved to Morgan County, Alabama, in the summer of 1818.

On April 6, 1820, Priscilla Turner Dancy died in Morgan County, Alabama (Find A Grave Memorial Number 32462536). She was buried in the Gunn Cemetery at Trinity in Morgan County, Alabama.

On February 6, 1822, William Dancy entered 80.24 acres of land in the West ½ of the Northwest ¼ of Section 17 of Township 5 South and Range 5 West in Morgan County, Alabama (Cowart, 1981).

Beginning in the 1820's, Captain William Dancy was a Justice of the Peace in Morgan County, Alabama. His duties as Justice of the Peace continued into the 1830's.

From 1827 to 1828, William Dancy was Junior Warden of The Rising Sun Masonic Lodge No. 29 in Decatur, Alabama. His brother, Colonel William Francis Dancy, served as the Worshipful Master of the Rising Sun Masonic Lodge Number 29 during the time William was Junior Warden.

On July 30, 1830, William Dancy entered 160.9 acres of land in the Southeast ¼ of Section 21 of Township 5 South and Range 5 West in Morgan County, Alabama (Cowart, 1981). On the same day, William Dancy entered 160.9 acres of land in the Northwest ¼ of Section 28 of Township 5 South and Range 5 West in Morgan County, Alabama (Cowart, 1981).

According to the 1830 Morgan County, Alabama Census, the William Dancy household contained the following: White Males 20-30: 4, 30-40: 1, 40-50: 1; White Females 15-20: 1, 50-60: 1. In 1803, William Dancy owned 63 Black slaves.

On March 16, 1832, William Dancy entered 80.24 acres of land in the West ½ of the Northwest ¼ of Section 29 of Township 5 South and Range 5 West in Morgan County, Alabama (Cowart, 1981).

On February 2, 1836, William Dancy died in Morgan County, Alabama. William was buried in the Gunn Cemetery at Trinity in Morgan County, Alabama (Find A Grave Memorial Number 32462637).

According to the Southern Advocate on February 2, 1836, "It is with the sincerest regret that we record the death of Capt. William Dancy which occurred on the 2nd inst. at his residence in Morgan County, Ala., aged 55 years and 6 months. He died of a chronic infection of the liver."

According to Yolanda Morgan Smith, as found in the abstract deed of Donald C. Sr. and Yolanda Smith, "William Dancy of Morgan County, Alabama, was the first person to purchase the land where we live from the United States Government after the Indians were removed. In our abstract, William bought the land we have in 1830. He also owned much land in this area east of Trinity. The cemetery where he was buried is just down Tower Street from our house about a mile or so; the cemetery is out in the middle of a field with large trees and undergrowth around it. Several years ago, Don, our family, and I cleaned the cemetery which was in bad condition. Piles of field stones were outside the fenced in part of the cemetery. The fenced in part of the cemetery was the graves of the Dancy family and other family members. There were depressions in the soil outside the fence assumed to be the graves of the Dancy slaves. Someone had piled the fieldstones which were assumed to be the headstones of slaves."

Colonel William Francis Dancy

William Francis Dancy (1780-1849) was the son of Francis Dancy and Mary Winfield Mason Dancy. He married Elizabeth Mason.

On December 24, 1822, Francis Dancy entered 80.14 acres of land in the East ½ of the Southwest ¼ of Section 6 of Township 8 South and Range 4 West in Morgan County, Alabama (Cowart, 1981). On the same date, Francis Dancy entered 80.26 acres of land in the East ½ of the Northeast ¼ of Section 1 of Township 8 South and Range 5 West in Morgan County, Alabama (Cowart, 1981).

On November 22, 1826, The Rising Sun Lodge Number 29 was organized in Decatur, Alabama. The following men signed as petitioners to the Grand Lodge of Ancient Free and Accepted Masons of the State of Alabama: Francis Dancy, Isaac Lane, Henry W. Rhodes, William Dancy, James T. Sykes, Gaius Kibby, Joseph Hersy, and Henry Adkins.

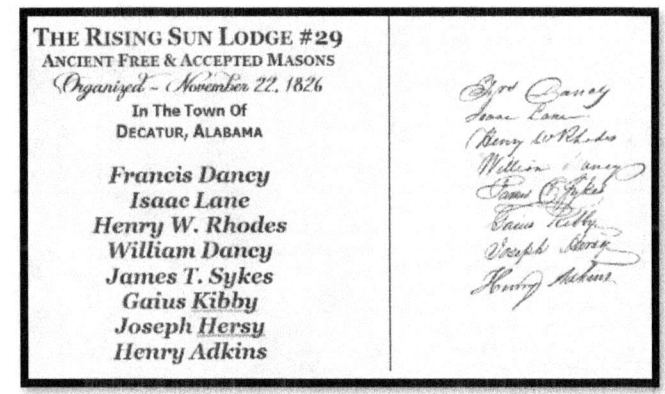

From the 1826 organization of the lodge until 1829, Francis Dancy was the first Worshipful Master of the Rising Sun Masonic Lodge Number 29 in Decatur, Alabama. Francis served three terms before the office was passed to James Fennel.

In 1829, Colonel William Francis Dancy completed his home in Decatur, Alabama. The house became the residence of his daughter Caroline Dancy and her husband Jonas C. Wood. Later, their daughter, Lavina Wood (11/21/1833-5/13/1888), and her husband, Dr. Thomas Gilchrist Polk, occupied the home.

According to the 1830 Morgan County, Alabama Census, the household of Francis Dancy had the following: White Males 10-15: 1, 20-30: 1, 40-50: 1; White Females 15-20: 2, 40-50: 1; Slaves: 13.

According to the 1830 Franklin, St. Mary's Parish, Louisiana Census, the Francis Dancy household had the following: White Males 5 total, the oldest was 40-50 years old; White Females None; Slaves: 50.

Beginning in 1830, Francis Dancy traveled between Decatur, Alabama, and St. Mary's Parish, Louisiana. Prior to moving to Louisiana in 1836, Francis established a sugar plantation there.

In the 1830 census of Morgan County, Alabama, and St. Mary's Parish, Louisiana, Francis Dancy was in both census records. In 1830, the household of Francis Dancy in Morgan County, Alabama, accounted for females, but there were no females in his household in St. Mary's Parish, Louisiana. There were also slaves at both locations with 50 slaves in Louisiana.

Around 1836, Colonel Francis Dancy moved from Decatur to St. Mary's Parish, Louisiana, to his sugar cane plantation. Colonel Dancy lived at Franklin in St. Mary's Parish, Louisiana; it is believed that he was a member of Franklin Lodge Number 57 in St. Mary's Parish. This Masonic lodge was the first in Louisiana to speak English; prior to establishing Number 57, all the other Louisiana lodges were speaking French.

Dancy-Polk House

Colonel Dancy built the Dancy-Polk House in Decatur, Alabama, which survived the Civil War. The home is listed in the National Register of Historical Places in Morgan County, Alabama. Lavina Woods Polk, granddaughter of Colonel Francis Dancy acquired the home and named it the Dancy-Polk House. Lavina married Thomas Gilchrist Polk from Maury County, Tennessee. Lavina and Thomas had several children.

At his death in 1849, Colonel William Francis Dancy received Masonic Rites at his funeral. It is believed that Colonel Dancy was buried on the Dancy Plantation grounds in Louisiana.

Wyatt Moye

After Martha Adams Moye died in 1845, Wyatt Moye married a second time to Mary Mason Dancy of the Dancy Plantation. This is believed to be the plantation of Colonel William Francis Dancy in St. Mary's Parish, Louisana.

According to the 1850 St. Mary's Parish, Louisana, Slave Schedules, Wyatt Moye and Company of the Dancy Plantation owned 119 Black slaves. Colonel Dancy died in 1849, and Moye probably took over the operation of his sugarcane plantation.

General Wyatt Moye (4/30/1793-10/21/1862) and Martha Adams Moye (2/9/1804-5/25/1845) had a daughter, Martha Caroline Moye, who married a William Francis Dancy on May 7, 1852; however, it is not known how he was related to Colonel William Francis Dancy of Decatur, Alabama, and St. Mary's Parish, Louisiana.

> **NOTICE.**
> WILL BE SOLD, at the Court House in Snow Hill, for ready money, on the second Monday in October, it being the first day of our Superior Court,
> **18 LIKELY NEGROES,**
> consisting of men, women, boys and girls—being perhaps as beautiful a lot of Negroes as ever went into any market. Those who wish to purchase will do well to attend. The sale will certainly take place.
> **WYATT MOYE**, Late Shff.
> September 8, 1829. 58vt*   of Greene County.

For many years, Wyatt Moye was a slave trader; he was known for taking North Carolina slaves and trading them in Mississippi and Louisiana. On September 8, 1829, Wyatt Moye was advertising in newspapers about the sale of Black slaves. On December 16, 1847, another advertisement mentions General Wyatt Moye dealing with slave trade.

> **TAKEN UP**
> AND committed to the jail of Davidson county, on the 29th of October, a negro man who says that his name is OWEN, and that he belongs to John Minsy, of Wayne county, and that B W Fields and Gen. Wyatt Moye, were taking him to the west when he made his escape. The said negro is about 22 or 23 years old, 5 feet 7 or 8 inches high, weighs about 160 lbs. The owner is requested to come forward, prove property, pay charges, and take him away, or he will be dealt with according to act of assembly.
> JOHN P. MABRY, Jailor.
> Lexington, N. C. Dec 16, 1847   37tf

On October 21, 1862, Wyatt died on the Dancy Plantation in St. Mary's Parish, Louisiana. After his death, Wyatt Moye was carried back to his home state of North Carolina. He was buried in the Calvary Church Cemetery at Tarboro in Edgecombe County, North Carolina (Find A Grave Memorial Number 24810019).

Sarah "Sallie" Winfield Dancy Sykes

On July 26, 1794, Sarah "Sallie" Winfield Dancy was born in North Carolina. She was the daughter of Francis Dancy Sr. and Mary Winfield Mason Dancy.

Sarah "Sallie" Winfield Dancy married Colonel James Turner Sykes. James was born in Virginia in 1799; he was the son of Dr. William Sykes and Burchett Lundy Turner from Greenville County, Virginia. Colonel James T. Sykes was a tall and handsome man; he commanded a regiment in the war of 1812 stationed at Norfolk, Virginia. James and Sallie lived about six miles west of Decatur.

Sarah "Sallie" Winfield Dancy Sykes and James Turner Sykes had the following children:
1. Dr. Francis "Frank" Winfield Sykes was born on April 19, 1819, in Chatham County, North Carolina; he married Susan Elizabeth Garth (1823-1875). Susan was the daughter of General Jesse Winston Garth; General Garth was a military leader, political figure, land baron with several plantations, owner of over 200 slaves, and a cotton planter. Frank and Elizabeth had a son John who died young and two daughters-Eunice Sykes Michie and Molly Sykes Groesbeck. In 1840, after graduating from Nashville and Transylvania Universities, Dr. Frank W. Sykes moved to Courtland in Lawrence County, Alabama. After purchasing the plantation of George W. Foster, Dr. Frank Sykes became a cotton planter and political figure; he served in Alabama House of Representatives and Senate. In the 1860 Lawrence County, Alabama, slave census, Frank and Sallie owned 58 black slaves. On January 6, 1883, Francis W. Sykes died at Decatur; he was buried in the Garth Cemetery at Decatur in Morgan County, Alabama (Find A Grave Memorial Number 21561527).
2. James Turner Sykes Jr. was born in Alabama in 1823; he married Sarah "Sallie" Ethelred Lundy (1828-1867). On December 13, 1852, James died at Aberdeen in Monroe County, Mississippi (Find A Grave Memorial Number 116166826).
3. Sarah Winfield Sykes Malone was born on August 23, 1827, in Alabama; in 1847, she married Samuel Booth Malone (1804-1863).

On April 5, 1854, Sarah died in Mississippi; she was buried in Friendship Cemetery at Columbus in Lowndes County, Mississippi (Find A Grave Memorial Number 12914909).

4. Andrew Jackson "Jack" Sykes was born in 1830; he married Emma Swoope. Emma was the daughter of John M. and Cynthia Early Swoope; John Swoope owned 129 slaves in 1850. In 1860, Dr. Jack Sykes owned 15 slaves; during the Civil War, he served as a surgeon. On April 8, 1887, Andrew Jackson "Jack" Sykes died at Courtland; he was buried in the Swoope-Ussery Cemetery in Lawrence County, Alabama (Find A Grave Memorial Number 26622080).

From December 4, 1818, through September 30, 1839, James T. Sykes entered some 1,135 acres in Townships 5, 6, 7 South and Ranges 1, 2, 3, 4, 5 West in Morgan County, Alabama (Cowart, 1981). The land he entered was scattered across Morgan County.

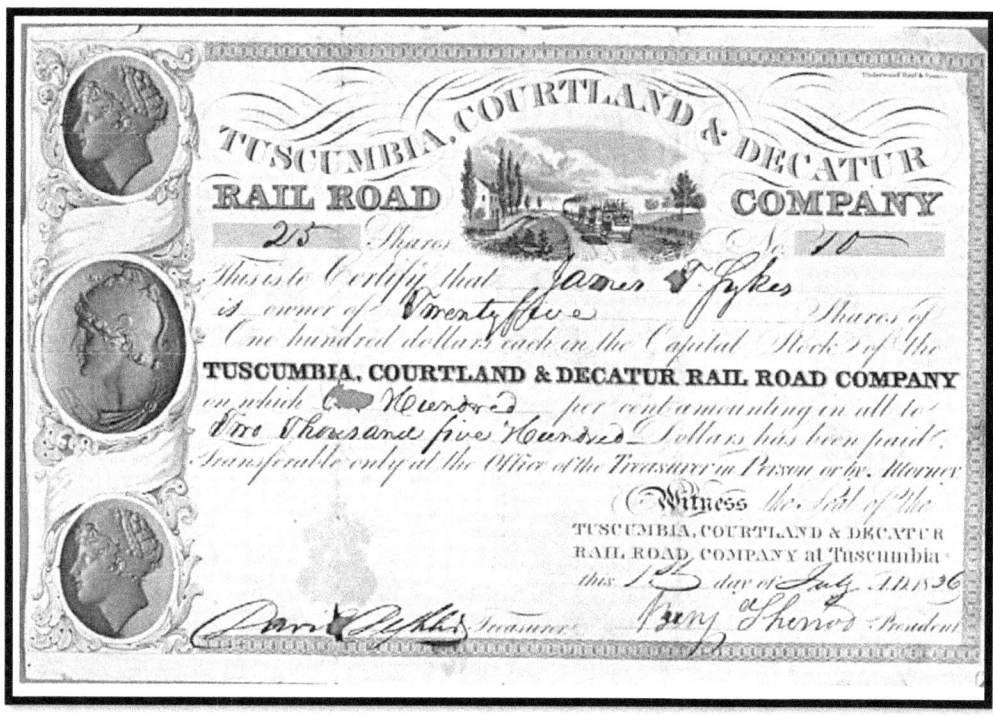

In 1828, Colonel Sykes was a member of the Alabama Legislature. For many years, he was president of the Branch Bank at Decatur. James was the third Worshipful Master of Rising Sun Lodge Number 29 in Decatur.

According to the 1830 Morgan County, Alabama Census, James T. Sykes owned 46 Black slaves. James Turner Sykes also owned 25 shares in the Tuscumbia, Courtland, & Decatur Railroad Company.

On January 29, 1835, at the age of 40 years, Sarah "Sallie" Winfield Dancy died in Decatur, Alabama. She was buried in Lafayette Street Cemetery at Decatur in Morgan County, Alabama (Find A Grave Memorial Number 11492219).

[A.]—*A table showing the liabilities of the president and directors of the branch of the Bank of the State of Alabama at Decatur, as drawers and acceptors of bills of exchange, both in their own and the names of their different firms, on the 1st January, 1st June, and 1st November, 1837.*

Names.	Liabilities on bills of exchange.			Am't of accommodation from 1st Nov. 1836, to 1st Nov. 1837.	Remarks.
	1st Jan. 1837.	1st June, 1837.	1st Nov. 1837.		
Horace Greene	$17,805 24	$19,859 61	$12,359 61	$32,664 85	
James Fennell	–	24,993 17	15,193 17	26,193 17	
Jesse W. Garth	8,700 00	9,114 78	3,814 78	17,814 78	
M. C. Houston	2,000 00	4,000 00	–	4,256 00	
James T. Sykes	39,876 86	45,161 58	9,745 33	47,779 35	Draft on Mobile for $10,000, deposited 8th February, 1837.
George Swink	22,575 91	28,500 00	9,500 00	41,575 91	
A. S. Christian	96,869 05	35,002 97	20,797 40	78,694 76	$22,000 draft placed to credit, 3d February, 1837.
Henry W. Rhodes	40,531 34	26,829 04	18,437 14	55,816 18	Deposited check on Mobile for $20,000, 2d February, 1837.
Isaac N. Owen	28,000 00	–	–	–	Resigned 22d February, 1837.
Robert H. High	22,700 00	31,687 13	–	33,934 13	Resigned 5th October, 1837.
Henry A. Bragg	8,000 00	8,000 00	–	11,000 00	
James Irwin	–	8,000 00	–	8,000 00	
Thomas Wilson	–	4,000 00	–	4,000 00	
M. B. Hampton	3,000 00	13,250 00	12,750 00	26,250 00	
M. P. T. Brindley	–	–	–	–	
J. W. Thomas	–	15,000 00	–	17,700 00	Elected 22d February, 1837.
William Saunders	–	–	–	–	Elected 5th October, 1837.
Benjamin Hubert	527 50	2,315 90	542 50	5,760 90	} Partners of A. S. Christian.
John C. Simpson	527 50	3,786 46	1,446 66	4,328 96	

In 1837, the brothers-in-law - Henry W. Rhodes and James T. Sykes - were wealthy land and slave owners in Morgan County, Alabama. In January 1837, according to the records of the Decatur branch of the Alabama State Bank, Henry W. Rhodes had $40, 531.34 and James T. Sykes had $39,876.86 in their bank accounts.

On June 25, 1849, James Turner Sykes, the husband of Sarah "Sallie" Winfield Dancy Sykes, died at Aberdeen, Mississippi. He was buried in the Odd Fellows Rest Cemetery in Monroe County, Mississippi (Find A Grave Memorial Number 13942253).

Martha Mason Dancy Rhodes

On March 14, 1797, Martha Mason Dancy was born to Francis Dancy Sr. and Mary Winfield Mason Dancy in Northampton County, North Carolina. On July 14, 1812, at 15 years old, Martha married Dr. Henry W. Rhodes in Northampton, North Carolina; he was born in North Carolina in 1791.

Martha Mason Dancy and Dr. Henry W. Rhodes had the following children:
1. Henry David Rhodes (1818-1866)
2. Sarah Evalina Rhodes Dancy (1820-1836)
3. Dewitt Clinton Rhodes (1830-1858).

On July 3, 1811, Henry W. Rhodes entered 160.68 acres of land in the Southeast ¼ of Section 5 in Township 4 South and Range 1 West in Madison County of Mississippi Territory (Cowart, 1979); therefore, by 1811, he was purchasing land in present-day North Alabama.

From July 11, 1818, through February 18, 1834, Dr. Henry W. Rhodes entered 1,705 acres of land in Townships 5, 6 West and Ranges 4, 5 South in Morgan County, Alabama (Cowart, 1981). On June 15, 1820, Henry W. Rhodes along with Jesse Winston Garth, McKinney Holderness, Isaac Lane, and George Peck entered 1,080 acres of land in Township 5 South and Range 4 West in Morgan County, Alabama (Cowart, 1981). On December 19, 1833, Henry W. Rhodes and his brother-in-law James T. Sykes entered 160 acres of land in Township 5 South and Range 5 West in Morgan County, Alabama (Cowart, 1981).

In June 1820, Dr. Henry W. Rhodes, Jesse Winston Garth, McKinney Holderness, Isaac Lane, and George Peck of the Decatur Land Company received patents for the land on which they would build the Town of Decatur. They would become known as the Founders of Decatur, Alabama. Dr. Rhodes was the first postmaster of Decatur.

On November 22, 1826, Dr. Henry W. Rhodes, William Francis Dancy, Col. Isaac Lane, William Dancy, James T. Sykes, Gaius Kibby, Joseph Hersy, Joseph Adkins organized a Masonic Lodge which would be chartered in 1827 as "The Rising Sun."

On December 8, 1826, Dr. Henry W. Rhodes served in the Alabama Legislature when an act incorporated the Town of Decatur.. During 1826, 1832, and 1835, Dr. Rhodes was Morgan County's representative to the Alabama Legislature.

From 1828-30, Dr. Henry W. Rhodes was elected and served on the Board of Trustees of the University of Alabama. He was a charter member on the Board of Directors of the Tuscumbia, Courtland & Decatur Railway Company. Dr. Rhodes was one of the first directors of the Decatur Branch of the Alabama State Bank.

In the 1830 Morgan County, Alabama Census, the household of Henry W. Rhodes had the following: White Males 0-5: 1, 10-15: 1, 20-30: 1, 30-40: 1 (Dr. Henry W. Rhodes); White Females: 0-5: 1; 10-15: 1; 30-40: 1 (Martha Mason Dancy Rhodes); Slaves: Males 46, Females 49, Total Slaves 95.

According to Early Settlers of Alabama, "Dr. Henry W. Rhodes…was quite wealthy and full of enterprise. He conceived the idea that the cotton planters should make their own bagging and rope, and actually commenced the business, raising the hemp on the river bottom just below Decatur, and erecting his factory and rope walk on the hill opposite. But he soon abandoned the business, as cotton bore a full price, and Kentucky could undersell him in bagging and rope. He moved to Mississippi about the same time with the Sykes. They had been cautious and left with estates unimpaired by the crash of 1837. But the doctor was embarrassed, although he had a large estate. He obtained large acceptances from B. L. Andrews, a Jew merchant of Mobile, and in return lent the merchant his name for a large amount, on accommodation paper. In consequence of the failure of a branch house in New Orleans, the house of B. L. Andrews went down also. Poor Andrews, when he heard of the failure he was so mortified at the loss of commercial honor, that he filled his pockets with the paper weights which lay on his office table, and went out on the wharf, and drowned himself. I deeply lamented his tragic end. I knew him well, having been a member of the Directory of the Bank of Mobile with him for some years, and learned to respect him as a

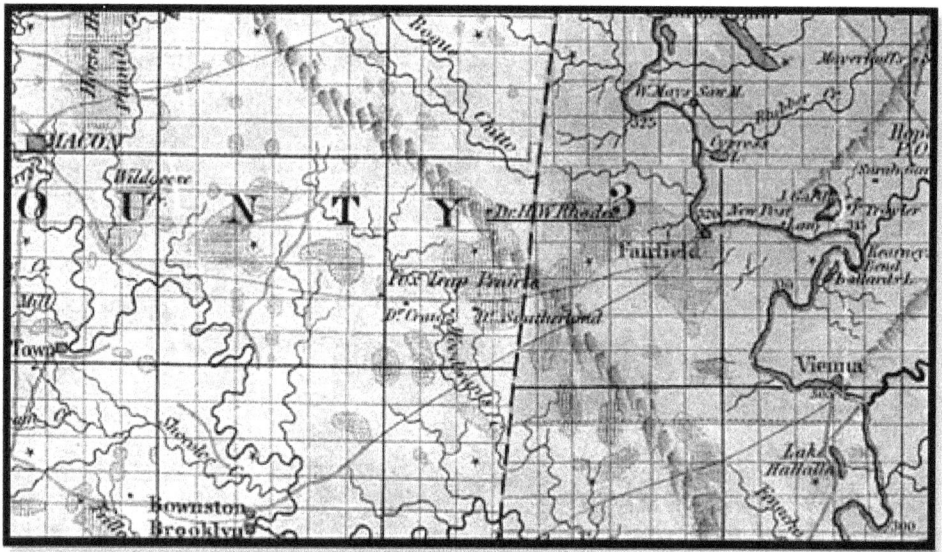

1838 Alabama map
Dr. Henry W. Rhodes
AL-MS state line

gentleman and an accomplished merchant. I never learned how Dr. Rhodes' estate wound up" (Saunders, 1899).

By 1838, Martha Mason Dancy Rhodes and Henry W. Rhodes owned land along the Alabama and Mississippi state lines; they moved southwest and settled near the state line. According to an 1838 map of Alabama, Dr. Henry W. Rhodes was located in the Fox Trap Prairie across the border from Noxubee County, Mississippi. Dr. Rhodes owned some 3,000 acres of land in the prairie area of the Alabama-Mississippi state lines.

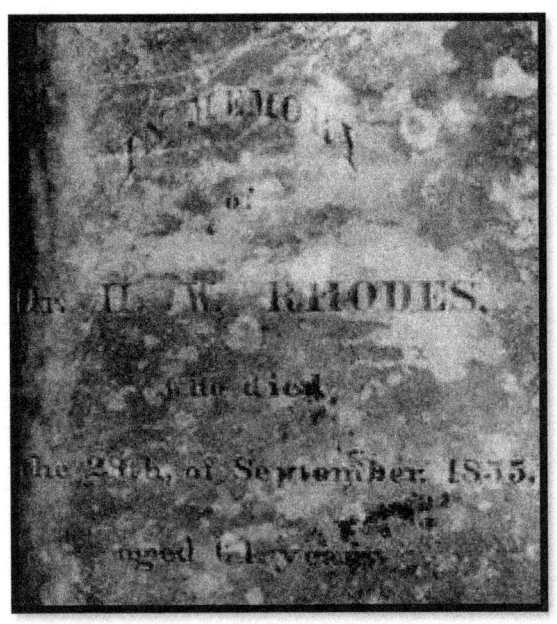

From Mississippi, it appears that Martha and Henry Rhodes eventually moved to Louisiana. On November 22, 1855, Martha Mason Dancy Rhodes died in Louisiana. Martha along with her son, Dewitt Clinton Rhodes, was buried in the Wells Cemetery in LeCompte Rapides Parish, Louisiana (Find A Grave Memorial# 28493345).

On September 28, 1855, at 64 years of age, Dr. Henry W. Rhodes died in Brazoria County, Texas. The inscription on his tombstone is as follows: "In Memory of Dr. H. W. Rhodes, who died the 28th of September, 1855, aged 64 years." He was buried in the Cedar Lake Cemetery in Brazoria, Brazoria County, Texas (Find A Grave Memorial Number 1299640876).

Davis, Riley S.

On October 2, 1839, Riley S. Davis married Francis S. Collier in Morgan County, Alabama. Riley S. Davis was represented on the list of Masonic officers during the first two decades. He was related to Fennel descendants, and had early holdings in the Trinity area.

According to the 1840 Morgan County, Alabama Census, the Riley S. Davis household had the following: White Males 0-5: 1, 5-10: 1, 30-40: 1; White Females 5-10: 1, 15-20: 1, 30-40: 1.

In 1840, Riley S. Davis owned 27 slaves with 13 being males and 14 being females. In the 1850 Morgan County, Alabama Slave Census, Riley S. Davis owned 16 slaves.

According to the 1850 Morgan County, Alabama, United States Census, Riley S. Davis of Somerville in Morgan County, Alabama, was a 47 year old white male born in Kentucky. Also listed in the household of Riley S. Davis were Sarah E. Collier, Female, 21, Alabama; Edward Collier, Male, 18, Alabama; John Collier, Male, 13 Alabama; William A. S. Collier, Male, 10 Alabama; Francis B. L. Collier, Female, 7, Alabama; and Natfield Collier, Male, 5, Alabama.

In 1860, Riley S. Davis died in Morgan County, Alabama. His grave site is not known.

The following synopsis was obtained from an article written by Gary Cosby Jr. of the Decatur Daily on June 23, 2009. "In the 1865 court records of Morgan County on Riley S. Davis' estate case file, $493 of uncirculated Confederate bills of various denominations in absolutely pristine condition was discovered. The money included a number of well used State of Alabama one dollar bills. In addition, the account ledger of Davis detailed the slaves by name and by value. When Davis passed away he had no will and his estate was settled by the Sheriff of Morgan County. At some point after his death, the slaves of Riley S. Davis were rented or hired out to various people around the county probably to pay off and settled his debts. The slaves included a 12 year old girl named Mary and a couple with seven children (Cosby, 2009)."

"A document filed in chancery court almost a month after the Civil War ended in 1865 gave an itemized list of people hiring slaves who had belonged to Davis, along with the amount of money that was due to his estate. The tally showed the file was $493 short. It was speculated that the clerk made up the difference with Confederate cash that was worthless because the war was either over or near its end. The like new condition of the cash suggested it came to the local court system directly from the Confederate Congress. The bills are in $1, $5, $10 and $50 denominations, and some had consecutive serial numbers (Cosby, 2009)."

Evans, Nathaniel

In 1797, Nathaniel Evans was born in East Tennessee. Nathaniel was the son of Joseph Evans and Elizabeth "Betsy" Earnest. Nathaniel Evans lived in Kentucky in his youth, and he moved with his family to Madison County of Mississippi Territory.

On January 29, 1818, Nathaniel Evans first married Jane Pride in Madison County. Jane was born January 29, 1800, in Blount County, Tennessee, to Burton Pride and Susan Bizwell.

Nathaniel Evans and Jane Pride Evans had the following children:
1. Hamilton P. Evans was born in 1822 in Morgan County, Alabama, and he died in 1862 in St. Francis County, Arkansas.
2. Martha B. Evans was born in 1824 in Morgan County, Alabama, and she died in 1916 at Mansfield in Tarrant County, Texas.
3. Franklin Evans was born in 1825 in Morgan County, Alabama.
4. Mary Ann Evans was born in 1826 in Morgan County, Alabama.
5. Nathaniel Evans Jr. was born in 1828 in Morgan County, Alabama, and he died in 1863 in Morgan County, Alabama.
6. Captain William Jefferson Evans was born about May 1830 in Morgan County, Alabama, and he died on July 29, 1916, at Purdon in Navarro County, Texas. William was buried in the Younger Cemetery at Silver City in Navarro County, Texas (Find A Grave Memorial Number 23928384).

7. Reuben was born about 1831 in Morgan County, Alabama, and he died at Baird in Callahan County, Texas.
8. Susannah Evans Williams was born in 1833, in Morgan County, Alabama. On January 22, 1851, Susannah married David Hughes Williams Jr.
9. Joseph Morgan Evans was born on June 15, 1836, in Morgan County, Alabama. He was named after his grandfather Joseph and his birth county of Morgan. Joseph served in the Confederate Army from DeSoto County, Mississippi. In the 1870s, Joseph and his wife Elvira Cook McDowell moved to Stephens County, Texas, where Joseph worked for many years as a stone mason in and around Breckenridge. On June 18, 1901, Joseph Morgan Evans died in Breckenridge, Texas. Joseph was buried in the Breckenridge Cemetery at Breckenridge in Stephens County, Texas (Find A Grave Memorial Number 82069291).

Probably by July 1818, based on land records, the family of Nathaniel Evans moved across the Tennessee River to Morgan County, Alabama. On July 20, 1818, Nathaniel Evans entered 159.95 acres of land in the Southwest ¼ of Section 8 of Township 6 South and Range 2 West in Morgan County, Alabama (Cowart, 1981).

About 1838, Jane Pride Evans died in Morgan County. She was probably buried somewhere around Somerville in Morgan County, Alabama.

On February 23, 1842, Nathaniel Evans married the widow Catherine Betts. On May 30, 1825, Catherine married Barbee Betts of Madison County, Alabama; he died in 1831 or 1832. Catherine and Barbee had two children: Barbee Betts and Martha Ann Betts.

Nathaniel Evans and Catherine Williams Betts Evans (1805-1871). They had the following children:
1. Clinton Evans (born about 1843)
2. John Freeman Evans (1847-1915);
3. Ann Catherine Evans Rash (1849-1900).

In the November 5, 1850, Somerville, Division 9, Morgan County, Alabama Census, Nathaniel Evans was a 55 year old White male born in

Tennessee; he was a farmer with an estate value of $6,000.00. Also listed in his household was the following: Catharine, 45, female, Virginia; Reuben, 19, male, farmer, Morgan County, Alabama; William, 18, male, farmer, Morgan County, Alabama; Joseph, 16, male, farmer, Morgan County, Alabama; Clinton, 7, male, Morgan County, Alabama; Freeman, 4, male, Morgan County, Alabama; Ann C., 2, female, Morgan County, Alabama; and Mary Ennis, 66 f, Tennessee. According to the 1850 Morgan County, Alabama Slave Schedule, Nathaniel Evans owned 47 slaves with 39 Black slaves and eight Mulatto.

In the 1850s, Nathaniel and Catherine moved to the part of Desoto County, Mississippi, that later became Tate County. They probably had a cotton plantation in Mississippi.

On November 8, 1871, at age 65-66, Catherine Williams Betts Evans died in Desoto County, Mississippi. She was buried in the Bethel Cemetery at Coldwater in Tate County, Mississippi (Find A Grave Memorial Number 3053119).

On January 14, 1877, Nathaniel Evans died at Senatobia in Tate County, Mississippi. He was buried in Bethel Cemetery at Coldwater in Tate County, Mississippi (Find A Grave Memorial# 30531122).

Fennel, Wiley

On March 29, 1773, Wiley Fennel was born to French Huguenot descendants in Southampton County, Virginia. Wiley was the son of John Fennell Jr. and Ann Powell of Northampton County, Virginia. Wiley probably had a brother John that went to Texas, and a brother James that entered land in Madison County of Mississippi Territory.

In 1776, Sarah "Sally" Fox, future wife of Wiley Fennel, was born in Brunswick County, Virginia. Sarah was the daughter of John and Selah Bonner Fox.

On January 9, 1800, Wiley Fennel married Sarah "Sally" Fox in Greenville County, Virginia. Wiley Fennel and Sarah "Sally" Fox Fennel had the following children:
1. John Allen Fennel was born in 1802 in Raleigh, North Carolina. John moved to Tennessee, then Texas; he died in Texas.
2. James Fennel was born on February 23, 1803, at Raleigh in Wake County, North Carolina, and moved with family to Morgan County, Alabama. James died on July 9, 1849, and was buried in the Fennel Cemetery in Morgan County, Alabama.
3. Celia Bonner Fennel was born May 19, 1805, at Raleigh in Wake County, North Carolina. In 1824, Celia married George Peck from Botetourt County, Virginia; George died in April 1826. Celia Fennel Peck and George Peck had a son John W. Peck (5/7/1825-11/26/1883) who became one of the wealthiest cotton planters in Morgan County, Alabama. In 1860 in Morgan County, Alabama, John W. Peck owned 27 slaves and 2,400 acres of land worth $30,000.00. On August 17, 1848, John married Sarah Elizabeth Love, daughter of William Love and Margaret Fennel. John W. Peck was buried in the Fennel Cemetery at Trinity in Morgan  County, Alabama (Find A Grave Memorial Number 16879439). On July 4, 1827, Celia married William Darwin (10/8/1799-8/22/1838). On March 18, 1849, Celia married Richard Moseley Bouldin (5/28/1801-8/2/1853); Richard was the son of Richard Bouldin and Elizabeth Moseley. Richard M. Bouldin was a slave owner, who was a first cousin to Green Bouldin. Richard had a very valuable group of slaves, several valued at $1,200.00 each as shown in his estate file in 1853. Celia died on October 2, 1882, at Pilot Point in Denton, Texas.

4. Ann Fennel was born on October 1, 1807, at Raleigh in Wake County, North Carolina. In 1826, Ann married Richard M. Bouldin (5/28/1801-8/2/1853). According to the 1840 Morgan County, Alabama Census, Richard M. Bouldin was between 30 and 40 years old. In his household, he had five Whites and 17 Black slaves. Ann Fennel Bouldin died on April 15, 1848, and was buried in the Fennel Cemetery at Trinity in Morgan County, Alabama.
5. Colonel Henry "Harry" W. Fennel was born about 1811 at Raleigh in Wake County, North Carolina. On April 20, 1835, Henry married Sarah Deloney in Lawrence County, Alabama. Henry died on August 24, 1869, at Decatur in Morgan County, Alabama.
6. Sarah A. Fennel Lane Morris was born on January 8, 1812, at Raleigh in Wake County, North Carolina. On March 18, 1830, Sarah married Jesse A. Lane in Morgan County, Alabama. In 1830, Jesse owned 12 slaves; he was buried in the Fennel Cemetery. On September 2, 1841, Sarah married Reverend Moses Strode Morris (Find A Grave Memorial Number 56820880) who was born in 1808; he died on December 13, 1849, after being shot and killed by Doctor Delony near Decatur. Moses S. Morris is buried in the Fennel Cemetery at Trinity. In 1860 in Morgan County, Sarah Fennel Lane Morris owned 11 slaves and 1,048 acres of land worth $20,000.00; she was among the wealthiest cotton planters in the county. Sarah died on July 11, 1878, and was buried in the Fennel Cemetery in Morgan County, Alabama.
7. Margaret Fennel Allen was born on May 27, 1814, at Raleigh in Wake County, North Carolina. On March 16, 1831, Margaret married William Wilburn Love in Morgan County, Alabama. On December 19, 1833, Margaret married John Franklin Allen in Morgan County. In 1850, John F. Allen owned 23 slaves. Margaret died on March 6, 1855; she was buried in the Fennel Cemetery in Morgan County, Alabama.
8. Mary Fennel was born on April 07, 1817, in Morgan County, Alabama. Mary died on August 3, 1838, at Huntsville in Madison County, Alabama; she was buried in the Fennel Cemetery at Trinity in Morgan County, Alabama.
9. Nelson Fennel Sr. was born in 1820 at Trinity in Morgan County, Alabama. Nelson first married a woman by the name of Julia. In the 1860 Lawrence County, Alabama Census, Nelson Fennel owned 23

slaves. On October 13, 1868, Nelson married Virginia Puryear at Courtland in Lawrence County, Alabama.

Prior to the 1816 Turkey Town Treaty, Wiley Fennel and his family came to Alabama from North Carolina. They first settled in the Guntersville area of Alabama. After the treaty removed the Cherokee Indians from the northwest Alabama, Wiley Fennel moved west along the Tennessee River into Morgan County where he purchased vast tracks of land west of Decatur.

On January 20, 1817, James Fennel entered 80.32 acres in the West ½ of the Southeast ¼ of Section 4 of Township 5 South and Range 1 East in Madison County of Mississippi Territory (Cowart, 1979). This James Fennel could have been the brother of Wiley Fennel.

On July 15, 1818, Wiley Fennel entered 878.5 acres of land around the mouth of Fox's Creek in Sections 30, 31, and 19 of Townships 4, 5 South and Range 5 West in Morgan County, Alabama (Cowart, 1981). The Wiley Fennell family first settled in northwestern corner of Morgan County, and then extended their land holdings into Lawrence and present-day Colbert Counties.

Wiley Fennel made his home some three miles west of Decatur where he operated a cotton plantation. Wiley built a summer home for his family that was called Summer Seat. The house was located south of the old stage coach road leading from Decatur to Courtland; the old road was originally an Indian trail known as the South River Road and became known as the Tuscumbia Road. The area was originally called Fennel's Turnout, but later, it became known as Trinity after Trinity Methodist Church located nearby.

Summer Seat was located northeast of the Fennel Family Cemetery; the home overlooked a deep valley known as Happy Hollow. In the early 1800's, the Methodist Church held summer camp revivals in the hollow.

Wiley Fennel was a business partner of George Peck, whose family were the first settlers, among the Kimbells and Darwins, in the regions inland from Finley Island, where Kimbells operated an early stagecoach inn on the present-day Highway 20 which was originally the South River Road, the Tuscumbia Road, old Courtland-Decatur Road, and Joe Wheeler Highway.

On December 23, 1826, Wiley Fennel died at age 53 at Trinity in Morgan County, Alabama. Wiley is buried in the east end of Fennell Cemetery, Group 4, Row 1, at Trinity (Find A Grave Memorial Number 16870039). His tombstone has the following: "In Memory of Willie Fennel, Born in Southampton Co, VA Died Dec 23d 1826 aged 53. This stone a tribute erected by his children."

According to the 1830 Morgan County, Alabama Census, the Sarah Fox Fennel household had the following: White Males 10-15: 1, 20-30: 3; White Females 10-15: 1, 15-20: 1, 50-60: 1. In 1830, Sarah Fennel owned 30 Black slaves consisting of 18 males and 12 females.

On August 1, 1831, Sarah "Sally" Fox Fennel, wife of Wylie Fennel, died at Trinity in Morgan County, Alabama (Find A Grave Memorial Number 16870030). Wiley and Sally Fennel were buried in the Fennel Cemetery on Trinity Mountain in Morgan County, Alabama.

James Fennell-Walnut Grove

On February 27, 1803, James Fennel was born in North Carolina. The parents of James Fennel were Wiley Fennel (3/29/1773-12/23/1826) and Sarah Fox Fennel (1776-9/1/ 1831).

On March 4, 1811, Mary Curtis King, future wife of James Fennel, was born near Raleigh, North Carolina. She was the daughter of Hartwell Richard King (1785-1841) and Burchet Curtiss King (1785-1872).

On September 24, 1829, James Fennel married Mary Curtis King; they lived in Summer Seat which became their summer home. The house was built by Wiley Fennel above a gorge known as Happy Hollow.

About 1829 around the time of his marriage, James Fennell purchased his Walnut Grove Plantation home from James T. Sykes. Walnut Grove was near present-day Town of Trinity in Morgan County, Alabama.

James Fennel and Mary Curtis King Fennel had the following children:

1. Alabama Fennel was born on July 26, 1830; she died on January 26, 1833 (Find A Grave Memorial Number 16870054).
2. Caroline Burchett Fennel was born on April 21, 1833; she died on July 19, 1846 (Find A Grave Memorial Number 16867009).
3. Celia Fennel Davis was born on February 16, 1836; she married Francis "Frank" Mark Davis. She died on April 30, 1894 (Find A Grave Memorial Number 14987912).
4. Ann Fennel Davis was born on July 17, 1839; she married Absalom Leonidas Davis. Ann died on May 19, 1905 (Find A Grave Memorial Number 16870086).
5. Susan Fennel Davis was born on December 27, 1841; she married John Summerfield Davis, 1827-1907. She died on March 1, 1905 (Find A Grave Memorial Number 14988100).
6. Margaret Fennel was born in 1845; she died on April 8, 1859 (Find A Grave Memorial Number 14988087).
7. James C. Fennel was born on October 9, 1846; on December 15, 1868, James "Jimmy" C. Fennel married Rebecca Delony. She was the daughter of Dr. Edward B. Delony and Nancy Emily Smith. On March 2, 1921, James C. Fennel died and was buried in King Cemetery in Colbert County, Alabama (Find A Grave Memorial Number 94477892).

On October 5, 1830, James Fennel entered 79.96 acres in the West ½ of the Northeast ¼ of Section 21of Township 6 South and Range 2 East in Madison County, Alabama (Cowart, 1979).

In 1830, James Fennel (1803-1849) served as the second Worshipful Master of Rising Sun Lodge Number 29; in 1827, the Masonic Lodge was chartered in Decatur.

On January 26, 1833, Alabama Fennel, daughter of James and Mary Curtis King Fennel died at just two and a half years old. Alabama was buried in the Fennel Cemetery near Summer Seat on Trinity Mountain.

In 1833, President Jackson authorized a state banking system and Decatur was chosen as the site of the first State Bank in North Alabama. Not only did James C. Fennell strongly support the establishment and construction of the bank, he owned the limestone rock quarry near Trinity that was used to make the five stone columns for the Decatur Branch of the Alabama State Bank. James Fennel provided the materials and Black slaves to work and make the limestone columns at his plantation quarry on Trinity Mountain. From the beginning of the bank until 1837, James Fennel was one of the twelve yearly elected directors of the Old State Bank and later served as bank president.

In October 1834, James Fennel traveled by stage to Washington where he met with President Andrew Jackson. He probably talked to President Jackson about the bank and plans for the railroad.

On December 14, 1834, the first railroad in the southeastern United States was completed from Tuscumbia to Courtland and finally to Decatur. James Fennell served as one of the Directors of the Tuscumbia, Courtland and Decatur Railway Company.

In 1836, Martin Van Buren was elected the United States President; he attended the dedication of the Decatur Branch of the Alabama State Bank. The event was a big celebration for the citizens of North Alabama. During dedication ceremonies for the bank, James Fennel freed the five Black slaves who had hand hewn the stone columns for the building. Fennel removed the shackles from his slaves and gave them their freedom because of their skillful stone work. From the start of the bank until 1837, James Fennel was one of the twelve directors that were elected on a yearly basis for the State Bank in Decatur; later, Fennel became the bank president.

James Fennel freeing slaves

On May 18, 1839, James Fennel, president of the Decatur bank, signed the conveyance of a home in Decatur called Riverview; the home was about 100 yards south of the Tennessee River. Supposedly, the home was constructed by John Sevier Rhea in 1836; Rhea was the grandson of John Sevier. Rhea got into financial difficulty and had to give up the home to the bank. Today, the home is known as the Rhea-Burleson-McIntire House.

In 1842, James Fennel was selected as the president of the Decatur Branch of the Alabama State Bank. He had several thousand dollars of deposits in the bank for an extended period of time.

On July 9, 1849, James Fennel died at age 46 at Trinity in Morgan County, Alabama. James was buried in the Fennel Cemetery, East End Plot, Group 4, Row 3 at Trinity in Morgan County, Alabama (Find a Grave Memorial Number 16867052).

Around 1854 after deeding Walnut Grove Plantation to her daughter Celia Fennel Davis, Mary Curtis King Fennel and her young children moved with her to LaGrange in Franklin County (present-day Colbert County, Alabama) near her childhood home. Mary purchased a two story brick home as a summer dwelling on LaGrange Mountain from her brother-in-law, Tignal Jones. She also had a fine home built near the foot of LaGrange Mountain.

On April 8, 1859, Margaret Fennel, youngest daughter of Mary Curtis Fennel died at the age of 14. She was buried in the Fennel Cemetery on Trinity Mountain near her two sisters and her father

On January 17, 1898, Mary Curtis King Fennel died at Leighton in Colbert County, Alabama. Mary was buried in the Fennell Cemetery at Trinity in Morgan County, Alabama (Find A Grave Memorial Number 14988072).

In the 1950's, Eleanor Massey Bridges was commissioned to paint a 35 foot by 18 foot mural in the rotunda of the old bank building. The mural depicted James Fennel freeing of the black slaves who built the building at the dedication of the old state bank in Decatur. Eleanor was a famous Alabama artist. When privately owned, the Old State Bank building was known as Leila Cantwell Seton Hall; the building is now a historical site.

Celia Fennel Davis-Walnut Grove

On July 6, 1851, Celia Fennel married Francis "Frank" Mark Davis from North Carolina. Frank was born on May 24, 1829; he attended school at LaGrange. Celia and Frank lived at the Walnut Grove home with the Mary Curtis King Fennel.

About 1854, Mary Curtis King Fennel, widow of James Fennel, deeded her Walnut Grove home to her oldest living daughter Celia Fennel Davis and her husband Francis "Frank" M. Davis.

According to the 1860 Morgan County, Alabama, Agricultural Census, Francis "Frank" Mark Davis owned 480 acres of improved land and 360 acres of unimproved land worth $15,000.00. Frank also had $450.00 worth of farming equipment and $2,500 worth of livestock.

On April 30, 1894, Celia Fennel Davis died and was buried in Fennell Cemetery (Find A Grave Memorial Number 14987912). On November 27, 1906, Francis "Frank" Mark Davis died. He was buried in the Fennell Cemetery at Trinity in Morgan County, Alabama (Find A Grave Memorial Number 14987905).

Francis "Frank" Mark Davis

About 1920, the Walnut Grove Plantation house burned down. The home was a total loss.

Ann Fennel Davis-Forest Home

On July 17, 1839, Ann Fennel was born. She was the daughter of James and Mary Curtis King Fennel.

On February 5, 1856, Ann Fennel, married Absalom Leonidas Davis, a graduate of LaGrange. He was the brother of Francis "Frank" Mark Davis who married Ann's sister, Celia.

After Ann married in 1856, Mary Curtis King Fennel, widow of James Fennel, deeded her daughter Ann Fennel Davis and her husband Absalom Leonidas Davis a 300 acre farm near Trinity. The tract of property was one of several contiguous acreages which Mary Curtis King Fennel gave to each of her children as they came of age and married.

Shortly after acquiring the property, Ann and Absalom built a fine house that they called Forest Home; it was also known as the Absalom L. Davis House. Their property was adjacent to the Walnut Grove home of her sister Celia Fennel Davis.

From 1856 through 1859, Absalom and Ann Fennel Davis completed and moved into Forest Home. During the same period, Ann Fennel Davis designed and laid out the geometrical garden immediately southwest of the house.

Gardens of Forest Home
Forest Home was located in the Southwest ¼ of Section 16 of Township 5 South and Range 5 West in Morgan County, Alabama. Forest Home faced south

toward the Trinity Road, from which it was originally approached by a half-mile long cedar lined lane.

Absalom Davis was a teacher at LaGrange College until it was destroyed during the Civil War. Absalom was also a cotton farmer and slave owner. According to the 1860 Morgan County, Alabama, Slave Schedule, Absalom Leonidas Davis owned 19 Black slaves.

During the 1870's, Absalom Davis became a leader of the Grange Movement of farmer advocacy. Cotton planters and farmers in the Tennessee Valley fought against the monopoly of trade, the decline in farm prices, and increasing freight rates.

Forest Home

On May 19, 1905, Ann Fennel Davis died at Trinity in Morgan County. She was buried in the Fennel Cemetery at Trinity, Alabama (Find A Grave Memorial Number 16870086).

On December 5, 1922, Absalom Leonidas Davis died in Morgan County. He was buried the Fennel Cemetery at Trinity, Alabama (Find A Grave Memorial Number 14985358).

After the deaths of Ann and Absalom, Forest Home became the residence of their son Jefferson S. Davis and his wife Mary Minor Davis (June 21, 1864-June 25, 1905).

Until 1973, Forest Home remained in the Davis family as a working cotton farm. Mrs. William E. Steed, daughter of Absalom and Ann Fennel Davis was the last of her Davis family to occupy the house.

In 1978, the Forest Home tract was sold by the Davis and Steed heirs. In 1979, Forest Home was listed on the Alabama Register of Landmarks and Heritage and the National Register of Historic Places in 1980. In 1991, Forest Home burned down.

Absalom L. Davis

Colonel Henry (Harry) W. Fennel

About 1811, Colonel Henry W. Fennel was born at Raleigh in Wake County, North Carolina. The parents of Henry W. Fennel were Wiley Fennel (3/29/1773-12/23/1826) and Sarah Fox Fennel (1776-9/1/ 1831).

On May 26, 1818, Sarah J. Delony, future wife of Henry Fennel, was born in Alabama. She was the daughter of Edward Delony and Margaret Fox.

On December 19, 1833, Henry Fennel entered 40 acres in the northeastern part of Lawrence County, Alabama. The land he entered was in the Northeast ¼ of the Northeast ¼ of Section 24 of Township 5 South and Range 6 West (Cowart, 1991).

On April 20, 1835, Colonel Henry W. Fennel married Sarah J. Delony in Lawrence County, Alabama. They had the following children who were born in Morgan County, Alabama.
1. Wylie Fennel was born in 1836.
2. Charles Fox Fennel was born on June 2, 1838; he served in the Confederate States of America Army. He died on July 17, 1890, and was buried in the Fennel Cemetery in Morgan County.
3. Benjamin Fennel was born in 1840.
4. Richard Oswell Fennel was born on June 14, 1842. He died on November 13, 1842, and was buried in the Fennel Cemetery.

On March 29, 1845, Sarah J. Delony Fennel died. After her death, Henry W. Fennel married a second time.

On November 03, 1846, Colonel Henry W. Fennel married Sarah "Sallie" Adaline Tucker in Limestone County, Alabama. She was born in Alabama. They had the following children in Morgan County:
1. Henry Fennel.
2. James Tucker Fennel was born on December 27, 1849, in Morgan County, Alabama. He died on July 2, 1904 in Morgan County.

Colonel Henry W. Fennel owned four shares of Memphis & Charleston Rail Road. He was an important figure in Morgan County, Alabama.

According to the 1850 Morgan County, Alabama Census, Page 203A, Henry W. Fennel was a 40 year old White male born in North Carolina. The following were listed in his household: Sarah, 22, Alabama; Wylie, 14, Alabama; Charles, 12, Alabama; Benjamin S., 10, Alabama; James, 6/12, Alabama.

The 1850 Morgan County, Alabama Slave Census, Division Number 10, William M. Dancy, Assistant Marshal, Page 853, November 13, 1850, Henry Fennel owned 30 Black slaves and five Mulatto slaves for a total of 35 slaves.

According to the 1860 North West Division, Morgan County, Alabama, United States Census, Henry Fennel was a 49 year old White male born in North Carolina. Also in his household was the following: Sallie A Fennel, Female, 30, Alabama; Benjamin S. Fennel, Male, 20, Alabama; Edward Fennel, Male, 7, Alabama; Sallie P. Fennel, Female, 5, Alabama; and, Henry W. Fennel, Male, 2, Alabama. In 1860, Henry W. Fennel of Morgan County, Alabama, owned 55 slaves.

According to the 1860 Morgan, Alabama, Agricultural Census, Henry Fennel owned 1,900 acres of improved land and 540 acres of unimproved land worth $17,000.00. He also owned $1,200.00 worth of farming equipment and $4,000.00 worth of livestock.

In the 1866 Alabama State Census, Henry Fennel was mentioned in Morgan County, Alabama, with Certificate Number 9334. This census was after the Civil War, but his personal and real estate values were not available.

On August 24, 1869, Colonel Henry W. Fennel died at Decatur in Morgan County, Alabama. There were no grave markers for Henry, but his two sons were buried in Fennel Cemetery in Trinity, Alabama.

Freeman, Reverend Fleming Fontaine

On May 29, 1791, Fleming Freeman was born in Wilkes County, Georgia; he was the son of Holman Freeman (1758-1817) and Peninah Walton Freeman (1772-1823). Fleming was the son of Colonel Holman Freeman of Revolutionary War fame in North Georgia, and Whig leader under Governor Elijah Clark. Fleming Freeman was the grandson of George Walton, a signer of Declaration of Independence. His siblings were Mary Ann Freeman Bibb (1788-1856) and John Walton Freeman (1793-1858).

On April 16, 1812, Fleming Freeman married Martha Dandridge Bibb; she was born on January 22, 1793. Martha was the sister to William Wyatt Bibb, the first territorial governor of Alabama.

Fleming and Martha had the seven children that did not live beyond their teenage years.
1. Edna Matilda Freeman Pollard (1814-1832), 18 years old.
2. Martha Penianah Freeman (1818-1823), five years old.
3. Fleming Joseph Freeman (1821-1838), 17 years old.
4. Alexander P. Freeman (1823-1831), eight years old.
5. John B. Freeman (1825-1832), seven years old.
6. Holman Freeman (1827-1832), five years old.
7. Charles P. Freeman (1833-1843), 10 years old.

Reverend Fleming Fontaine Freeman

According to the 1830 Morgan County, Alabama Census, Fleming Freeman had the following in his household: White Males 0-5: 2, 5-10: 2, 30-40: 1; White Females 15-20: 1, 30-40: 1; Slaves: Males 27, Females 26, Total Slaves 53.

Between 1830 and 1835, Fleming Freeman and his family moved with his slaves to Montgomery, Alabama, to continue extensive cotton farming operation. The Freeman family moved with members of the family of his wife-the Bibb family. About 1835, Fleming Freeman lived in a Federal-style house in Montgomery County that became known as the Freeman House. At the start of the Civil War, the Freeman House served as the Executive Mansion of the Confederacy.

The first White House of the Confederacy had several owners over the years as follows: William Knox, George Matthews, Fleming Freeman, Joseph S. Winter, Mr. Galloway, Colonel Edmund Harrison, William Crawford Bibb, and others before the State of Alabama purchased the home in 1920. Fleming Freeman was the uncle by marriage of William Crawford Bibb, son of John Dandridge Bibb.

On February 4, 1835, at the age of 42, Martha Dandridge Bibb Freeman died at Montgomery in Montgomery County, Alabama. She was buried in the Oakwood Cemetery in Montgomery (Find A Grave Memorial Number 92446704).

Later that year of 1835, Fleming married Nancy Freeman (1795-1875). They had a daughter, Mary Anne Elizabeth Freeman (1836-1841). Based on census records, it appears that the Fleming Freeman family remained in Montgomery County, Alabama, from the 1830s through 1860s.

According to the 1850 Montgomery County, Alabama, Slave Census, Fleming Freeman owned 135 Black slaves. He was among the largest slave holders in the county.

According to the 1860 District 1, Montgomery, Alabama, United States Census, Fleming Freeman was a 69 year old White male born in Georgia. Also in his household was Nancy Freeman a 60 year old White female born in Georgia.

In 1860, Fleming Freeman owned 179 Black slaves to work his cotton plantation. He was tied as the fourth largest slave holder in Montgomery County, Alabama, in 1860. Also, in 1860, three members of the Bibb Family were listed in the largest slave holders in Montgomery County: B. H. Bibb owned 125 slaves; J. D. Bibb owned 56 slaves; and, J. B. Bibb owned 53 slaves.

In the 1870 Alabama Census, Fleming Freeman was 79, and Nancy was 70. Sometimes after the Civil War, Fleming Freeman he moved to Talladega County, Alabama.

On November 7, 1875, Fleming Freeman died in Talladega County, Alabama. He was buried in the Oak Hill Cemetery at Talladega in Talladega County, Alabama, (Find A Grave Memorial Number 72184280).

Garner, Lawson William

On April 29, 1799, Lawson Garner was born in Rutherford County, North Carolina. He was the grandson of Charles Garner, a Revolutionary War soldier.

In 1810, Lawson Garner was enumerated in the census of Warren County, Kentucky. By 1816, he and his family were in Franklin County, Tennessee.

On July 10, 1818, Lawson Garner entered the West ½ of Southeast ¼ of Section 13, Township 7, Range 3 West in Morgan County, Alabama, for a homestead. From that first land entry in 1818 and until 1853, Lawson entered some 1,200 acres in Morgan County, Alabama (Cowart, 1981).

Around 1818, Lawson Garner built a log cabin on his original land entry west of Somerville and began to acquire farmland. He continually enlarged his home, built slave cabins, and a kitchen behind his plantation house. He was involved in Baptist Church, Democratic Party, and civic organizations. He provided a cemetery for his slaves.

Around 1826, Lawson Garner married Jane Langham. Jane was born on October 11, 1803, and they had the following children:

1. Mary Ann Garner Bean was born on February 2, 1827; in 1844, she married Major Benjamin F. Bean. Mary died on January 8, 1898, and was buried in the Bean Cemetery at Decatur in Morgan County, Alabama (Find A Grave Memorial Number 31785347).

2. Celia Jane Garner Ford was born on March 5, 1829; in 1858, she married Jonathan Ford who was born in South Carolina on June 30, 1813. The father of Jonathan Ford was Middleton Ford (12/11/1790-1854); his mother was Jane Reeves who was born in South Carolina in 1794. The siblings of Jonathan Ford were: James Ford-twin (1813-1884); Telitha Ford McCrary (1825-1908); and William Green Ford (6/18/1828-1858). Judge Jonathan Ford was a slave owner who had a cotton plantation near the old North Alabama Regional Hospital. He represented Morgan County in the Secession Convention that started on January 7, 1861, in Montgomery, Alabama; he opposed secession for any reason. Celia Jane Garner Ford died on May 10, 1879, and she was buried in the Mount Pisgah Cemetery at Decatur in Morgan County, Alabama (Find A Grave Memorial Number 12199083). In 1880, Jonathan Ford married Alice Kelly. Jonathan died on December 5, 1884, at the age of 71 years, five months, and five days. He was buried in Mount Pisgah Cemetery at Decatur in Morgan County, Alabama.
3. Thomas Daniel Garner was born on February 15, 1831; on April 19, 1854, he married Nancy Susan E. Bean, daughter of William and Nancy Bean. Thomas died on Feburary 21, 1903, and was buried in Hopewell Baptist Church Cemetery at Danville in Morgan County, Alabama (Find A Grave Memorial Number 51646633).
4. John E. Garner was born on January 15, 1833. John died on June 23, 1852, and was buried in the Garner Cemetery Number 1 at Somerville in Morgan County, Alabama (Find A Grave Memorial Number 31356524).
5. Zerelda Jane Garner Witt was born on May 31, 1835; she married Jeremiah Witt (1833-1926). Zerelda died on September 15, 1882, and was buried in Quitman Cemetery in Cleburne County, Arkansas (Find A Grave Memorial Number 80717337).
6. Robert "Bob" Lawson Garner was born on October 2, 1835. Robert died on May 14, 1898, and was buried in Garner Cemetery Number 1 at Somerville in Morgan County, Alabama (Find A Grave Memorial Number 31356706).
7. Hezekiah Franklin Garner was born on May 28, 1838. Hezekiah died on January 4, 1870, and was buried in Garner Cemetery Number 1 at

Somerville in Morgan County, Alabama (Find A Grave Memorial Number 31356726).
8. Kate E. Garner Freeman was born in 1840; she married Zenas Frederic Freeman (1826-1872). Kate died in 1924, and she was buried in the Topeka Cemetery in Shawnee County, Kansas (Find A Grave Memorial Number 15707605).
9. Sarah F. Garner Robinson was born on April 26, 1843; she married Madison B. Robinson (1838-1925). Sarah died on January 12, 1926, and was buried at Mount Zion Baptist Church Cemetery at Hartselle in Morgan County, Alabama (Find A Grave Memorial Number 6573246).
10. Sidney F. Garner Robinson was born on May 27, 1849; she married James Henry Robinson (1841-1925). Sidney died on June 23, 1926, and was buried in Falkville City Cemetery at Falkville in Morgan County, Alabama (Find A Grave Memorial Number 19850603).

In 1840, Lawson and his wife Jane Langham Garner joined the Baptist Church. Most of their children were Baptist.

In 1850 Morgan County Slave Schedule, Lawson Garner owned 64 Black slaves and four Mulatto slaves for a total of 68 slaves. In 1850, the farm of Lawson Garner was worth $5,000.00.

According to the 1860 Eastern Division, Morgan, Alabama, United States Census, Lawson Garner was a 62 year old White male born in North Carolina. Also living in the household of Lawson Garner was the following: Robert Garner, Male, 24, Alabama; Sarah F. Garner, Female, 17, Alabama; Ellen V. Garner, Female, 14, Alabama; and, Sidney F. Garner, Female, 11 Alabama.

The 1860 Morgan County Slave Schedule was taken on July2, 1860, and July 10, 1860. On pages 282B and 283A, Lawson Garner was listed with a total of 69 slaves which included 30 males and 39 females. Five of his slaves were Mulatto.

On April 11, 1860, Jane Langham Garner, wife of Lawson Garner died. She was buried in Garner Cemetery Number 1 at Somerville in Morgan County, Alabama (Find A Grave Memorial Number 31356443).

According to the 1860 Morgan, Alabama, Agricultural Census, Lawson Garner owned 825 acres of improved land and 1,875 acres of unimproved land worth $13,500.00. He also owned $350.00 worth of farming equipment and $3,315.00 worth of livestock.

On November 9, 1863, Lawson Garner died without a will. He was buried in Garner Cemetery Number 1, Somerville, Morgan County, Alabama (Find A Grave Memorial Number 31356411). He shares a tombstone with Jane Garner and John E. Garner. The four sided stone has names on three sides; the top of tombstone has been broken.

Garner Cemetery Number 2 is on Sample Road near Somerville in Morgan County, Alabama. The cemetery was originally for the slaves of the Lawson Garner plantation, and still used for burials. The cemetery can be found by taking Highway 36 east to Poor House Road, turn right, go 1¼ mile to Sample Road and turn right. Cemetery is on the right side of road as the road curves to go around the cemetery.

Garth, Jesse Winston

On October 17, 1788, Jesse Winston Garth was born in Albemarle County, Virginia. He was the son of Thomas Garth (1758-1834) and Susanna Dourrett (?-1829); they lived on a cotton plantation near Charlottesville in Albermarle County, Virginia. Jesse Winston Garth was the grandson of Thomas and Judith Bowcock Garth of Virginia, and he was the grandson of Richard and Elizabeth Davis Dourette, III, who lived in Albemarle County, Virginia.

As a young man, Jesse Winston Garth was six feet four inches tall. He was of Celtic stock which included Welch and French Huguenot ancestry.

In 1809, Jesse Winston Garth was admitted to the bar after studying law in Charlottesville, Virginia. He began his law practice in Charlottesville.

In the War of 1812, Jesse Winston Garth served on the coast in the Virginia militia. During the campaign, Jesse was promoted to major. Before the end of the War of 1812, he received the rank of general.

In 1815, Jesse Winston Garth was elected to represent Albemarle County in the Virginia legislature. While serving as a representative of Virginia, Jesse he met the Honorable John Tyler who became president of the United States. President Tyler and Jesse W. Garth had a lifelong personal and political friendship.

In 1817 after losing a Virginia election, Jesse Winston Garth left Virginia and moved to Missouri to be near his brother who was living there. Prior to leaving Virginia, he donated the land where the University of Virginia was built. He migrated to St. Louis, Missouri, but he stayed only one winter because of the severe cold climate of St. Louis during the winter months.

General Jesse Winston Garth

In June 1817, Jesse Winston Garth moved from St. Louis to Cotaco County (present-day Morgan), Alabama. He became a cotton planter and owned the largest number of slaves in the county. In addition to cotton farming, he engaged in practicing law for a short period prior to concentrating on his cotton plantation. He became one of the largest planters in the State of Alabama.

Jesse Winston Garth was first married to Elizabeth Brown. They had one son together.

From June 20, 1818, through July 27 1818, General Jesse Winston Garth entered about 1,666 acres of land in Morgan County, Alabama (Cowart, 1981).

Most of the land that General Garth entered in 1818 was along the Tennessee River in Township 5 South and Range 4 West.

From September 11, 1818, through November 30, 1818, Jesse Winston Garth entered about 2,607 acres of land in Lawrence County, Alabama. Most of the land was entered as Garth and Anderson (Cowart, 1991). It is believed that Charles Anderson was the partner of Jesse W. Garth; Charles Anderson was listed as entering land in some of the same areas.

From 1819 through 1821, Jesse Winston Garth represented Morgan County, Alabama, in the Alabama Legislature. In 1819, he served with Micajah Vaughn and John McCorley. In 1820, Jesse served with McKinney Holderness, and John Taylor Rather. In 1821, Garth served with McKinney Holderness, and Horatio Philpot.

In 1819, Jesse Winston Garth helped develop the constitution of Alabama, and he was elected president of the first Alabama State Senate. He served in both the Senate and House of Representatives as a representative of Morgan County, Alabama.

On June 5, 1820, General Jesse Winston Garth along with Henry W. Rhodes, Isaac Lane, McKinney Holderness, and George Peck entered 1,085 acres of land in Morgan County, Alabama (Cowart, 1981). The land was in Sections 7, 16, 17, and 18 of Township 5 South and Range 4 West and became part of present-day Decatur.

Jesse Winston Garth, Isaac Lane, McKinney Holderness, George Peck, and Dr. Henry Rhodes were the first directors of Decatur Land Company which laid out the streets in Decatur. Only Jesse Winston Garth remained in the Decatur area and built one of the largest cotton plantations in Morgan County; George Peck died in 1826, and the other three cotton planters left the area for farming lands opening up father west.

On August 23, 1821, Jesse Winston Garth married Unity Spottswood Dandridge in Morgan County, Alabama. She was the daughter of Nathaniel West Dandridge (1762-1847) and Sarah Watson Dandridge (1758-1814), who lived in

Hanover County, Virginia. Unity was the granddaughter of Governor Spottswood of Virginia, and related to Martha Dandridge Washington and Dolly Madison.

Nathaniel West Dandridge, father of Unity Spotswood Dandridge Garth, was born in King William County, Virginia, to Nathaniel West Dandridge and Dorothea Spotswood. Nathaniel first married Martha H. Fontaine, and they had seven children. He then married Sarah Watson, and they had six children. In 1841 Nathaniel West Dandridge passed away in Pontotoc, Mississippi.

Jesse Winston Garth and Unity Spottswood Dandridge had the following children:
1. Susan Elizabeth Garth was born on August 13, 1823; she married Dr. Francis Winfield Sykes, son of James T. Sykes. Susan died on November 16, 1875, and was buried in the Garth Cemetery in Decatur (Find A Grave Memorial Number 21561481).
2. Sarah Dandridge Garth was born on May 20, 1825; she married Dr. Charles Fenton Mercer Dancy, son of William and Priscilla Turner Dancy. Sarah and Charles Dancy were the parents of Unity and Mary Lou Dancy. Sarah died on February 9, 1908, and was buried in the Garth Cemetery in Decatur (Find A Grave Memorial Number 21570851).
3. Colonel William Willis Garth was born on October 28, 1826, in Morgan County; on June 21, 1855, he married Maria Eliza Rearn (1832-1917). William died on February 25, 1912, and was buried in Maple Hill Cemetery in Huntsville (Find A Grave Memorial Number 6420426).
4. Mary "Mollie" Frances Garth married Confederate General John Gregg in 1858 in Morgan County, Alabama; he was born in Lawrence County, Alabama. After their marriage, John and Mary moved to Fairfield in Freestone County, Texas; in July 1861, John Gregg organized the 7th Texas Infantry. On October 7, 1864, General John Gregg was killed in action in the Battle of Richmond. During the chaos of the Civil War, Mary traveled from the home of her father in Decatur to Virginia to recover the body of her husband. With the body of her husband, she traveled to land in Aberdeen, Mississippi, that was owned by her father; here she buried her husband and spent the remainder of her days. On June 15, 1897, Mary died and was laid to

rest by her beloved husband, General John Gregg. They are buried in the Odd Fellows Rest Cemetery at Aberdeen in Monroe County, Mississippi (Find A Grave Memorial Number 6191234).
5. Jesse Winston Garth Jr., was elected to the state legislature from Morgan County in 1853; he married Virginia Manning in Decatur.

General John Gregg

From 1828 through 1830, Jesse Winston Garth represented Morgan County, Alabama, in the Alabama Legislature. During his term in the Alabama legislature, Jesse served with Benajah S. Bibb, James T. Sykes, Thomas McElderry, Horatio Philpot, John T. Rather, and Daniel E. Hickman. In 1830, Jesse Winston Garth was defeated for Congress by the Honorable Samuel W. Mardis.

According to the 1830 Morgan County, Alabama Census, the household of Jesse Winston Garth had the following: White Males 0-5: 2, 40-50: 1; White Females 05: 1, 5-10: 2, 10-15: 1, 30-40: 1. In 1830, Jesse Winston Garth had 136 Black slaves with 65 males and 71 females.

From August 3, 1830, through September 3, 1839, General Jesse Winston Garth entered some 3,250 acres of land in Morgan County, Alabama (Cowart, 1981). He was one of the largest land owners in Morgan County, Alabama.

On October 24, 1833, Unity Dandridge Garth passed away in Morgan County, Alabama. She was buried in the Garth Family Cemetery at Decatur in

Morgan County, Alabama (Find A Grave Memorial Number 21570594). The inscription at her grave follows: "Rest in peace, wife of General Jesse Winston Garth, daughter of Nathaniel West Dandridge, born in Hanover, County, Virginia, died in Morgan County, Alabama."

In 1834, when the Rising Sun Masonic Lodge Number 29 was built in Decatur, General Jesse Winston Garth was the secretary and an active member of the lodge. He was one of the founders of Decatur, and a director of the Decatur Land Company.

In an 1837 survey map of the Morgan County area, the home of General Jesse Winston Garth was the only structure featured in Decatur. General Garth was considered one of the most prominent leaders in Decatur

In 1840, Jesse Winston Garth was elected President to the Decatur branch of the Alabama State Bank. He also served as one of the first directors of the bank. General Garth was one of the promoters and builders of the bank.

According to the 1840 Morgan County, Alabama Census, the Jesse Winston Garth household had the following: White Males 10-15: 1, 50-60: 1, 70-80: 1; White Females 10-15: 1, 15-20: 1. In 1840, Jesse Winston Garth owned 167 Black slaves with 97 males and 70 females.

On December 4 and 5, 1845, General Jesse Winston Garth entered 640 acres of land in Morgan County, Alabama (Cowart, 1981). Most of the land was in Township 5 South and Range 5 West.

Around 1846, Jesse Winston Garth became an advocate for the Memphis and Charleston Railroad which would connect the Mississippi River to the Atlantic Coast. He purchased $60,000.00 of stock in the railroad project.

From October 14, 1847, through September 7, 1853, General Jesse Winston Garth entered an additional 200 acres of land in Morgan County, Alabama (Cowart, 1981).

According to the 1850 Morgan County, Alabama Slave Schedule, Page number 889, Jesse Winston Garth owned 88 Black and one Mulatto slave for a total of 89 slaves. Also in the 1850 Morgan County, Alabama Slave Schedule, Page number 893, Jesse W. Garth owned 92 Black slaves and eight Mulatto slaves for a total of 100; therefore, in 1850, he owned 189 slaves.

In 1850, Jesse Winston Garth had $150,000.00 in personal property and real estate valued at $75,000.00. The total value of his estate in 1850 was $225,000.00 making him one of the wealthiest cotton planters in Morgan County, Alabama.

By 1853, General Jesse Winston Garth had entered a total of some 6,841 acres of land in Morgan County, Alabama. In addition, he had entered some 2,607 acres of land in Lawrence County, Alabama; therefore, his cumulative land holdings in Morgan and Lawrence Counties were nearly 9,500 acres.

On October 13, 1855, a train named General Garth in honor of General Jesse Winston Garth arrived in Huntsville on the newly laid tracks of the Memphis and Charleston Railroad. A spectator called the event one of the greatest day in the history of Huntsville since John Hunt.

In 1857, the rail line supported by General Jesse Winston Garth was completed from Memphis to Charleston, South Carolina. This was the first railroad in the United States to connect the Atlantic Ocean to the Mississippi River. The General Garth train was the first train to arrive at the Memphis and Charleston Headquarters, and Thomas Dunn served as the first railroad agent.

On April 5, 1859, a beloved female slave by the name of Charlotte died. Charlotte was originally the property of Unity Dandridge Garth; after her death, she was buried in the Garth Family Cemetery. Some believe that she was the mother of a child of Jesse Winston Garth. Her monument reads as follows: "To the memory of Charlotte, a faithful slave, a sincere friend. She was born upon the estate of Nathaniel W. Dandridge, Hanover City, Va., and died 5th of April 1859, aged 50 years. Cheerfully, affectionately, faithfully she discharged the various duties of life." Her stone was thought to have been erected by Jesse Winston Garth.

According to the 1860 Morgan County, Alabama, Slave Schedules, Jesse Winston Garth owned 182 slaves. Those slaves were housed in 40 slave cabins on his plantation.

According to the 1860 Morgan County, Alabama, Agricultural Census, Jesse Winston Garth owned 1,000 acres of improved land and 1,700 acres of unimproved land worth $15,000.00. He also owned $200.00 worth of farming equipment and $4,000.00 worth of livestock.

According to the 1860 Morgan, Alabama, Agricultural Census, Agent J. E. Stalbrooks for Jesse Winston Garth owned 4,300 acres of improved land and 2,700 acres of unimproved land worth $20,000.00. He also owned $200.00 worth of farming equipment and $7,000.00 worth of livestock.

In 1861, Garth was too old to serve in the Union or Confederate armies. Two of his nephews from Lawrence County fought for the Confederacy.

On September 7, 1867, Jesse Winston Garth died at the age of seventy-nine, at the house of his son at Huntsville in Madison County, Alabama. He was buried in Garth Cemetery in Southwest Decatur near Danville Road in Morgan County, Alabama (Find A Grave Memorial Number 21546755).

Prior to his death in 1867, Jesse Winston Garth, as many other slave holding plantation owners, suffered severe economic losses after the devastation caused by the Civil War. He lost his slaves; therefore, the free labor force of slaves to work his cotton plantation was no longer available. In spite of these losses, Jesse Garth left his two sons and four daughters wealthy primarily due to the accumulation of his vast land holdings in the area.

By 1880, the Jesse Winston Garth plantation house was gone. Records were not available on the demise of the Garth plantation home.

In 1932, Unity D. Dancy, granddaughter of Jesse Winston Garth, was the last burial that occurred in the Garth Family Cemetery. A stone wall surrounds the cemetery, which has burials dating to the 1840s. An eight foot high iron and chain link fence on top of the stone wall surrounds the Garth Cemetery.

Around 1936, the second home of Jesse Winston Garth known as Cotton Gardens was lost to history. The Garth Cotton Gardens plantation mansion was submerged when Wheeler Dam was constructed and the backwaters covered the site.

Garth Cemetery

The Garth Cemetery was part of a 20 acre tract held in trust by Garth descendants. Supposedly, Winston Garth, who died on December 31, 1932, had the deed to the remaining 20 acres of land that was once part of one of the largest cotton plantations in Morgan County, Alabama.

However, today, the cemetery now comprises less than an acre. The cemetery is accessed by a private driveway 1/4 mile north of the intersection of Eighth Street and Memorial Drive S.W. in Decatur. The cemetery has not been maintained with vegetation taking over the graves; it has been vandalized with broken tombstones and damage to the surrounding stone walls and fencing.

Garth, William Willis

On October 28, 1828, William Willis Garth was born in Morgan County, Alabama. He was the son of Jesse Winston Garth (1788-1867), the largest slave holder in Morgan County, Alabama, and Unity Spotswood Dandridge Garth (1799-1833).

As a young student, William Willis Garth studied at Lagrange, Emory, and Henry Colleges in Virginia; he studied law at the University of Virginia. After completing his degrees, Garth was admitted to the Alabama bar. He first settled in Morgan County, then Lawrence County, and finally in Madison County where he practiced law at Huntsville, Alabama.

According to the 1850 Morgan County, Alabama, United States Census, William W. Garth was a 23 year old White male born in Alabama. Also living in his household was the following: Jesse W. Garth, Male, 61, Virginia; Mary J. Garth, Female, 21 Alabama; and Jesse W. Garth, Male, 20, Alabama.

On June 21, 1855, William Willis Garth married Maria Eliza Fearn in Madison County, Alabama. Maria was born on January 9, 1832; she was the daughter of Thomas Fearn (1789-1863) and Sallie Bledsoe Shelby Fearn (1806-1842). William and Maria had a son, Winston Fearn Garth (1856-1932).

According to the 1860 Lawrence County, Alabama Census, Household 238, William Willis Garth was a 33 year old male lawyer born in Alabama with a personal and real estate values of $35,000.00 and $52,000.00. Also living in his household was the following: Mariah, 28, Female, Alabama; and Winston, 3, Male, Alabama.

William Willis Garth

In the 1860 census, some of the neighbors of William Willis Garth were as follows by household number: House 233, William Cravens, Dentist; House 234, Andrew Jackson Sykes, Physician; House 235, Fortunatus Shackelford McMahon, Physician, and William Jackson McMahon, Physician; House 240, William P. McMahon, Lawyer; House 241, William Stuart Bankhead, Planter; House 242, James Edmonds Saunders, Planter; House 244, Frank Jones, Planter; and House 246, Willis Watkins, Planter. Most of his neighbors were very wealthy slave owning land barons living in and near Courtland in Lawrence County, Alabama.

In the 1860 Lawrence County, Alabama, Slave Schedules, Page 166, William Willis Garth owned 59 Black slaves. William and his slaves were probably living and cotton farming some of the 2,600 acres of land in Lawrence County, Alabama, that his father Jesse Winston Garth had entered from September through November of 1818.

From 1861 through 1865 during the Civil War, William Willis Garth served as a Lieutenant Colonel with the staff of General James Longstreet in the Confederate States Army. At the start of the Civil War, Garth was probably living in Lawrence County, Alabama.

According to the 1870 United States Census, William Garth was a 43 year old white male from Alabama. Also living in his household was the following: Mariah Garth, Female, 38, Alabama; Winston Garth, Male, 13, Alabama; Lucy Fearn, Female, 27, Alabama; Fearn Steele, Male, 13, Texas; Dinah Brandon, Female, 65, Tennessee; Susan Carter, Female, 24, Alabama; John Higgins, Male, 60, Alabama; Caledonia Higgins, Female, 55, Alabama; and Robert Higgins, Male, 15, Alabama.

In 1876, William Willis Garth was elected as a Democratic representative to the Forty-fifth United States Congress. From March 4, 1877, through March 3, 1879, William Willis Garth served as a representative of the Sixth Congressional District of Alabama in the United States House of Representatives.

In 1878, William Willis Garth was defeated for reelection to the United States Congress. After completing his term of office, Garth resumed his law practice in Huntsville, Alabama.

According to the 1880 Huntsville, Madison County, Alabama, United States Census, William W. Garth (October 28, 1828-February 25, 1912) was a 53 year old white male lawyer born in Alabama; his father and mother were born in Virginia. Also in his household was the following: Maria F. Garth, Wife, Female, 47, Alabama; Winston F. Garth, Son, Male, 23, Alabama; and Kate W. Steele, Niece, Female, 10.

On February 25, 1912, William Willis Garth died at Huntsville in Madison County, Alabama. He was buried in Maple Hill Cemetery in Huntsville (Find A Grave Memorial Number 30691913).

On March 6, 1917, Maria Eliza Fearn Garth died at Huntsville in Madison County, Alabama. She was buried in Maple Hill Cemetery in Huntsville (Find A Grave Memorial Number 6420426).

Humphreys, Dr. Carlisle

Carlisle Humphreys was born between 1780 and 1790. He was the son of John Humphreys, and grandson of William Humphreys.

On August 6, 1811, John Humphreys entered 161 acres of land in the Southeast ¼ of Section 20 of Township 3 South and Range 1 West in Madison County of Mississippi Territory. On the same date, John Humphreys entered 40 acres of land in the Northwest ¼ of Southeast ¼ of Section 20 of Township 4 South and Range 1 West in Madison County of Mississippi Territory (Cowart, 1979). On August 6, 1811, John Humphreys of Lincoln County, Tennessee, entered 163.92 acres of land in the Southeast ¼ of Section 29 of Township 1 South and Range 1 East in Madison County of Mississippi Territory (Cowart, 1979).

On March 4, 1816, Dr. Carlisle Humphreys married Harriet A. Campbell in Rhea County, Tennessee; she was born in 1798. Harriet was the daughter of Judge David Campbell of the United States District Court of East Tennessee, and Elizabeth Campbell. Dr. Carlisle Humphreys first wife Eliza was the sister of Harriet.

Dr. Carlisle Humphreys and Harriet A. Campbell Humphreys had the following children:
1. Elizabeth Humphreys died in 1839.
2. David Campbell Humphreys
3. Dr. William Carlisle Humphreys, born in 1823, lived in Georgia.
4. James Alexander Humphreys lived in Georgia.
5. Samuel B. Humphreys lived in Texas.

Around 1817, Dr. Carlisle Humphreys moved to Morgan County, Alabama. He moved to north Alabama near his father John Humphreys.

On February 23, 1818, John Humphreys entered 159 acres of land in the Northwest ¼ of Section 29 of Township 4 South and Range 4 West in Limestone County, Alabama (Cowart, 1984).

On March 14, 1827, Dr. Carlisle Humphreys married Ann Roby in Morgan County, Alabama. His first wife had died prior to his marriage to Ann Roby.

According to the 1830 Morgan County, Alabama Census, the Carlisle Humphreys household had the following: White Males 0-5: 1, 5-10: 1, 10-15: 1, 40-50: 1; White Females 10-15: 1, 20-30: 1; Slaves: None.

According to the 1840 Morgan County, Alabama Census, the Carlisle Humphreys household had the following: White Males 5-10: 1, 10-15: 1, 15-20: 1, 20-30: 1, 50-60: 1; White Females 30-40: 1. He owned 22 Black slaves with 14 males and 8 females.

On February 26, 1842, Dr. Carlisle Humphreys died. After his death, his wife Ann Roby Humphreys remarried.

On April 23, 1843, Ann Roby Humphreys married Jonathan Burleson. Jonathan and Ann Burleson had one son Roby Burleson.

In 1876, Ann Roby Humphreys Burleson died in Morgan County, Alabama. She was buried in the Burleson-Stephenson Cemetery at Decatur in Morgan County, Alabama (Find A Grave Memorial Number 142551440).

David Campbell Humphreys

On November 9, 1817, David Campbell Humphreys was born in Morgan County, Alabama. He was the son of Dr. Carlisle Humphreys and Harriet A. Campbell Humphreys.

In 1843, David Campbell Humphreys served Madison County, Alabama, as a member of the Alabama House of Representatives. He also served in that position in 1849, 1853, and 1868.

On October 22, 1845, David Campbell Humphreys married Margaret McLeod. David C. Humphreys and Margaret McLeod Humphreys had the following children: George McLeod Humphreys, Sallie Humphreys, Kate F. Humphreys May, Helen Humphreys, and David Campbell Humphreys Jr.

In 1848, David Campbell Humphreys built his home in Madison County, Alabama. He had a private practice as a lawyer in Huntsville, and was a cotton planter and slave owner in Madison County, Alabama.

On July 10, 1857, and March 16, 1859, David C. Humphreys entered land in Madison County, Alabama. In 1860, David Campbell Humphreys owned 93 Black slaves in Madison County, Alabama. From 1850 through 1861, he was an extensive cotton planter in Madison County.

During the Civil War (1861-1865), David Campbell Humphreys rose to the rank of colonel for the Confederate States of America. He tried to prevent Alabama succeeding from the Union prior to the Civil War. During the war, he was unsuccessful in bringing Alabama back into the Union.

On April 22 1870, David Campbell Humphreys was nominated by President Ulysses Grant for Associate Justice on the United States District Court

David Campbell Humphreys Home

for the District of Columbia. He was confirmed by the Senate on May 10, 1870. He served as a United States Federal Judge until his death. On July 2, 1879, David Campbell Humphreys died in Fairfax County, Virginia. He was buried at Alexandria in Fairfax County, Virginia.

On August 3, 1977, the David Campbell Humphreys House in Huntsville, Alabama, was placed on the National Register of Historic Places.

Johnson, Benjamin

On October 12, 1795, Benjamin Johnson was born in Greensville County, Virginia. His parents were David Johnson and Winnifred Sledge.

According to the 1830 Morgan County, Alabama Census, the household of Benjamin Johnson had the following: White Males 0-5: 2, 30-40: 1; White Females 0-5: 2, 5-10: 2, 20-30: 1. Benjamin Johnson owned nine slaves with six males and three females.

On December 2, 1833, Benjamin Johnson married Harriet Owens in Morgan County, Alabama. Their children were Sarah A. Johnson Wiggins (1827-1880) and Benjamin Williamson Johnson (1834-1890).

According to the 1840 Morgan County, Alabama Census, the household of Benjamin

Johnson had the following: White Males 5-10: 1, 10-15: 2, 40-50: 1; White Females 0-5: 2, 5-10: 2, 10-15: 1, 15-20: 1, 30-40: 1. Benjamin Johnson owned 23 slaves with 13 males and 10 females.

According to the 1850 Morgan County, Alabama Slave Census, Benjamin Johnson owned 18 slaves.

On July 25, 1853, Benjamin Johnson died in Morgan County, Alabama. He was buried in Chestnut Grove Cemetery at Decatur in Morgan County, Alabama (Find A Grave Memorial Number 11461949).

Kimbell, Edmond and James

Edmond and James Kimbell were the sons of James and Frances Kimbell. They were born in Warren County, North Carolina. Edmund Kimbell was born on July 30, 1779, and James Kimbell was born on May 2, 1781.

In 1818, the Kimbell, Burt, Murphey, and Moseley families migrated to Morgan County, Alabama, from North Carolina. On July 15, 1818, all four families entered land in Township 5 South and Range 5 West in Morgan County, Alabama (Cowart, 1981).

Edmond Kimbell

Edmond Kimbell entered the following tracts of land in Morgan County, Alabama (Cowart, 1981):
1. July 15, 1818, 160.40 $^{3/4}$ acres, SW¼, Section 8, T5S, R5W.
2. May 17, 1831, 158.36½ acres, SW¼, Section 5, T5S, R5W.
3. May 17, 1831, 160.58$^{3/4}$ acres, NE¼, Section 7, T5S, R5W.
4. May 17, 1831, 160.40$^{3/4}$ acres, NW¼, Section 8, T5S, R5W.

According to the 1830 Morgan County, Alabama Census, Edmund Kimble had the following in his household: White Males 0-5: 1, 5-10: 1, 50-60: 1; White Females 5-10: 1, 10-15: 1, 15-20: 1, 20-30: 1, 40-50: 1; Slaves Males 1, Females 3, Total Slaves: 4.

In the 1840 Morgan County, Alabama Census, the Edmund Kimble household had the following: White Males 10-15: 2, 15-20: 1, 30-40: 1, 60-70: 1 (1770-1780); White Females 10-15: 1, 20-30: 1, 50-60: 1; Slaves: Males 13, Females 8, Total Slaves: 21.

In the 1850 Morgan County, Alabama, United States Census, House Number 307, listed to following: Edmund Kimbell, Male, Age 71, White, North Carolina; William Kimbell, Male, 24, Alabama; Parlunna Kimbell, Female, 33, Alabama; Martha Kimbell, Female, 25 Alabama; James J. Murphy, Male, 29, Alabama.

According to the 1850 Morgan County, Alabama Slave Census, Edmund Kimbell owned 28 slaves. His slaves were used to farm cotton on his plantation west of Decatur.

Edmund Kimbell was the husband of Elizabeth M. Tunstall, and he was a brother to James Kimbell. Edmond Kimbell ran an inn on the stage coach road that was located just west of the cemetery. The road was originally an Indian trail called the River Road, but later, it was known as the Tuscumbia Road.

On October 17, 1854, Edmund Kimbell died in Morgan County, Alabama. He was buried on his own property in the Kimbell Cemetery at Trinity in Morgan County, Alabama (Find A Grave Memorial Number 20794967).

James Kimbell

In 1818, James Kimbell came to Morgan County, Alabama, with family and friends of the Burt, Murphey, and Moseley families. He entered the following tracts of land in Morgan County, Alabama (Cowart, 1981).
1. July 15, 1818, 161.45¼ acres, NE¼, Section 10, T5S, R5W.
2. July 15, 1818, 161.45¼ acres, SE¼, Section 10, T5S, R5W.

According to the 1830 Morgan County, Alabama Census, James Kimble had the following in his household: White Males 0-5: 1, 15-20: 1, 40-50: 1; White Females 0-5: 1, 5-10: 1, 40-50: 1; Slaves: Males 16, Females 11, Total Slaves: 27.

In the 1840 Morgan County, Alabama Census, the James Kimble household had the following: White Males 10-15: 1, 20-30: 1, 60-70: 1; White Females 10-15: 1, 15-20: 1, 50-60: 1; Slaves: Males 20, Females 16, Total Slaves: 36.

On April 8, 1841, James Kimbell died at Trinity in Morgan County, Alabama. He was buried in the Kimbell Cemetery (Find A Grave Memorial Number 20664742).

Kimbell Cemetery

Kimbell Cemetery, also known as Wimbley Cemetery, was located on land originally purchased by Edmond Kimbell. The cemetery is on the Alabama Historical Cemetery Listing at 1001 Red Hat Road, Trinity, in Morgan County, Alabama.

In the Kimbell Cemetery, a monument contains the following:
1. Mary Burt Kimbell, Daughter of James and Nancy Kimbell, Born Sep 1, 1817, Died Sep 10, 1826.
2. Nancy Kimbell, Who was born in Halifax Co, NC, Oct 24, 1785, Died as the Christian only death, Jan 4, 1855, Aged 69 yr, 2 mo, 11 da, (Wife of James Kimbell. Her name was Nancy Burt, born in Halifax County, North Carolina, and daughter of William Burt Sr. and Elizabeth Hurt. She was a distant cousin to John and Hardy Burt).
3. James Kimbell, Who was born in Warren Co, NC, May 2, 1781, Died as the Christian only death, Apr 8, 1841, (Son of James and Frances Kimbell, brother of Edmond and Nathan Kimbell, wife Nancy Burt).
4. James Hurt Kimbell, Son of James and Nancy Kimbell, Born Nov, 22, 1819, Died Aug. 22, 1825.

The beautiful old cemetery located on property purchased by United Launch Alliance, formerly Boeing, is surrounded by a rock wall and an iron fence. The Kimbell Cemetery was abandoned for many years, and many of the huge tombstones have been vandalized and broken. It contains 37 known burials with the five earliest burials being March 1823, July 1824, October 1824, August 1825, and September 1826.

The following are graves that have been recorded in the Kimbell Cemetery:
1. Davis, Elizabeth Murphey (Find A Grave Memorial Number 20668693), b. Jun. 29, 1786 d. Jul. 27, 1824.
2. Hill, Temperance Murphey (Find A Grave Memorial Number 34758503), b. May 4, 1814 d. Oct. 1, 1836.
3. Kimbell, Dr. Dewitt C. (Find A Grave Memorial Number 20906933), b. Oct. 31, 1827 d. Nov. 13, 1857.
4. Kimbell, Edmond(Find A Grave Memorial Number 20794967), b. Jul. 30, 1779 d. Oct. 17, 1854.
5. Kimbell, Edwin N. G. (Find A Grave Memorial Number 20664280), b. Sep. 26, 1826 d. Nov. 14, 1887.
6. Kimbell, Elizabeth M. Tunstall (Find A Grave Memorial Number 20794732), b. Dec. 4, 1787 d. Nov. 14, 1849.
7. Kimbell, Frances (Find A Grave Memorial Number 20668476), b. 1750 d. Mar., 1823.
8. Kimbell, James (Find A Grave Memorial Number 20664742), b. May 2, 1781 d. Apr. 8, 1841.
9. Kimbell, James Hurt (Find A Grave Memorial Number 20664695), b. Nov. 22, 1819 d. Aug. 22, 1825.
10. Kimbell, Mary Burt (Find A Grave Memorial Number 20664594), b. Sep. 1, 1817 d. Sep. 10, 1826.
11. Kimbell, Nancy Burt (Find A Grave Memorial Number 20664928), b. Oct. 24, 1785 d. Jan. 4, 1855.
12. Kimbell, Sally B. (Find A Grave Memorial Number 20668398), b. Feb. 23, 1810 d. Aug. 31, 1831.
13. Kimbell, William R. B. (Find A Grave Memorial Number 20794775), b. May 2, 1821 d. Jul. 5, 1853.
14. Kimble, Anna Dent (Find A Grave Memorial Number 20906963), b. Nov. 14, 1856 d. Oct. 25, 1857.
15. Kimble, Perlimney (Find A Grave Memorial Number 20906900), b. Feb. 21, 1813 d. May 25, 1856.
16. Lile, Samuel K. (Find A Grave Memorial Number 20794757), b. 1830 d. Oct. 25, 1850.
17. McDaniel, Sarah A. Kimbell (Find A Grave Memorial Number 20663929), b. Feb. 28, 1829 d. Apr. 7, 1890.

18. Minor, Ann Eliza Moseley (Find A Grave Memorial Number 20759718), b. Apr. 4, 1835 d. Oct. 12, 1869.
19. Moseley, Edmond Kimbell (Find A Grave Memorial Number 20683498), b. 1845 d. Sep. 6, 1849.
20. Moseley, Frances A. Kimbell (Find A Grave Memorial Number 20759689), b. Jan. 31, 1817 d. Aug. 15, 1859.
21. Moseley, Mary Ophelia (Find A Grave Memorial Number 20683460), b. 1840 d. Sep. 4, 1845.
22. Murphey, Eliza M. Kimbell (Find A Grave Memorial Number 20668531), b. Apr. 4, 1808 d. Aug. 10, 1832.
23. Murphey, George (Find A Grave Memorial Number 20683410), b. Apr. 7, 1774 d. Aug. 11, 1846.
24. Murphey, George Steptoe (Find A Grave Memorial Number 20794995), b. Aug. 28, 1852 d. Jan. 22, 1853.
25. Murphey, Julia Longstreet (Find A Grave Memorial Number 20812401), b. May 1, 1826 d. Jun. 9, 1854.
26. Murphey, Mary Frances (Find A Grave Memorial Number 20683302), b. Jan. 24, 1817 d. Oct. 17, 1838.
27. Murphey, Mary Louise (Find A Grave Memorial Number 20812436), b. Nov. 7, 1853 d. Jul. 13, 1854.
28. Murphey, Mary P. Kimbell (Find A Grave Memorial Number 20668648), b. Jul. 11, 1788 d. Oct. 13, 1824.
29. Murphey, Mary Reid (Find A Grave Memorial Number 20683340), b. 1772 d. Jan. 20, 1855.
30. Murphey, Nathan Kimbell (Find A Grave Memorial Number 20812566), b. Mar. 29, 1810 d. Nov. 11, 1858.
31. Murphey, Patience (Find A Grave Memorial Number 20683378), b. 1776 d. Jan. 24, 1855.
32. Murphey, Temperance Hill (Find A Grave Memorial Number 20668746), b. May 4, 1814 d. Oct. 1, 1836.
33. Murphey, Williamson (Find A Grave Memorial Number 20668572), b. 1794 d. Aug., 1842.
34. Murphy, Dr William E. (Find A Grave Memorial Number 20812498), b. Mar. 19, 1819 d. Sep. 21, 1889.
35. Nevill, William B. Jr. (Find A Grave Memorial Number 20664474), b. Apr. 16, 1817 d. Sep. 12, 1831.

36. Pride, George W. (Find A Grave Memorial Number 20812542), b. Oct. 15, 1851 d. Jul. 3, 1883.
37. Wilson, Eliza Rebecca Kimbell (Find A Grave Memorial Number 20664318), b. Oct. 28, 1828 d. Aug. 28, 1861.

Kolb, James

James Kolb was born in York County, South Carolina, and died 1807 in York County, South Carolina. He had some children who migrated south with his son Joseph living in Morgan County, Alabama.

James married Elizabeth who was born about 1754 in York County, South Carolina. From 1759 through 1760, James Kolb served in the Colonial Army during the Cherokee Rebellion. James owned land in what was "Old Ninety Six" District of South Carolina.

James Kolb was listed in the 1790 Census of York County, South Carolina. The census indicates James Kolb and his wife Elizabeth had four sons and six daughters.

The known children of James Kolb and Elizabeth were as follows:
1. Mary Kolb was born about 1772 in York County, South Carolina. She married William Love, and her date of death is unknown.
2. Margret Kolb was born on February 14, 1774, in York County, South Carolina. In 1797, Margret married William Feemster; he was born June 2, 1774. Around 1820, William and Margret Kolb Feemster moved to Monroe County, Mississippi. William died on October 2, 1856, and Margret died on June 5, 1860; they were buried in the Feemster Cemetery.
3. Catharine Kolb was born on March 9, 1775, in York County, South Carolina. Catharine first married Josiah Minter; after he died, she married William Clinton. Her date of death is unknown.
4. Ruth Kolb was born about 1776; she died on December 6, 1824.
5. Silas Kolb was born May 8, 1778 in York County, South Carolina; he died on September 23, 1850 in Lowndes County, Mississippi.
6. Elizabeth Kolb was born about 1780; she married Stephenson Lawson.

7. Jean Kolb was born about 1780 in York County, South Carolina; she married Samuel Smith.
8. Joseph Kolb was born in 1786 and died in 1843.

On December 13, 1802, James Kolb made a will that was probated on June 1, 1807, in York County, South Carolina. He named his second wife and children as his heirs.

Joseph Kolb

On May 8, 1786, Joseph (Joe) Kolb was born in York County, South Carolina. The father of Joseph was James Kolb. Joseph inherited the 319 acre family plantation from his parents.

By 1818, based on land records and the inscription on his tombstone, Joseph Kolb moved from South Carolina to Morgan County, Alabama. In the land records, his name was spelled Kolb, Kobb, or Cobb; the different names may possibly be recorded incorrectly by a misunderstanding of the clerk in the probate office of Morgan County, Alabama.

Joseph Kolb married Rachel Boyd; she was born on July 11, 1805, to Nancy Boyd (1771-1867). Joseph and Rachel had the following children:
1. James L. Kolb (November 15, 1823-November 17, 1857)
2. Nancy E. Kolb Thompson (July 31, 1824-January 31, 1864)
3. Joseph C. Kolb (September 2, 1828-December 7, 1864)
4. Rachel Catherine Kolb Gill (September 16, 1830-April 1, 1857)
5. Dr. David G. Kolb (September 11, 1835-October 3, 1863).

From 1818 through 1831, Joseph Kolb entered some 1,340 acres of land in Morgan County, Alabama. The peak of his cotton farming operation with some 50 Black slaves was around the 1840s.

Starting on July 9, 1818, Joseph Kolb entered the following tracts of land in Morgan County, Alabama (Cowart, 1981):
1. July 9, 1818, w/William Rainey, 110 acres, NW, Sec 2, T6S, R3S;
2. July 9, 1818, 159.88 acres, NW¼, Section 12, T6S, R3S;
3. July 9, 1818, 79.94 acres, W½ of SE¼, Section 12, T6S, R3S;

4. July 9, 1818, 159.92$^{3/4}$ acres, NW¼, Section 13, T6S, R3S;
5. July 12, 1830, 79.94 acres, E½ of SE¼, Section 12, T6S, R3S;
6. July 12, 1830, 79.94 acres, W½ of SE¼, Section 11, T6S, R3S;
7. July 12, 1830, 93 acres, W part of W part, Section 1, T6S, R3S;
8. July 12, 1830, 79 acres, part of NE¼, Section 11, T6S, R3S;
9. July 26, 1830, 79 acres, part of NE¼, Section 11, T6S, R3S;
10. March 15, 1831, 87.50 acres, W part of E part, Section 1, T6S, R3S;
11. July 12, 1831, 231 acres, E fraction part, Section 2, T6S, R3S;
12. July 12, 1831, 100 acres, S part of SW fraction ¼, Section 2, T6S, R3S.

According to the 1830 Morgan County, Alabama Census, Joseph (Joe) Kolb had the following in his household: White Males 0-5: 1, 5-10: 1, 15-20: 1, 40-50: 1 (Joseph would have been 44 in 1850); White Females 0-5: 1, 5-10: 1, 20-30: 1; Slaves: Males 15, Females 6, Total Slaves: 21.

In the 1840 Morgan County, Alabama Census, the household of Joseph Kolb had the following: White Males 5-10: 1, 10-15: 1, 15-20: 1, 20-30: 1, 40-50: 1, 50-60: 1 (Joseph would have been 54 in 1840); White Females 5-10: 1, 10-15: 1, 15-20: 1, 20-30: 1, 30-40: 1; Slaves: Males 25, Females 24, Total Slaves: 49.

On July 29, 1843, Joseph (Joe) Kolb died in Morgan County, Alabama. His wife erected a tombstone in memory of her beloved husband. The inscription on the stone is as follows: "Joseph Kolb was born in South Carolina May 8, 1786, and came to Alabama in 1818. Departed this life July 29, 1843, in the 58 year of his life."

Joseph Kolb was buried in the Kolb Cemetery at Somerville in Morgan County, Alabama. The grave of Joseph Kolb was covered by a box tomb (Find A Grave Memorial Number 33488360).

After the death of her husband Joseph Kolb, Rachel Boyd Kolb married John E. McCroskey. John was born on October 11, 1802.

According to the 1850 Morgan County, Alabama Slave Census, Page number 905, November 1, 1850, Joseph Kolb owned 11 Black slaves and two Mulatto slaves for a total of 13 slaves. Since Joseph Kolb died in 1843, the person listed must have been his son Joseph C. Kolb. Also in 1850, James Kolb, who was one of the sons of Joseph, owned 19 Black slaves and one Mulatto slave for a total of 20 slaves.

According to the 1860 Morgan County, Alabama, Agricultural Census, John E. McCroskey, husband of Rachel Boyd Kolb McCroskey, owned 300 acres of improved land and 360 acres of unimproved land worth $6,600.00. John also had $300.00 worth of farming equipment and $400 worth of livestock.

On May 27, 1862, John E. McCroskey, second husband of Rachel, was also buried in Kolb Cemetery in Morgan County, Alabama. In addition, the children of Joseph and Rachel Kolb were buried in the Kolb Cemetery.

On January 30, 1863, Rachel Boyd Kolb McCroskey died at Somerville in Morgan County, Alabama (Find A Grave Memorial Number 32517818). She was buried in the Kolb Cemetery at Somerville close to her two husbands.

Rachel Catherine Kolb Gill

On November 19, 1845, Rachel Catherine Kolb married Dr. William Gardner Gill. She was daughter of Joseph and Rachel Boyd Kolb who lived at Somerville in Morgan County, Alabama. Joseph and Rachel Kolb were originally from South Carolina.

William Gardner Gill was born on April 14, 1819, in Franklin County, Tennessee, to Daniel (1793-1858) and Catherine Threat Gill of Dinwiddie County, Virginia. At nineteen years old, William attended school in Athens, where he studied medicine. On March 4, 1843, William Gill graduated with the highest honors from the Louisville Medical College.

After his marriage to Rachel Catherine Kolb, Dr. William Gardner Gill practiced medicine in Somerville, Alabama. The Rachel Kolb Gill family continued to live in the Somerville area for many years.

In 1850, Dr. William G. Gill owned 18 Black slaves, and in 1860, he owned 36 slaves. Before the Civil War, Dr. Gill owned a plantation of nearly five thousand acres.

Prior to her death on April 1, 1857, Rachel Catherine Kolb Gill give birth to seven children: Margaret C. Gill, Rachel C. Gill, Martha E. Gill, Nancy Eloise Gill, William Gill, Etta Gill, and Elizabeth J. Gill.

On November 19, 1857, Dr. Gill married Elizabeth J. Evans, the daughter of Major Isaac Evans. They had eight children, but all died in infancy except three sons: William Robert Gill, Clarence Gill, and Eugene Gill.

According to the 1860 Morgan County, Alabama, Agricultural Census, Dr. William Gardner Gill owned 40 acres of improved land and 1,400 acres of unimproved land worth $12,000.00. John also had $500.00 worth of farming equipment and $2,500.00 worth of livestock.

In 1871, Dr. Gill and his family moved to Decatur, Alabama. Dr. Gill was president of the Morgan County Medical Association and served as United States Medical Examiner for North Alabama.

On October 15, 1888, Doctor William Gardner Gill died during a yellow fever epidemic in Decatur along with four other doctors. He was buried in the Decatur City Cemetery in Morgan County, Alabama.

Sons of Joseph Kolb in Morgan County

Joseph Kolb had three sons listed in the records of Morgan County, Alabama. These sons were James Kolb, David G. Kolb, and Joseph C. Kolb.

In the 1850 Morgan County, Alabama, Slave Schedules, James Kolb, son of Joseph Kolb, owned 20 Black slaves. James probably inherited his slaves after the death of his father in 1843.

On November 19, 1852, Joseph C. Kolb, son of Joseph Kolb, entered 39.01 acres of land in the Northwest ¼ of Southeast ¼ of Section 7 of Township 6 South and Range 2 West in Morgan County, Alabama (Cowart, 1981). Joseph C. Kolb was probably listed as Joseph Kolb in the 1850 census.

According to the 1860 Morgan County, Alabama, Slave Schedules, David G. Kolb, son of Joseph Kolb, owned 41 Black slaves. David appears to be the largest slave holder of the sons of Joseph.

According to the 1860 Morgan County, Alabama, Agricultural Census, David G. Kolb, agent for James McDowell, owned 350 acres of improved land and 900 acres of unimproved land worth $15,000.00. David G. Kolb also had $300.00 worth of farming equipment and $200.00 worth of livestock.

Lacy, John

In 1766, John William Lacy was born in Halifax, Virginia; John came to Mississippi Territory with two of his brothers, Hopkins and Theophilis "Thomas," who were also born in Virginia. The three Lacy brothers were the sons of Theophilus and Martha Cocke Lacy, and they are the namesake of Lacey's Spring in Morgan County, Alabama.

On March 18, 1813, Hopkins Lacy entered 179.7 acres of land in Section 4 of Township 6 South and Range 1 East in Madison County of Mississippi Territory (Cowart, 1979). On July 6, 1818, Hopkins Lacy entered 320 acres of land in Morgan County, Alabama; 160 acres were in Section 34 of Township 5 South and Range 1 West, and the other 160 acres were in Section 12 of Township 6 South and Range 1 West (Cowart, 1981).

On July 7, 1818, Theophilius "Thomas" Lacy entered 159.7 acres of land in the Southeast ¼ of Section 1 of Township 6 South and Range 1 West in Morgan County, Alabama (Cowart, 1981).

On August 31, 1818, John Lacy entered 80 acres of land in the Northeast ¼ of Section 19 of Township 6 South and Range 1 West in Morgan County. On October 15, 1818, John Lacy entered 80 acres of land in the East ½ of the Northeast ¼ of Section 2 of Township 6 South and Range 1 West in Morgan County, Alabama (Cowart, 1981).

On November 13, 1826, John Lacy died at Lacey's Spring. John was buried in the Bartee Cemetery at Lacey's Spring near the intersection of Highways 36 and 231.

The two brothers of John Lacy, Hopkins and Theophilius, are also buried in the Bartee Cemetery. Hopkins was born in Virginia, and he died on February 9, 1831, and Theophillus died on August 31, 1831, at the age of 67 years.

Thomas Henderson Lacy

On June 11, 1806, Thomas Henderson Lacy was born at Richmond in Rockingham County, North Carolina. The parents of Thomas were John William Lacy and Mary "Polly" Henderson; her parents were Thomas Henderson and Jane Martin. Mary was born on January 16, 1785, at Lincoln in Rockingham County, North Carolina.

On March 17, 1803, John married Mary Polly Henderson in Rockingham County, North Carolina. Their children were:
1. Theophilus, born January 1, 1804, in Rockingham County, N. C., died February 10, 1874, at Huntsville, Ala., married (1) Mary W. Harris, (2) Frances Hardeman Binford;
2. Thomas Henderson, married Mary McClelland; Frances Hardeman, born 1810, died young;
3. Alexander H., born 1814, married Sallie Wall;
4. John Lacy removed to Madison County, Ala., and owned land in both Madison and Morgan Counties.

In 1834, Thomas H. Lacy married Mary Elizabeth McCellan in Alabama. On July 27, 1817, Mary was born in Blount County, Tennessee.

The children of Thomas H. and Mary Elizbeth M. Lacy were Alice Lee Lacy, Theophilius "Theo" Lacy, Laura Frances Lacy, John H. Lacy, Bessie Lacy, Charles McCellan Lacy, Thomas H. Lacy, and Alex H. Lacy.

According to the 1850 Morgan County, Alabama, Slave Schedules, Thomas H. Lacy owned 33 Black slaves. Sometime after 1850, Thomas Lacy moved to Arkansas.

By 1860, Thomas and his family were living in Arkansas. In 1863, Thomas H. Lacy passed away in Arkansas.

Lane, Joseph

On April 8, 1761, Joseph Lane was born in Wake County, North Carolina. In 1784, Joseph Lane was married to Pherebee Hunter in Wake County, North Carolina. Pherebee was born on June 25, 1765; she was the daughter of Isaac Hunter Sr. and sister of Isaac Hunter Jr. and Alexander Hunter who married Patience Jones and Frances Alley Jones.

Joseph Lane and Pherebee Hunter Lane had the following children who were born in Wake County, North Carolina:
1. Delilah Lane was born on December 14, 1785.
2. Isaac Lane was born on February 12, 1787.

3. Martha Patsy Lane was born on November 20, 1789.
4. Joseph Lane was born on May 12, 1792.
5. Jonathan Lane was born in May 1794.
6. Rebecca Lane was born on January 8, 1803.
7. Jesse Lane was born on April 20, 1808. In 1836, Jesse was buried Lane or Grayson Cemetery, Trinity, Morgan County, Alabama (Find A Grave Memorial Number 40671998).
8. Pherebee Lane was born about 1810.

In 1817, Joseph Lane Sr. moved near Trinity in Morgan (then Cotaco) County, Alabama. He and his family settled west of present-day Decatur, Alabama, where he left his will.

On May 20, 1825, Joseph Lane made his last will and testament as follows: "I, Joseph Lane Sen'r of Morgan County State of Alabama, being of sound mind and memory do make publish and deliver this my last will and Testament in the words and form following (to wit):

Item 1st - I give and bequeath to my daughter Jane _?_igh one hundred dollars to her and her heirs forever.

Item 2nd - I give and bequeath to my son Jesse A. Lane my quarter section of land on which I now live with all the improvements thereon to him and his heirs forever, reserving to my beloved wife Phebe Lane her dower in said land.

Item 3rd - I give also to my son Jesse A. Lane one bed and furniture, one horse worth one hundred dollars to him and his heirs forever.

Item 4th - I give to my beloved wife Pherebe Lane all my household and kitchen furniture except that I have already disposed of.

Item 5th - It is my will and desire that my river tract of land shall be sold by my executor at public sale and the proceeds of said sale applied to the paying out and patenting the tract of land on which I now live.

Item 6th - It is my will and desire that all my other property of what kind so ever after paying all my just debts shall be equally divided between my beloved wife Pherebee Lane, my daughter Pherebee Lane, my daughter Rebecca Lane and son Jesse A Lane except that the value of the property heretofore given to my wife Pherebee Lane is to be taken from her share in this division.

Item 7th - It is my will and desire that all the property herein given to my wife Pherebee Lane or which may fall to her in a division between her and my other legatees shall belong to her during her natural life or widowhood and after her death or marriage shall be equally divided between my other legatees herein named.

Item 8th - the reason I have not given property by this will to my daughters Delia Burt, my son Isaac Lane, my daughters Patsy Burt, my son Joseph Lane and my son Jonathan Lane is that I have given to them heretofore property of equal value.

Item 9th - I nominate and appoint my sons Joseph Lane and Jonathan Lane my true and lawful executors to this my last will and Testament hereby revoking all former wills and Testaments and public saying and declaring this my last will and Testament this 20th day of May 1825."
Jos. Lane (seal),

Signed sealed and delivered in the presence of Joseph Lane, Jr., John, Davis, George Damien, Stephenson Hood; State of Alabama, Morgan County, at a special Orphans Court held for that purpose.

I, Stephen Heard, Judge of Morgan County Court, do hereby certify that the foregoing last will and testament of Joseph Lane Senior, deceased, was proved before me by the subscribing witnesses thereto & that the Testator was of sound mind & memory at the time of the execution thereof Given under my hand and seal this 2nd day of February 1826.
Stephen Heard (seal), Judge of Morgan County Court

On November 28, 1825, Joseph Lane died in Morgan County, Alabama. On October 11, 1826, Pherebee Hunter Lane died in Morgan County, Alabama. They were buried in the Lane Cemetery (also known as Grayson Cemetery) on the Red Hat Road near Trinity in Morgan County, Alabama.

Joseph Lane Jr.

According to the 1830 Morgan County, Alabama Census, Joseph Lane had the following in his household: White Males 5-10: 1, 10-15: 2, 15-20: 1, 30-40: 1; White Females 15-20: 2, 30-40: 2; Slaves: Males 11, Females 9, Total Slaves: 20.

In the 1840 Morgan County, Alabama Census, the only Lanes were Jonathan and Sarah. The rest of the Lane family had died or moved away from Morgan County, Alabama.

Delia Lane Burt

On December 14, 1785, Delia Lane was born in Wake County, North Carolina. The parents of Delia Lane Burt were Joseph Lane and Pherebe Hunter Lane, daughter of Isaac Hunter Sr. Delia's parents and siblings all relocated to Morgan County, Alabama, from North Carolina.

On July 11, 1781, Captain John Burt, husband of Delia Lane, was born in Wake County, North Carolina. He was the son of John Burt Jr. who was born about 1750 in Virginia, and died about 1823 in Wake County, North Carolina. His mother was Priscilla Senter Hardy who was born about 1760. John Jr. and Priscilla were married around 1778 in Wake County, North Carolina; she died about 1820. On November 30, 1805, John Burt Jr. entered 60 acres on Little White Oak Creek in Wake County, North Carolina. His land joined the property lines of his father John Burt Sr. (born circa1750).

On February 14, 1809, Delia Lane married Captain John Burt. After their marriage, Captain John Burt of Cumberland County, North Carolina, was listed as serving in the War of 1812. According to the muster rolls of the soldiers in the militia of North Carolina during the War of 1812, John was listed a captain in the 2nd Regiment which was organized in August 1814.

By 1818 based on land records, Delia Lane Burt and her husband John Burt were living in Morgan County, Alabama. Delia Lane Burt and Captain John Burt and had the following children:
1. Sarah Burt was born on April 26, 1811, probably in Wake or Cumberland County, North Carolina; she died on June 17, 1830.

2. Mary Ann Burt was born on June 30, 1813, probably in Wake or Cumberland County, North Carolina; she died before 1860 in Morgan County, Alabama.
3. Martha Burt was born on March 27, 1815 probably in Wake or Cumberland County, North Carolina.
4. Joseph Burt was born on August 18, 1817; he died after 1860 probably in Alabama.
5. Henry (Harry) Augustus Burt was born on December 22, 1819; he died on January 8, 1890.
6. John Lane Burt was born about 1821and died after 1860.
7. William Hardy Burt was born on October 17, 1821; he died on July 16, 1893.

On July 15, 1818, John Burt entered 79.18 acres in the east ½ of the southeast ¼ of Section 5 of Township 5 South and Range 5 West in Morgan County, Alabama (Cowart, 1981). From July 22, 1830, through June 2, 1831, John Burt entered an additional 431 acres adjacent to his original land entry; his land was near Fox's Creek and the Tennessee River.

According to the 1830 Morgan County, Alabama Census, the household of John Burt had the following: One male 5-10 (probably William Hardy Burt), two males 10-15 (probably Henry "Harry" Augustus Burt and John L. Burt), one male 40-50 (probably Captain John Burt), one female 10-15 (probably Martha Burt), one female 15-20 (probably Mary Ann Burt), one female 40-50 (probably Delia Lane Burt). Listed directly above John Burt in the census was Jesse A. Lane, brother of Delia Lane Burt. According to the 1830 Morgan County, Alabama Census, John Burt owned 15 black slaves.

On July 27, 1831, Hardy Burt, John Burt, James Burt, and Isaac Lane purchase 80.18 acres of land in the west ½ of the northwest ¼ of Section 34 in Township5 South and Range 6 West in Lawrence County, Alabama; the number of the certificate or warrant was 4190 (Cowart, 1991). Hardy, John, and James Burt were probably brothers; on March 12, 1811, Hardy Burt married Martha "Patsey" Lane in Wake County, North Carolina. Isaac Lane was a brother to Delia Lane Burt, wife of John Burt.

According to the 1840 Morgan County, Alabama Census, the household of John Burt had the following: Two males 10-15, one male 20-30, one male 60-70, one female 10-15, and one female 50-60. In 1840 Morgan County, Alabama Census, John Burt is also listed with 22 slaves.

On August 21, 1841, Captain John Burt died in Morgan County, Alabama. He was probably buried in the Lane Cemetery in Morgan County.

In the 1850 Morgan County, Alabama Census, the following members of the Burt family were slave owners:
1. Ann G. Burt owned 15 slaves; in 1860, she owned 400 acres of land worth $4,000.00.
2. Henry A. Burt owned 10 slaves; in 1860, he owned 270 acres of land worth $4,050.00.
3. John L. Burt owned 11 slaves; in 1860, he owned 300 acres of land worth $7,000.00.
4. Joseph J. Burt owned 7 slaves; in 1860, he owned 160 acres of land worth $1,500.00.
5. William H. Burt owned 9 slaves.

In the 1850 Morgan County, Alabama Census, Delia Lane Burt was listed living in the household of her son, William H. Burt. On March 18, 1857, Delia Lane Burt died in Morgan County, Alabama.

Isaac Lane

On February 12, 1787, Isaac Lane was born in Wake County, North Carolina. He was the eldest son of Joseph and Pherebee Hunter Lane.

On January 11, 1810, Isaac Lane married Mary "Polly" Hunter Pride (1788-1862); she was born on June 14, 1788, in Raleigh, North Carolina. Mary's parents were Edward Pride and Sarah "Sally" High. Edward was born on November 30, 1755, in Chesterfield, Virginia, and died February 7, 1839, at Tuscumbia. Sarah was born July 28, 1759, in Prince George County, Virginia (later became Dinwiddie County), and she died on October 25, 1821, at Decatur in Morgan County, Alabama.

Isaac and Polly Pride Lane had the following children:
1) Wylie Pope Lane (1810-1837).
2) Sarah Pride Lane Gillespie (1812-1835).
3) Isaac Hunter Lane (1815-1831).
4) Mary Lane Goodloe (1817-1847) was the oldest living child, and she died at 30 years of age (Find a Grave Memorial Number 125235945).
5) Joseph Lane (1829).
6) Edward Pride Lane (1831-1852).

In 1817, Colonel Isaac Lane, Mary (Polly) Pride Lane, and their families moved from Wake County, North Carolina, to the area west of Decatur in Morgan County, Alabama, and settled near Trinity. At the time of their move, the Lanes came as a family unit in a wagon train along Indian trails and roads.

Beginning in February 1818, Isaac Lane entered some 3,360 acres in Lawrence, Limestone, and Morgan Counties of North Alabama. Over 2,500 acres of the land that Isaac entered were in Morgan County with most of the property in Township 5 South and Range 5 West (Cowart, 1981, 1984, and 1991).

In 1820, Isaac Lane was one of the five trustees of the original Decatur Land Company. Isaac Lane was the fourth Worshipful Master of Rising Sun Lodge Number 29 in Decatur.

In the 1830 Morgan County, Alabama Census, Isaac Lane, the son of Joseph, had the following in his household: White Males 10-15: 1, 15-20: 1, 40-50: 1; White Females 10-15: 1, 15-20: 1, 40-50: ; Slaves: Males 16, Females 12, Total Slaves: 28.

In 1832, Isaac Lane was on the board of directors of the newly created Decatur Bank. In 1834, Colonel Isaac Lane served as a state representative from Morgan County in the Alabama Legislature.

Noah (servant), Isaac Lane, Henry Clay (horse), Polly Lane, Venus (dog)

Around 1837, Colonel Isaac and Polly Lane moved to Franklin County (now present-day Colbert) and began building their Lane Springs Plantation house just west of Natchez Trace. Earlier, Isaac had entered some 6,030 acres in the area near the Natchez Trace and the Tennessee River.

By 1850, Isaac Lane was one of the wealthiest cotton planters and largest land holders in North Alabama. According to the 1850 Franklin County, Alabama, Agricultural Census, Colonel Isaac Lane owned 1,400 acres of improved land and 65,000 acres of unimproved land with a value of $50,000. His farm equipment was worth $1,000 and he owned $5,585 worth of livestock. In 1850, Isaac owned 106 Black slaves and much of his livestock consisted of many fine racing horses.

In 1851, Isaac Lane hired William Frye an Austrian artist from Huntsville to paint a twelve by nine foot Lane Family portrait at Lane Springs in Franklin (Colbert) County, Alabama. The frame of the painting was gold leafed. Henry

Clay's saddle was a deep rich tan on two blankets of dark red and blue. Noah's coat was tan over black pants and jackct. The Lane Family portrait hung in the parlor of the Lane Springs Plantation Mansion.

In 1858, the will of Colonel Isaac Lane indicated that he owned about 150 black slaves. According to the 1860 census records, Isaac owned 124 black slaves, and his estate was value at $250,000. Prior to his death in 1862, Isaac Lane owned vast tracts of land in Alabama, Mississippi, Louisiana, Arkansas, and Texas.

Lewis, Owen

Owen Lewis and Sarah Perkins Lewis were the parents of Nicholas Lewis and Harding Perkins Lewis of Morgan County, Alabama. Owen and Sarah Perkins Lewis were from Virginia.

Nicholas Lewis

In 1783, Nicholas Lewis was born in Buckingham County, Virginia. He was the son of Owen and Sarah Perkins Lewis.

About 1805, Nicholas Lewis married Ann Meriwether in Virginia. They had the following children: Sarah Perkins Lewis, Emaline Lewis, Nicholas Lewis, Daniel Owen Lewis, and Arthur Meriwether Lewis.

In the 1810 and 1820, Nicholas Lewis and Ann Meriwether Lewis were listed in the census records of Buckingham County, Virginia. In May 1820, Nicholas Lewis applied for a ferry license and began Lewis' Ferry operations. After 1820, Nicholas Lewis moved to Morgan County, Alabama.

In May 1828, Nicholas Lewis received a grant from the United States of America for 160 acres for river improvement. This was the beginning of the development of Talucah Landing. Lewis owned a large warehouse and the first cotton gin at Talucah. He constructed a wooden chute to carry baled cotton from the warehouse to the docks below.

In the 1830 Morgan County, Alabama Census, the Nicholas Lewis household had the following: White Males 40-50: 1; White Females None; Slaves: Males: 33, Females: 18, Total Slaves: 51; Free Persons of Color: 4.

From August 11, 1830, through April 12, 1838, Nicholas Lewis entered some 740 acres of land in Townships 5, 6 South and Ranges 1, 2 West in Morgan County, Alabama (Cowart, 1981). Some say that Nicholas Lewis owned some 3,013 acres located in Morgan and Madison Counties of Alabama. After his death, the property of Nicholas Lewis was described in a court case as 2,237 acres along the Tennessee River in Madison and Morgan Counties of North Alabama.

According to the 1840 Morgan County, Alabama Census, Nicholas Lewis had the following in his household: White Males 50-60:1; White Females 60-70: 1; Slaves: Males 39, Females 27, Total Slaves: 66 with 40 of those slaves working in agriculture.

According to the 1850 Somerville, Morgan County, Alabama, United States Census, House Number 385, Nicholas Lewis was living in Somerville and listed as a 67 year old White male born in Virginia. Also living in his household was Walter Grantland a 40 year old male born in Virginia. According to the 1850 Morgan County, Alabama Slave Schedule, Nicholas Lewis owned 92 Black slaves and eight Mulatto slaves for a total of 100 slaves.

Arthur Meriwether Lewis was executor of the will of his uncle Nicholas Lewis. The following was a portion of the last will and testament of Nicholas Lewis of the County of Morgan and State of Alabama. ... "But of the residue given as above to my said two brothers I do will that there shall be excepted and reserved therefore the negro slaves hereinafter named and the balance left after taking on said slaves to be divided equally and above my slave Bob and his wife, Lindy Nelson and his wife Amy, Thornton his wife Mary, and Ruckers an old man, all of whom are now on my plantation in Morgan County, Alabama, and have served me with much fidelity and feeling a strong attachment for them, I would direct my executor to emancipate them if I believed their happiness would be thereby prompted, but trusting that my said Zachariah and his two sons will faithfully observe my wishes in relation to said slaves, I give them to my said brother, he should survive me during his life time, and at his death to his said two sons if he should not survive me then directly to his two sons and to the survivors of them. And I hereby will that said negroes to be paid each annually the following sums namely, to Bob, Lindy each ten dollars also to Nelson, Amy, Thornton, and Mary each ten dollars and to Ruckers fifteen dollars. Said sum to be paid by my said brother Zachariah or the said John O. Lewis, Zachariah Lewis sons of my said brother Zachariah. And if at any time my said brother or his said sons should think the happiness of said slaves would be promoted by removing them to a free state or territory I wish them to have it done. I hereby revoke all former wills by me made."

On October 1, 1856, Nicholas Lewis died in Morgan County, Alabama. He was buried in the Lewis Family Cemetery at Valhermoso Springs in Morgan County, Alabama (Find A Grave Memorial Number 356552100).

According to the 1860 Morgan County, Alabama, Agricultural Census, John O. Lewis and Zachariah Lewis owned 1,300 acres of improved land and 1,330 acres of unimproved land worth $18,000.00. They also had $1,000.00 worth of farming equipment and $4,000.00 worth of livestock.

Harding P. Lewis

Harding P. Lewis was born in Albemarle County, Virginia. He married Ann Lewis and they had the following children: Sarah P. Lewis Rodgers, Emaline M. Lewis Walker, Arthur M. Lewis and Daniel O. Lewis.

After 1820, Hardin and Ann Lewis along with his brother Nicholas Lewis moved to Morgan County Alabama. Before 1827, Hardin and Ann Lewis died in Morgan County, Alabama. After their deaths, Nicholas Lewis was made guardian of the children.

On January 18, 1826, the following was an inventory of property belonging to the estate of Hardin P. Lewis by Administrator Nicholas Lewis: "First 21 Negroes as follows Jim, Lucy, Richard, Harry, Lonmon, King, Elvey with two children, Nancy with three children, Lucky with one child, Fanny with three children, and Sarah with two children. Six head of horses, one mule, two heifers, 16 pounds of corn, five hoes, three plows, one lot of gear, crosscut saw, three bridles, three singletrees, four geres and three Clovis, one hand saw, lot of tea ware, table, two dozen silver teaspoons, one silver ladle, one jug canister, one tea pot, one lot ware, one fine gold watch, three beds, furniture, Stays Harness, 20 yard of baling, 1 trunk, 1 harness, 10 Chairs, 1 side saddle, 2 spinning wheels, 1 loom, 1 mans saddle, Pigging Trays, Sifters, 1 pair steel yards, 2 augers, 1 shot gun, 1 lot castings, 1 foot lute, 1 D Knife, 3 bushels of salt, 1 lot of pork, 1 large slap bottle, 1 padlock, 1 wagon, 9 stacks fodder, 7 head of fat hogs, 20,000 pounds of seed cotton, 16 head stock hogs."

In the year 1827, a total of $822.00 was earned from the hiring out of the slaves of the estate of Hardin P. Lewis: Richard to William King for $106.00; Lonnon to Whitfield Rogers 105.00; Louis to S. B. Walker 100.00; Harry to James to D. Ballew 110.50; King to W. W. Rogers 64.00; Elvey and child to Wm. King 46.00; Vickey and child to W. W. Rogers 89.00; Nancy and child to S. B. Walker 60.00; Lemming to W. W. Rogers 40.00; Ceyer to 10.00; Fanny and child to S. B. Walker $53.75.

On January 1, 1828, John McKinzie, William Thompson, William Read, William King divided the estate of Hardin P. Lewis among his children: Sarah P. Lewis Rodgers, Emaline M. Lewis Walker, Arthur M. Lewis and Daniel O. Lewis as follows:
1. Emaline M. Lewis Walker drew lot number one amounting to $1,390.00 for the following slaves: Nancy, Cate, Richard, and Lemor-$500.00; Evey and her child-$500.00; Michel-$175.00; Richard Junior-$115.00; Lee-$200.00.
2. Sarah P. Lewis Rodgers drew lot number two amounting to $1,350 for the following slaves: Nancy Lewis-$450.00; Susan-$375.00; Porter-$275.00; Macojok-$175.00; Mary Tom-$175.00.
3. Daniel O. Lewis drew lot number three amounting to $1,075.00 for the following slaves: Namely-$400.00; Nancy-$400.00; Mitchel-$125.00; Archelias-$100.00; James-$350.00.
4. Arthur M. Lewis drew lot number four amounting to $1,375.00 for the following slaves: Landon-$450.00; King-$300.00; Flemon-$275.00; Lucy Ann-$125.00; Fanny and her child Roseta-$125; Hanah-$100.00

On March 24, 1830, Nicholas Lewis appeared before Judge Charles W. Peters, County Court of Morgan County, Alabama Nicholas made oath that

$570.59 1/3 was the dividend of the personal estate of Harding P. Lewis, deceased.

After reaching adulthood, the surviving children of Harding P. Lewis moved to Sumter County, Alabama. They became cotton planters and engaged in the horse racing business.

Arthur Meriwether Lewis

Arthur Meriwether Lewis was born about November 12, 1818; he was the son of Harding P. Lewis and Ann Lewis. On January 4, 1839, Arthur Meriwether Lewis married Sarah Cato Chaney.

According to the 1850 Marengo County, Alabama Census, the Lewis household had the following: Arthur M. Lewis, 36, Male, White, Virginia; Sarah C., 25, Female, White, Alabama; Owen, 8, Male, White, Alabama; Ophelia, 6, Female, White, Alabama; Olivia, 3, Female, White, Alabama; Sarah, 2, Female, White, Alabama; Agnes 7 Months, Female, White, Alabama.

In the 1860 Marengo County, Alabama Census, the household of Arthur M. Lewis had the following: Arthur M. Lewis, 41, Male, White, planter, $50,000, $200,000, Virginia; Sarah C., 35, Female, White, Alabama; Owen, 18, Male, White, Alabama; Ophelia, 16, Female, White, Alabama; Olivia, 14, Female, White, Alabama; Greenberry, 8, Male, White, Alabama; Arthur, 7, Male, White, Alabama Alabama, 5, Female, White, Alabama Carolina, 3, Female, White, Alabama.

On November 26, 1860, at age 42 years and 14 days, Arthur M. Lewis died in Marengo County, Alabama. He was buried in the small Lewis Family Cemetery near Highway 28 on the south side of Jefferson in Marengo County, Alabama.

Lile, Samuel

Samuel Lile married Ann Harrison. They lived in North Carolina prior to moving to Morgan County, Alabama.

Samuel Lile and Ann Harrison Lile were the parents of four children:
1. Peyton Harrison Lile was born on October 12, 1794, in Wake County, North Carolina. On May 19, 1870, Peyton died at Aberdeen in Monroe County, Mississippi.
2. Mary Lile (High).
3. Thomas Lile(1804-1863).
4. William Lile.

In 1815, Samuel Lile left his land holdings in North Carolina and moved south to Mississippi Territory. With his wife, Ann Harrison Lile, and their four children, Samuel Lile scouted out fertile ground just south of the Tennessee River and established one of the first plantations near what would become Trinity, Alabama.

On June 23, 1821, Samuel Lile did a Last Will and Testament that was recorded in the court records of Morgan County, Alabama. Before the end of September, 1821, Samuel and Ann had both passed away leaving their eldest children to run the estate.

Samuel died in 1821 in Morgan County, and he was buried in the Lile Cemetery number 2 at Trinity in Morgan County, Alabama (Find A Grave Memorial# 43777526). In 1821, Ann Harrison Lile died, and she was buried in Lile Cemetery #2 at Trinity in Morgan County, Alabama, but she has no tombstone.

Lile, Peyton

On October 12, 1794, Peyton Harrison Lile was born in Wake County, North Carolina. Peyton married Mary C. Kimbell (1806-1878); she was born in Warren County, North Carolina.

Peyton Harrison Lile and Mary C. Kimbell Lile had the following children.
1. Peyton Harrison Lile
2. Mary Ann Lile Ewing (1827-1884)
3. Edward P Lile (1841 ____)

4. Frances Adelia Lile Benson (1844-1921)

According to the 1830 Morgan County, Alabama Census, the Peyton Lile household had the following: White Males 30-40: 1; White Females 0-5: 1, 20-30: 1; Slaves: Males 12, Females 9, Total Slaves: 21.

In the 1840 Morgan County, Alabama Census, the household of Peyton Lile had the following: White Males 0-5: 1, 5-10: 1, 40-50: 1; White Females 10-15: 1, 30-40: 1; Slaves: Males 19, Females 15, Total Slaves: 34.

Between 1840 and 1850, the family of Peyton Harrison Lile moved from Morgan County, Alabama, to Monroe County, Mississippi. Many families left Morgan County, Alabama, during the same period and settled in various counties of southeast Mississippi.

In the 1850 Monroe County, Mississippi Census, Peyton H. Lile owned 51 slaves. The 1850 Monroe County, Mississippi, United States Census, House Number 576 had the following: Peyton Lile, Male, Age 55, White, North Carolina; Mary C. Lile, Female, 44, North Carolina; William H. Lile, Male, 12, Alabama; Edward B. Lile, Male, 9, Alabama; and Frances A. Lile, Female, 6, Alabama.

On May 19, 1870, Peyton Harrison Lyle died at Aberdeen in Monroe County, Mississippi. Peyton was buried in the Odd Fellows Rest Cemetery at Aberdeen in Monroe County, Mississippi (Find A Grave Memorial Number 114552344).

On November 5, 1878, Mary C. Kimbell Lile died at Aberdeen in Monroe County, Mississippi. She was buried in the Odd Fellows Rest Cemetery at Aberdeen in Monroe County, Mississippi (Find A Grave Memorial Number 46823958).

On November 8, 1878, the following was given in the Aberdeen Weekly, "We regret to record the death of Mrs. Mary C. Lile, widow of the late Mr. Peyton Lile. She leaves a large circle of friends and relations to cherish her memory and mourn her death."

Thomas Lile

On March 23, 1804, Thomas Lile was born in North Carolina. In 1824, Thomas Lile of Trinity married America M. Allison at age 13; she was born on January 1, 1811, in Madison County, Alabama.

America M. Allison, wife of Thomas Lile, was the daughter of John Allison (1770-1810) and DuAnna Hewlett Allison (1787-1879) of Virginia. On January 15, 1810, John Allison Sr. entered 161.40 acres of land in the Northwest ¼ of Section 32 in Township 3 South and Range 1 West in Madison County of Mississippi Territory. John and Duanna Hewlett Allison were among the earliest settlers in Madison County.

Based on census records, it appears that Thomas Lile and America M. Allison Lile had the following children:
1. John Allison Lile was born in 1825.
2. Virginia E. Lile was born in 1827.
3. William E. Lilewas born in 1829.
4. Antonett A. Lile was born in 1832.
5. Du Ann L. Lile was born on August 23, 1833, and she died on August 13, 1853.
6. Thomas Lile was born in 1836.
7. Victoria Louisa Lile was born in 1839, and she died on September 22, 1863, at 24 years of age.
8. Samuel J. Lile was born on October 25, 1839, and he died on November 16, 1864.
9. Susan J. Lile was born about 1840.
10. Lucian J. Lile was born on March 9, 1842, and he died on October 12, 1867.
11. Virginia G. Lile was born on March 25, 1844, and she died on September 24, 1848.

According to the 1830 Morgan County, Alabama Census, Thomas Lile owned 19 slaves. On May, 30, 1830, Thomas Lile first entered 80.49 acres of land in East½ of the Northwest ¼ of Section 18 in Township 5 South and Range 5 West in Morgan County, Alabama (Cowart, 1981).

On May 17, 1831, Thomas Lile entered 160.98 acres of land in the Northeast ¼ of Section 18 in Township 5 South and Range 5 West in Morgan County, Alabama (Cowart, 1981).

In 1833, Thomas Lile helped establish the first state bank of Alabama at Decatur in Morgan County, Alabama. He also helped organize one of the earliest schools in near his plantation.

In the 1840 Morgan County, Alabama Census, Thomas Lile owned 30 Black slaves. He probably inherited his slaves after the death of his parents.

According to the 1850 Trinity, Morgan County, Alabama Census, Thomas and America (Allison) Lile household had the following: Thomas Lile, 46, Male, Farmer, North Carolina; America M. Lile, 39, Female, Alabama; John A. Lile, 26, Male, Farmer, Alabama; William E. Lile, 21, Male, Farmer, Alabama; Virginia E. Lile, 23, Female, Alabama; Antonett A. Jones, 18, Female, Alabama; Thomas B. L. Jones, 2/12, Male, Ala; Du Ann Lile, 16, Female, Alabama; Thomas Lile, 14, Male, Alabama; Victoria L. Lile, 12, Female, Alabama; Susan J. Lile, 11, Female, Alabama; Lucian J. Lile, 8, Male.

In 1850, the farm of Thomas Lile was worth $10,000, and he owned 52 slaves; 49 were Black and three were Mulatto. On September 19, 1853, Thomas Lile entered 40.14½ acres of land in the Northwest ¼ of Northwest ¼, Section 30 in Township 5 South and Range 5 West in Morgan County, Alabama (Cowart, 1981).

The 1860 Morgan County, Alabama Census had the following for the Thomas Lile household: Lile, Thomas, 56,Male, Farmer, 27,000, 70,000, North Carolina; Lyle, America L., 49, Female, Housewife, Alabama; Lyle, Thomas B. Jr., 24, Male, Farmer, 15,000, Alabama; Victoria L., 21, Female, Seamstress, 14,000, Alabama; Samuel J., 20, Male, Farmer, 13,000, Alabama; Lucian J., 18, Male, Student, 12,000, Alabama, Student in last year Morgan County, Alabama. According to the 1860 Morgan County, Alabama, Slave Schedule, Thomas Lile owned 21 male and 24 female slaves. Of the 45 slaves, 43 were Black and two were Mulattos.

According to the 1860 Morgan County, Alabama, Agricultural Census, Thomas Lile owned 560 acres of improved land and 800 acres of unimproved land worth $30,000.00. He also had $700.00 worth of farming equipment and $2,700.00 worth of livestock.

During the Civil War, Thomas Lile was a Unionist and was saddened by his three sons who fought for the Confederacy. Thomas died in Morgan County, Alabama, during the middle of the war.

On October 29, 1863, at age 59 years, seven months and six days, Thomas Lile died at Trinity in Morgan County, Alabama. Thomas Lile was buried in the Lile Cemetery number 2 at Trinity in Morgan County, Alabama (Find A Grave Memorial Number 32606973)

On September 15, 1867, America M. Allison Lile died in Morgan County, Alabama; she was the wife of Thomas Lile. She was buried in the Lile Cemetery number 2, at Trinity in Morgan County, Alabama (Find A Grave Memorial Number 32607027).

The following are markers in the Lile Cemetery: Lile, in memory of Ben and Eliza A., 1860 D, Colored servant of John A. Lile, The tall, the wise, the reverend head, must lie as low as ours. Lile, Adeline (Black slave), b 1844, d, Lile, Uncle Nick (Black slave), b Oct 2, 1842, d Aug 20, 1908, Lile, May Belle, b Sep 30, 1858, d Jan 25, 1913, wife of Jim Lile, Jones, Mary Lyle, John Allison, b 1825, d 1883, Blalock, Sarah C, dau of Joseph K. and Sally Blalock.

John Allison Lile

John Allison Lile was the son of Thomas Lile and America M. Allison Lile. John was born about 1825 in Morgan County, Alabama.

The 1860 Morgan County, Alabama Census had the following for John Allison Lile: Lile, John A., 35, Male, Farmer, 20,000 Real Estate, 50,000 Personal Property, Alabama; Lile, Louisa M., 21, Female, Housewife, Alabama; Lile, John L., 2, Male, Alabama; Lile, William M., 1, Male, Alabama; Cooper, Herrod, 50, Male, Overseer, 1200, South Carolina.

According to the 1860 Morgan County, Alabama, Agricultural Census, John Allison Lile owned 600 acres of improved land and 600 acres of unimproved land worth $20,000.00. He also had $1,000.00 worth of farming equipment and $3,500.00 worth of livestock.

McClanahan, Sarah

Sarah Moore McClanahan was born on February 20, 1760; on May 6, 1788, she married Alexander McClanahan Sr. Alexander was born on February 20, 1755; he was from Botetourt, Virginia.

Sarah Moore McClanahan and Alexander McClanahan had the following children.
1. John McClanahan was born about 1789; he married Elizabeth Barnett on October 2, 1819.
2. Elisabeth McClanahan was born on Wednesday, December 22, 1790; she married Andrew Neeley on May 11, 1813.
3. James McClanahan was born on Wednesday the December 26, 1792. At 33 years old, James McClanahan died in Morgan County, Alabama, at the house of his mother on May 20, 1825.
4. Mary McClanahan was born on Sunday the February 8, 1795; she married Elisha Moore on March 5, 1815.
5. William McClanahan was born on Wednesday the April 12, 1797; he married Jane Childers on August 28, 1823. At 31 years old, William McClanahan died at his residence in Morgan County, Alabama, on August 18, 1827.
6. Alexander McClanahan Jr. was born on Sunday, April 10, 1799, in Tennessee. In 1860, Alexander McClanahan owned 280 acres of land in Morgan County.
7. Elijah McClanahan was born on Sunday, September 14, 1800, in Tennessee; he married Marjory Childers. In 1860, Elijah McClanahan owned 480 acres of land in Morgan County.
8. Margaret A. McClanahan married M. V. Denton on February 26, 1837.
9. Peggy Ann McClanahan was born on Sunday, August 20, 1808.

On May 5, 1824, at 69 or 70 years old, Alexander McClanahan Sr. died at his residence in Morgan County, Alabama.

According to the 1830 Morgan County, Alabama Census, Sarah McClanahan was 60 to 70 years old and owned no slaves. By 1840, she became a slave owner or a son living with her was a slave owner.

In the 1840 Morgan County, Alabama Census, the household of Sarah McClanahan had the following: White Males: 30-40: 1; White Females: 10-15: 1, 60-70: 1; Slaves: Males 13, Females 10, Total Slaves: 23.

On June 13, 1856, Sarah McClanahan, at age eighty eight years, appeared before the Justice of the Peace of Morgan County, Alabama. Sarah McClanahan made her oath in order to obtain the benefit of the an act of Congress passed July 7, July 1838, that granted half pay to certain widows. Sarah stated that she was the widow of Alexander McClanahan who was a soldier or private in Captain David May Company of Botetourt Militia in the State of Virginia in the Revolutionary War.

Alexander was at the Battle of Guilford Court House on March 15, 1781, and served in the war for a term of at least six months. Sarah declared that her name was Sarah Moore before she was married to Alexander McClanahan on May 6, 1788, and that Alexander McClanahan died on May 5, 1824.

McClanahan, John

John McClanahan was the son of Alexander McClanahan and Sarah Moore McClanahan. On October 2, 1819, John McClanahan married Elizabeth Barnett in Morgan County, Alabama.

In the 1830 Morgan County, Alabama Census, the household of John McClanahan had the following: White Males 0-5: 1, 5-10: 1, 10-15: 1, 15-20: 2, 40-50: 1; White Females 5-10: 1, 10-15: 1, 15-20: 1, 40-50: 1. In the 1830 census, John was not listed with slaves.

According to the 1840 Morgan County, Alabama Census, the household of John McClanahan had the following: White Males 10-15: 1, 20-30: 1, 50-60: 1;

White Females 0-5: 2, 5-10: 1, 15-20: 1, 20-30: 1, 40-50: 1; Slaves: Male 20, Females 22, Total Slaves: 42.

In the 1860 North West Division of Morgan County, Alabama, United States Census, John McClanahan was a 70 year old White male born in North Carolina. Also in his household was the following: John Bodery, Male, 56 North Carolina; Frank Easley, Male, 25, Alabama; John H. Edmonson, Male, 25, Tennessee; John B. Mason, Male, 55, Virginia.

On January 10, 1866, John McClanahan died in Morgan County, Alabama. His burial site was not available.

Menefee, Thomas

On March 8, 1779, Thomas Menefee was born in Virginia. Thomas was the son of John Menefee and Frances Rhodes Menefee. In 1785, the Menefee family moved from Virginia to Knox County, Tennessee. On May 14, 1812, Thomas Menefee married Lucy Sutherland Paine in Knox County, Tennessee. Lucy was a widow with one child. Thomas Menefee fathered nine children.

In 1823, Thomas Menefee moved his family from Tennessee to Morgan County, Alabama. They probably settled near Decatur where he entered land. On July 28, 1830, Thomas Menefee entered $160.40^{3/4}$ acres of land in the Southwest ¼ of Section 27 in Township 5 South and Range 5 West in Morgan County, Alabama (Cowart, 1981).

According to the 1830 Morgan County, Alabama Census, the Thomas Menifee household had the following: White Males 0-5: 3, 5-10: 2, 10-15: 1, 20-30: 1, 50-60: 1; White Females 5-10: 2, 10-15: 3, 30-40: 1, 60-70: 1; Slaves: Males 15, Females 14, Total Slaves: 29.

In 1830, with a group composed of the Menefee and Sutherland family members, Thomas Menefee traveled to Texas to settle in the colony of Stephen F. Austin in what is now Jackson County, Texas. John Sutherland Menefee and

George Menefee were two sons of Thomas Menefee that fought in the Texas Revolution.

Probably the Tom Menefee born in Alabama was one of the sons of Thomas Menefee. Tom Menefee was mentioned in the death records of Adline Summerford who was born in 1848. Adline listed her father as Tom Menefee; she died on February 15, 1928, at Toney in Limestone County, Alabama.

On December 29, 1858, Thomas Menefee died at his home in Jackson County, Texas. The location of his burial site was not available.

Moseley, William Sr.

On July 3, 1776, William Moseley Sr. was born at Buffalo Creek in Charlotte County, Virginia. He was the son of Captain Edward Moseley and Amey Green Moseley of Virginia.

On August 17.1797, William Moseley Sr. married his first wife Ann in Halifax, Virginia; William later married Temperance Vaughn. William and Temperance had their first child in 1810 probably in present-day Limestone County, Alabama.

On September 11, 1809, William Moseley Sr. entered 159.36 acres of land in the Southwest¼ of Section 36 of Township 1 South and Range 3 West in Limestone County of Mississippi Territory (Cowart, 1984). On April 19, 1814, William Moseley Sr. entered 159.36 acres of land in the Northeast¼ of Section 36 of Township 1 South and Range 3 West in Limestone County of Mississippi Territory (Cowart, 1984). By 1814, William Moseley had purchased 318.72 acres of land in Limestone County of Mississippi Territory.

On February 2, 1818, William S. Moseley and Thomas T. Moseley entered 158.24 acres of land in the Northwest¼ of Section 10 of Township 4 South and Range 2 West in Madison County of Alabama Territory. They paid $3.12½ per acre for the land (Cowart, 1979). On July 15, 1818, William Moseley Sr. entered 161.23¼ acres of land in the Southwest¼ of Section 11 of Township 5 South and Range 5 West in Morgan County, Alabama (Cowart, 1981).

According to the 1830 Morgan County, Alabama Census, the William Moseley had the following: the total number of White males in the household was eight with the oldest White male being 50-60 years old (Wm Moseley Sr.); the total White females in household was four with the oldest White female being 40-50 years old. The household had 86 slaves which included 45 males and 41 females.

On July 19, 1830, William Moseley Sr. entered $80.61^{5/8}$ acres of land in the West ½ of the Southeast ¼ of Section 11 of Township 5 South and Range 5 West in Morgan County, Alabama (Cowart, 1981).

On December 12, 1830, William Moseley Sr. died at his home at Decatur in Morgan, Alabama. He was buried in the Moseley/Decatur Cemetery in Morgan, Alabama. In 1951, the Moseley/Decatur Cemetery was moved.

According to the 1840 Morgan County, Alabama Census, the following were found in the household of Temperance Moseley (Widow of Wm. Moseley Sr.): White Males 15-20: 1, 20-30: 1; White Females 10-15: 1, 50-60: 1; Slaves: Males 22, Females 21, Total Slaves: 43.

William Moseley Jr.

On August 24, 1810, William Moseley Jr. was the first child born to William Moseley Sr. and Temperance Vaughn Moseley. He was probably born in Limestone County of Mississippi Territory (present-day Limestone County, Alabama).

On May 2, 1831, William Moseley Jr. entered 161.23¼ acres of land in the Northeast¼ of Section 11 of Township 5 South and Range 5 West in Morgan County, Alabama (Cowart, 1981). On June 23, 1831, William Moseley Jr. entered 8.02 acres of land south of the Tennessee River in Section 1 of Township 5 South and Range 5 West in Morgan County, Alabama (Cowart, 1981). On the same date, William Moseley Jr. entered 100.90 acres of land south of the Tennessee River in Section 2 of Township 5 South and Range 5 West in Morgan County, Alabama (Cowart, 1981).

During 1831 after the death of his father, William Moseley Jr. added 270.15½ acres of land to the Moseley Plantation. In the 1840 census, the Moseley Plantation had 43 Black slaves, but by 1860, William Jr. had accumulated 94 slaves to work his plantation. William Moseley Jr. took over responsibilities and ownership of the Moseley plantation which thrived prior to the Civil War.

According to the 1850 Morgan County, Alabama, United States Census, House Number 290, William Moseley Jr. was a 40 year old white male born in Tennessee. Living with him was his mother Temperance Vaughn Moseley who was a 64 year old female born in Virginia. In the 1850 Morgan County, Alabama, Slave Schedule, William Moseley Jr. owned 48 Black and 2 Mulatto slaves for a total of 50 slaves.

On November 13, 1855, William Moseley Jr. married Martha Adelia Pryor Kimbell in Morgan County, Alabama. Martha was born on July 9, 1825. On May 1, 1859, Martha Adelia Pryor Kimbell Moseley died in Morgan County, Alabama.

According to the 1860 Morgan County, Alabama, United States Census, the following were in the Mosley household: William Moseley, 49, Male, Farmer, $22,000.00 real estate, $115,650.00 personal worth, Tennessee; Temperance Moseley, 76, Female, Housekeeper, Virginia; William, Male, 3; Samuel Hefley, 25, Male, Overseer, Alabama; William M. High, 17, Male, Alabama, Student.

In the 1860 Morgan County, Alabama, Slave Schedule, William Moseley owned 91 Black and 3 Mulatto slaves for a total of 94 slaves-of the slaves, 49 were female and 45 male. Also in the 1860 agricultural census, William Moseley owned 680 acres of improved land and 428 acres of unimproved land worth $22,000.00. He also owned $500.00 worth of farming equipment and $3,000.00 worth of livestock.

The 1870 Morgan County, Alabama, United States Census had the following for the household of William Moseley Jr.: William Moseley Jr., Male, 59, White, Tennessee; Jesse Moseley, Female, 13, Alabama; Hettie Moseley, Female, 11, Alabama; Harry Moseley, Male, 30, Maryland; Cora Moseley, Female, 6, Alabama; Fanny Green, Female, 70, Virginia; Hannah Green, Female, 25, Alabama.

On February 27, 1899, William Moseley Jr. died. William Moseley Jr. was 88 years of age when he died of senility. He was widowed. William Moseley Jr. was buried in Decatur City Cemetery at Decatur in Morgan County, Alabama (Find A Grave Memorial Number 68268470).

In 1951, Chemstrand bought the Moseley property. The Moseley Cemetery on the property had to be moved to the Decatur City Cemetery.

Today in the Trinity and Decatur area, many Black folks have the last name Moseley. They are probably descendants of the slaves of the William Moseley family.

Other Moseleys

John P. Moseley

In the 1840 census, John P. Moseley lived near Temperance Moseley. According to the 1840 Morgan County, Alabama Census, the John P. Moseley household had the following: White Males 0-5: 1, 20-30: 1; White Females 0-5: 2, 20-30: 1; Slaves: Males 9, Females 11, Total slaves: 20. In 1850, John P. Moseley had 22 slaves, and in 1860, he had 34 slaves.

According to the 1860 Morgan, Alabama, Agricultural Census, John P. Moseley owned 600 acres of improved land and 500 acres of unimproved land worth $15,000.00. He also owned $500.00 worth of farming equipment and $3,500.00 worth of livestock.

Drury V. Moseley

In 1850, Drury V. Moseley owned 15 slaves in Morgan County. In 1860, Drury had 31 slaves. According to the 1860 Morgan, Alabama, Agricultural Census, Drury V. Moseley owned 500 acres of improved land and 500 acres of unimproved land worth $20,000.00. He also owned $600.00 worth of farming equipment and $3,470.00 worth of livestock. Based on land value, Drury V. Moseley was one of the wealthiest men of Morgan County, Alabama.

Murphey, George

On April 7, 1774, George Murphey was born in Franklin County, North Carolina. George married Mary "Polly" Kimbell; their daughter was Temperance Murphey Hill (1814-1836).

By 1809, Robert, Elijah, John and William Murphey of North Carolina had entered land in Madison County of Mississippi Territory. On August 22, 1809, Robert and Elijah Murphey entered 162.35 acres in the Southeast ¼ of Section 10 in Township 2 South and Range 1 West (Cowart, 1979). On September 18, 1809, John Murphy entered 157.56 acres in the Northeast ¼ of Section 24 in Township 1 South and Range 1 West in Madison County of Mississippi Territory (Cowart, 1979). These Murphey settlers were probably the kinfolks of George Murphey who settled in Morgan County, Alabama.

On July 15, 1818, George Murphey entered 159.48½ acres in the northeast ¼ of Section 6 in Township 5 South and Range 5 West in Morgan County, Alabama (Cowart, 1981). His neighbors included John Burt, William Whitaker, Edmond Kimbell, Isaac Lane, Smith Murphey, William Moseley, John McKinley, and Henry W. Rhodes.

By 1818, George Murphey had staked his claim to land in Morgan County, Alabama; some historians indicate that he first migrated to Madison County from North Carolina. George and family settled near the river in the Fox's Creek drainage in northwest Morgan County, Alabama. Since George Murphy was a cotton planter, he moved to the area in search of fertile soil for cotton production.

Around 1824, George Murphey with the help of his slaves built the Murphey House on his property between the River Road and Tennessee River west of Decatur. He had moved with several other families and friends to northwest Morgan County from North Carolina. George Murphey and his wife, Mary, constructed their Tidewater cottage with a hall and parlor layout which was a design that was common in North Carolina but rare in North Alabama. The house eventually passed to William, the son of George and Mary Kimbell Murphey.

In the November 5, 1824, edition of the Huntsville Democrat, the following was written about the death of the wife of George Murphey: "Murphey, Mary P., Died in Morgan County, Alabama, on the 13th inst. after a short illness, Mrs. Mary P. Murphey, aged 36 years, consort of Mr. George Murphy, left five little children."

According to the 1830 Morgan County, Alabama Census, the George Murphey household had the following: White Males 10-15: 1, 20-30: 1, 50-60: 1; White Females 5-10: 1, 10-15: 1, 50-60: 1; Slaves: Males 11, Females 20, Total Slaves: 31.

In the 1840 Morgan County, Alabama Census, the household of George Murphy had the following: White Males 20-30: 1, 60-70: 1; White Females 15-20: 1, 40-50: 1, 50-60: 1; Slaves: Males 16, Females 15, Total Slaves: 31.

On August 11, 1846, George Murphey died at Trinity in Morgan County, Alabama. He was buried in a box tomb in the Kimbell Cemetery at Trinity in Morgan County, Alabama. The Kimbell Cemetery contains the remains of many of the cotton planters and plantation owners of northwest Morgan County, Alabama.

Dr. William E. Murphey

On March 19, 1819, William E. Murphey was born in Franklin County, North Carolina. He was the son of George and Mary Kimbell Murphey.

Around 1823 or 1824, the Doctor William Murphey House was built by his father George Murphey; however, the home was named in honor of Dr. William E. Murphey. The Murphey Plantation was located on the north side of present-day Alabama Highway 20 near Trinity and consists of some 1,520 acres of land.

In 1846 after the death of his parents, George and Mary Kimbell Murphey, Dr. William E. Murphy inherited the Murphey Plantation which included the house and land. The wife and two children of Dr. William E. Murphy died young.

According to the 1860 Morgan County, Alabama, Slave Schedules, Dr. William E. Murphey owned with 52 Black slaves. The Murphey Plantation produced about 70 bales of cotton annually.

According to the 1860 Morgan County, Alabama, Agricultural Census, William E. Murphy owned 800 acres of improved land and 720 acres of unimproved land worth $20,000.00. He also had $750.00 worth of farming equipment and $3,400.00 worth of livestock.

Prior to and during the Civil War, Dr. William E. Murphey was opposed to secession. It was believed that Dr. Murphey hid runaway slaves on his plantation as they tried to get to Decatur to join the Union Army.

In the 1870s, Dr. Murphey married a second time to Annie Lindsay. Details of his second marriage were not available.

On September 21, 1889, at the age of 70, Dr. William E. Murphey died in LaGrange, Georgia. He was buried in the Kimbell Cemetery at Trinity in Morgan County, Alabama (Find A Grave Memorial Number 20812498). Dr. Murphey had no heirs.

Murphy House

In 1988, the Murphey House was listed on the National Register of Historic Places. The Dr. William E. Murphey House, a historic residence near Trinity, Alabama, was one of the earliest examples of Atlantic Seaboard type building in Alabama. The Alabama Historical Commission presented Nucor Steel with its Distinguished Service Award for the company's efforts in restoring the historic Murphey House.

In 1986, the Murphey House was listed on the National Register of Historic Places. On April 27, 2011, tornadoes destroyed Murphy House.

Smith Murphey

Smith Murphy of Morgan County, Alabama, lived adjacent to George Murphey. By 1840, Smith Murphey was not on the Morgan County Census.

On July 15, 1818, Smith Murphey entered 159.48½ acres of land in the Southwest¼ of Section 6 in Township 5 South and Range 5 West in Morgan County, Alabama (Cowart, 1981). Smith and George Murphey entered land in the same area on the same date in Morgan County; Smith and George were probably brothers.

According to the 1830 Morgan County, Alabama Census, the Smith Murphy household had the following: White Males 30-40: 1 (Smith Murphy); White Females 0-5: 1, 15-20: 1, 20-30: 1; Slaves: Males 13, Females 13, Total Slaves: 26.

Orr, Christopher

On October 1, 1754, Christopher Orr was born in Augusta County, Virginia; he was the son of Robert Orr and Charlotte Green Orr. Robert was of Scots Irish ancestry from Ballygowan, Ireland, and he died 1779 in Johnston County, North Carolina. Christopher Orr served in the American Revolution from North Carolina along with five of his brothers.

On August 27, 1778, Christopher Orr married Martha "Patty" Watkins, the daughter of Reese Watkins, in Wake County, North Carolina. Martha was born March 16, 1761, in Augusta County, Virginia.

Christopher Orr and Martha Watkins had nine of 11 children who settled in Lawrence and Morgan Counties of North Alabama:

1. Sarah Orr was born on September 25, 1779, in Wake County, North Carolina. Sarah married Robert Barber, son of George and Margaret Watkins Barber. Sarah died January 6, 1853.

2. Philip Orr was born on January 7, 1781; he married Elizabeth Davis in 1812. Philip married Niri Rucker on December 12, 1820; they lived in Coweta County, Georgia. Philip died on April 11, 1841, and Niri died in the 1860s.
3. Ann Nancy Orr was born on December 11, 1782. Ann married John Gibson about 1798; he was born on May 11, 1774. By 1820, they were living in Lawrence County, Alabama. In 1820, John owned 15 slaves. Ann Nancy Orr died on September 21, 1823, and John Gibson died on August 8, 1837.
4. Mary "Polly" Orr was born on March 11, 1785; she married Reverend Sylvanus Gibson Jr., brother of John Gibson. Sylvanus was born on November 24, 1783, in Wilkes County, Georgia. Mary and Sylvanus owned some 820 acres about two miles west of Speake School on Highway 36 in Lawrence County, Alabama. In 1850, Sylvanus owned 16 black slaves, and in 1860, Mary owned 14 slaves. On July 25, 1851, Sylvanus Gibson Jr. died and Mary "Polly" Orr Gibson died October 20, 1874; they are buried just a few yards north of Highway 36 at their home place.
5. John Orr was born on April 16, 1787; he married Eady Stone on January 14, 1813. John married Elsey Freeman on February 1, 1820. In the early 1820s, John and Elsey moved to Morgan County, Alabama. According to the Morgan County Census, John owned 28 slaves in 1830, 37 slaves in 1840, and 32 slaves in 1850. Elsey died around 1848, and John died around 1854 in Morgan County.
6. Jonathan Orr was born December 26, 1789; he married Sarah Allen Glenn on October 18, 1822. Jonathan settled in Morgan County, Alabama, and he died on April 29, 1857.
7. Jacob Orr was born on December 11, 1790; he married Elizabeth Wise on February 14, 1818. She may have been Elizabeth Davis Wise, daughter of William Davis. They settled in Morgan County, Alabama; Jacob died in 1839.
8. Margaret Orr was born on December 26, 1791; she married Drury Stovall on February 21, 1809. Margaret died on May 19, 1841. Drury Stovall was a slave owner; in 1830, he owned eight slaves. In 1840, Drury owned 16 slaves, and in 1850, he owned 22 slaves. Drury died in July 1864.

9. Watkins Orr was born on December 12, 1793; he married Cynthia Reeves on January 7, 1822. They settled Morgan County, Alabama; Watkins died on November 29, 1849.
10. Martha Orr was born on January 1, 1799; she married David Johnson on November 20, 1815. They settled in Georgia.
11. Elizabeth Orr was born on October 1, 1801; she married Henry J. Wise on January 5, 1825. They settled in Georgia.
12. Olive Orr was born February 9, 1803; she married Robert Malone Johnson on September 10, 1819. They settled in Lawrence County, Alabama; Olive died on May 3, 1862.

On October 1, 1830, Martha "Patty" Watkins Orr died, and Christopher Orr died on October 5, 1830. They were living on Long Creek in Wilkes County, Georgia.

Several children of the Christopher and Martha Orr family came to Lawrence County and Morgan County, Alabama. Many of the Orr Family originally settled around a creek that became known as Crowd Around Creek or Crowd About Creek. The creek was named because of so many family members settling near the creek before dispersing to surrounding farms.

John Orr

On April 16, 1787, John Orr was born in Wilkes County, Georgia. He was the son of Christopher Orr and Martha "Patty" Watkins Orr.

On January 14, 1813, John Orr married Eady Stone who probably died before 1820. On January 31, 1820, John Orr married the second time to Elsey Freeman. The children of John and Elsey were Frances Elizabeth Orr, Simeon Watkins Orr, and George Christopher Orr who died young.

According to the 1830 Morgan County, Alabama Census, the John Orr household had the following: White Males 5-10: 2, 20-30: 1, 40-50: 1; White Females 5-10: 2, 30-40: 1, 60-70: 1. John owned 28 Black slaves in 1830.

In the 1840 Morgan County, Alabama Census, the household of John Orr had the following: White Males 15-20: 1, 20-30: 4, 50-60: 1; White Females 20-30: 2, 40-50: 1, 70-80: 1; Slaves: Males 16, Females 21, Total Slaves: 37.

In the 1850 Morgan County, Alabama Slave Census, John Orr owned 32 slaves. John died around 1854 in Morgan County, Alabama.

Frances Elizabeth Orr

On July 12, 1836, Frances Elizabeth Orr married William W. Roby in Morgan County, Alabama. Frances was born on December 9, 1820, in Wilkes County, Georgia; she was the daughter of John Orr and Elsey Freeman Orr. Frances and William had five children-three girls and two boys.

According to the 1840 Morgan County, Alabama Census, the William W. Roby household had the following: White Males 0-5: 1, 20-30: 1; White Females 0-5: 1, 15-20: 1 (Frances Elizabeth Orr); Slaves: Males 18, Females 14, Total Slaves: 32.

By 1854, William W. Roby and Frances Elizabeth Orr Roby lived in Noxubee County, Mississippi. They moved from Morgan County, Alabama, to Noxubee County, Mississippi, between 1840 and 1854.

In the 1860 Noxubee County, Mississippi, Slave Schedules, William W. Roby owned 67 slaves. At the time, he was living in District 3 which was the same district as his brother-in-law Simeon Watkins Orr.

Colonel Simeon Watkins Orr

On December 19, 1822, Simeon Watkins Orr was born in Morgan County, Alabama. His parents were John Orr and Alicy "Elsey" Rousseau Freeman Orr.

On August 19, 1842, Simeon Watkins Orr entered 40 acres in the Northwest ¼ of the Southeast ¼ in Section 34 of Township 7 South and Range 4 West in Morgan County, Alabama (Cowart, 1981). Therefore, between 1842 and 1854, Simeon moved to Noxubee County, Mississippi.

According to the 1860 Noxubee County, Mississippi Census, Simeon Watkins Orr was a 37 year old farmer born in Alabama with a personal value of $67,000.00 and a real estate value of $94,000.00. His wife Mary was 28 years old and born in South Carolina. They had two sons-John who was nine months old and born in Mississippi, and William who was three years old.

In 1860 the Noxubee County, Mississippi, Slave Schedules, Simeon Orr owned 76 slaves. He was obviously a cotton planter, in addition to raising and trading in a lot of livestock.

On December 5, 1872, The Weekly Clarion in Jackson, Mississippi, published the following: "The Columbus Index reports that Colonel Simeon Orr, the great stockraiser (sic) died at his home in Brooksville, Noxubee County, on last Thursday morning of consumption." Simeon Watkins Orr was only 49 years old at the time of his death.

Jonathan Orr

On December 26, 1789, Jonathan Orr was born in Wilkes County, Georgia. He was the son of Christopher Orr and Martha "Patty" Watkins Orr.

On October 18, 1822, Jonathan Orr married Sarah Allen Glenn who was born on April 4, 1800, in Oglethorpe County, Georgia. Sarah was the daughter of John and Mary Brooks Glenn.

Jonathan and Sarah were married by Reverend Sylvanus Gibson; Jonathan Gibson, the son of Sylvanus, married Susan Ann Glenn. Jonathan Orr and Sarah Allen Glenn Orr became the in-laws of Jonathan Gibson who married Susan, the sister of Sarah.

Jonathan and Sarah Glenn Orr were the parents of 11 children who were born in Morgan County, Alabama, as follows:
1. John Christopher Orr was born on February 7, 1824. John married Eleanor Freeman on December 9, 1845; she died on November 1, 1856. John married Ailsie Freeman, the sister of his deceased wife. In 1850, John C. Orr owned eight Black slaves. In 1860, John C. Orr owned 23 Black slaves and 1,100 acres of land valued at $5,000.00.

On April 18, 1899, John died, and he was buried in the Orr Family Cemetery.
2. William Watkins Orr was born on December 6, 1825. William married Elizabeth Jane McDaniel on April 6, 1852; she was born on September 17, 1833, and died on August 20, 1912. In 1860, William Watkins Orr owned 20 black slaves. William died on April 14, 1895. William and Elizabeth were buried in the Orr Family Cemetery.
3. Philip Lewis Orr was born on November 29, 1827; he married his first cousin Frances "Fannie" Lucinda Orr on October 20. 1854. In 1860, Philip owned 17 black slaves and 1,600 acres of land worth $6,600.00 with $5,875.00 worth of livestock. Philip died on February 24, 1891, and Fannie died on February 5, 1903. Philip and Frances are buried in the Orr Family Cemetery.
4. Jonathan Gibson Orr was born on June 17, 1834; he married Martha "Mattie" Helen Burleson on December 20, 1860. In 1860, Jonathan G. Orr owned 7 slaves. On December 11, 1905, Jonathan died in Morgan County, Alabama, and Martha died on April 20, 1923; they were buried in the small Orr Cemetery at Danville.
5. Daniel Jonathan Orr was born on August 28, 1837; he married Sarah Lane Wiggins (1837-1899). Daniel died on March 26, 1897, and he was buried in Orr Cemetery number 1.
6. Sarah Ann "Sallie" Glenn Orr was born on August 22, 1839; she married Dabney Adair Burleson. In 1860, Dabney owned eight Black slaves. On July 31, 1908, Sarah died, and Dabney died on July 24, 1912. They were buried in the Bethel Cemetery near Hartselle in Morgan County, Alabama.
7. Henrietta Orr was born in 1846; she never married. In 1860, Henrietta C. Orr was listed in the census records of Morgan County owning five Black slaves (maybe different Henriettas). Henrietta Orr died before 1870.
8. Robert Orr died young with birth and death unknown.
9. Martha Orr died young with birth and death unknown.
10. Mary Elizabeth "May" Orr died young with birth and death unknown.
11. Henry Orr died young with birth and death unknown.

According to the 1830 Morgan County, Alabama Census, the Jonathan Orr household had the following: White Males 0-5: 2, 5-10: 1, 15-20: 1, 30-40: 1; White Females 0-5: 1, 20-30: 1; Slaves: Males 8, Females 8, Total Slaves: 16.

In the 1840 Morgan County, Alabama Census, the household of Jonathan Orr had the following: White Males 0-5: 1, 5-10: 1, 10-15: 2, 15-20: 1, 20-30: 1, 50-60: 1; White Females 0-5: 1, 40-50: 1; Slaves: Males 17, Females 13, Total Slaves: 30.

The 1850 Morgan County, Alabama United States Census, House Number 182 had the following: Jonathan Orr, Male, 60, White, Georgia; Sarah A. Orr, Female, 50, Virginia; William W. Orr, Male, 24, Alabama; Phillip L. Orr, Male, 22 Alabama; Jonathan G. Orr, Male, 16, Alabama; Daniel D. Orr, Male, 13, Alabama; Sarah A. Orr, Female, 10, Alabama; Henrietta M. Orr, Female, 4, Alabama; Sarah O. Gibson, Female, 16 Alabama; Mary Gibson, Female, 23, Georgia. In the 1850 Morgan County, Alabama Slave Census, Jonathan Orr owned 43 slaves.

On April 28, 1857, Jonathan Orr died and was buried in the Orr Cemetery Number 1 at Danville in Morgan County, Alabama (Find A Grave Memorial Number 32783678). The inscription on his tombstone states, "Died in his 68th year, leaving a wife and seven children to mourn his death. He was a friend to the needy. We trust he has gone to meet his reward in heaven. May we all meet there."

At the time of his death in 1857, Jonathan Orr owned 16,054 acres of land in North Alabama with 14, 920 of those acres located in Morgan County; therefore, he was the largest antebellum land owner in Morgan County, Alabama (Burleson, 2020). Jonathan was also considered one of the wealthiest men of Morgan County, Alabama.

In the 1860 Morgan County, Alabama, Slave Schedules, Sarah A. Orr owned 26 Black slaves. Probably some of the 43 slaves that she and her husband Jonathan owned in 1850 were given to their children.

According to the 1860 Morgan County, Alabama, Agricultural Census, Sarah A. Orr owned 600 acres of improved land and 1,720 acres of unimproved land worth $10,000.00. She also had $200.00 of farm equipment and $1,600.00 worth of livestock.

On July 27, 1878, Sarah Allen Glenn Orr died in Morgan County, Alabama. She was buried in the Orr Cemetery number 1 at Danville in Morgan County, Alabama (Find A Grave Memorial Number 32738392).

Watkins Orr

On December 12, 1793, Watkins Orr was born in Wilkes County, Georgia. He was the son of Christopher Orr and Martha "Patty" Watkins Orr.

On January 7, 1822, Watkins Orr married Cynthia Reeves; they moved from Wilkes County, Georgia, to Morgan County, Alabama, in the early 1820s.

Watkins and Cynthia Reeves Orr had the following known children:

1. Watkins Orr Jr. married Margaret Hodges in Morgan County, Alabama, on March 24, 1842.
2. Sarah Elizabeth Orr (October 24, 1822-February 6, 1844) married John Troup on August 22, 1842. In 1840, John Troup Jr. owned 39 Black slaves, and in 1850, he owned 36 slaves.
3. Willis F. Orr (September 1, 1824-July 2, 1900) married Temperance Bean on November 20, 1844. Willis owned 20 Black slaves in 1850; in 1860, he owned 42 slaves and 1,400 acres of land plus $3,000.00 worth of livestock in Morgan County.
4. James Christopher Orr (July 22, 1827-October 11, 1836).
5. Joseph Orr (July 21, 1832-September 21, 1842).
6. Simeon W. Orr (February 10, 1838-October 11, 1903) married Nettie Leeper.

According to the 1830 Morgan County, Alabama Census, the household of Watkins Orr had the following: White Males 0-5: 1, 5-10: 1, 30-40: 1; White Females 5-10: 1, 20-30: 1; Slaves: Males 6, Females 2, Total Slaves: 8.

In the 1840 Morgan County, Alabama Census, Watkins Orr had the following living in his household: White Males 0-5: 1, 15-20: 1, 40-50: 1; White Females 15-20: 1, 30-40: 1; Slaves: Males 10, Females 17, Total Slaves: 27.

On November 29, 1849, Watkins Orr Sr. died in Morgan County, Alabama. He was buried in the Hopewell Cemetery east of Danville in Morgan County, Alabama.

In the 1850 Morgan County, Alabama, Slave Schedules, Cynthia Orr owned 14 Black slaves. In the 1860 slave schedules, Cynthia owned 36 slaves.

According to the 1860 Morgan County, Alabama, Agricultural Census, Cynthia Orr owned 300 acres of improved land and 600 acres of unimproved land worth $5,000.00. She also had $100.00 of farm equipment and $1,550.00 worth of livestock.

On June 13, 1863, Cynthia Reeves Orr died in Morgan County, Alabama. Cynthia was buried in the Hopewell Cemetery east of Danville in Morgan County, Alabama.

Patterson, Andrew "Andy" McDonald

On June 12, 1820, Andrew McDonald "Andy" Patterson was born in Morgan County, Alabama. He was the son of Malcolm Patterson and Margaret Dinsmore Patterson.

On September 15, 1818, Malcolm Patterson first entered land in Morgan County, Alabama. On December 9, 1818, James Dinsmore entered land adjacent to Malcolm Patterson who entered the adjacent property on the same date. James Dinsmore had 11 slaves in the 1830 census.

The home of Andrew "Andy" McDonald Patterson was on the southeast edge of the Town of Falkville in Morgan County, Alabama; Andy was one of the founders of Falkville. The Patterson house was built of thick oak logs and stood two stories high. The lumber on the interior walls was hand planed with the chinked logs visible on the upper floor. The outside had huge chimneys with the outside logs covered with plank siding. In 2016, the Patterson House was in ruin, deteriorating, and falling in due to decay.

On February 13, 1843, Andrew McDonald Patterson married Jane Turney; she was born on January 2, 1820, in Morgan County, Alabama. Jane was the daughter of Joseph Turney who settled in Gandys Cove of Morgan County in 1818. Joseph was a large land holder with some 1,400 acres most of which was entered in 1818. Joseph Turney was also cotton planter and slave owner; he had 12 slaves in 1840, 18 slaves in 1850, and 10 slaves in 1860.

Andrew "Andy" McDonald Patterson and Jane Turney Patterson had the following children:
1. Joseph Patterson was born about 1846.
2. America H. Patterson was born about 1847.
3. Malcifa D. F. Patterson was born about 1849.
4. Andrew Patterson was born about 1852.

According to the 1850 Morgan County, Alabama Census, House Number 251, the Patterson household had the following: Andrew M. L. Patterson, Male, 28, White, Alabama; Jane Patterson, Female, 30, Alabama; Joseph M. G. Patterson, Male, Alabama; America H. Patterson, Female, 4, Alabama; Malikijah Patterson, Male, 2, Alabama. In the 1850 Morgan County, Alabama, Slave Census, District 10, Wm. M. Dancy Asst. Marshal, Andrew M. Patterson owned 3 Black slaves.

In the 1860 South West Division, Morgan County, Alabama, United States Census, the Andrew M. Patterson had the following: A. M. Patterson, Male, 39, White, Alabama; Jane Patterson, Female, 40, Alabama; Joseph M. Patterson, Male, 15, Alabama; America H. Patterson, Female, 13, Alabama; M. D. F. Patterson, Male, 11, Alabama; Andrew Patterson, Male, 9, Alabama.

According to the 1860 Morgan County, Alabama, Agricultural Census, Andrew "Andy" McDonald Patterson owned 300 acres of improved land and 1,000 acres of unimproved land worth $2,000.00. He also had $400.00 of farm equipment and $2,000.00 worth of livestock.

During the Civil War 1861-1865, Captain Andrew "Andy" McDonald Patterson was a captain in the famous Fifth Alabama Cavalry, Confederate States of America. He was the half-brother of Colonel Josiah Patterson, who was perhaps the most noted native son of Morgan County who served the Confederacy.

The 1870 Morgan County, Alabama, United States Census had the following: Andy Patterson, Male, 50, White, Alabama; Jane Patterson, Female, 57, Alabama; Joseph Patterson, Male, 24, Alabama; Malcifa Patterson, Male, 21, Alabama; Andrew Patterson, Male, 18 Alabama.

On February 12, 1875, Jane Turney Patterson died in Morgan County, Alabama. Jane was buried in the Turney Cemetery in Morgan County, Alabama. The Turney Cemetery is near Gandys Cove Methodist Church in Morgan County, Alabama; the cemetery is 200 yards off Gandys Cove Road.

On October 22, 1879, Andrew M. Patterson married Sarah Louisa Robinson in Morgan County, Alabama; Sarah was born on April 15, 1842. They had the following children:

1. Priscilla Patterson (November 22, 1880-August 16, 1882) was 21 months old (Find A Grave Memorial Number 33457687).
2. Martha Louisa Patterson was born on October 5, 1882.
3. Margaret Jane "Jennie" Patterson (May 2, 1884-September 2, 1887) was three years and 4 months old (Find A Grave Memorial Number 33457714).

On August 17, 1891, Captain Andrew McDonald "Andy" Patterson died at 70 years, 2 months, and 5 days at Falkville in Morgan County, Alabama (Find A Grave Memorial Number 33457505). He was buried in the Patterson Family Cemetery at Falkville in Morgan County, Alabama. The Patterson Cemetery is about ¼ mile south of the Falkville City Cemetery on the west side of the Patterson house place.

On August 20, 1891, <u>The Alabama Enquirer</u> had the following: "Captain Andy Patterson of Falkville, died at his home last Monday, Aug., 17th, with congestion of the bowels. He was seventy one years old last June. He was buried at Falkville, Tuesday in the presence of a large concourse of relatives and friends. He was an excellent citizen and his death will be greatly regretted. He was a brother to Col. Josiah Patterson, of Memphis, Tenn. who was present at his burial."

On March 16, 1919, Sarah Louisa Robinson Patterson died in Morgan County, Alabama. She was buried next to her husband in the Patterson Family Cemetery at Falkville in Morgan County, Alabama (Find A Grave Memorial Number 33457647).

Perry, Aaron

In 1824, the Aaron Sr. and Mary Kerr Perry family and their slaves moved from North Carolina to Morgan County, Alabama. Aaron Perry Sr. was a cotton planter and slave owner.

According to the 1830 Morgan County, Alabama Census, the Aaron Perry household had the following: White Males 20-30: 2; 60-70: 1(Aaron Perry, Sr.); White Females 50-60: 1; Slaves: Males 7, Females 16, Total: 23.

In December 1833, the following was a court case that Aaron Perry filed against Augustin Hewlett: "On December 23, 1833, Aaron Perry hired two slaves to Augustin Hewlett and others. Hewlett agreed to pay $150 for the pair and to return them by December 25 of the next year. One of the slaves, Fanny, died in June. Hewlett permitted the other slave to visit Perry, who detained him.

Judge Hopkins ruled that Hewlett still owed Perry the agreed upon price, despite the death of Fanny. On the other hand, Hewlett's debt was discharged because Perry detained the other slave before the expiration of the agreement (Perry vs. Hewlett, 5 Porter 318, 1837)."

According to the 1840 Calhoun (Benton) County, Alabama Census, the Aaron Perry household had the following: White Males 60-70: 1; 70-80: 1; White Females 15-20: 1; 30-40: 2; 70-80: 1. Slaves: Males: 8, Females: 7, Total Slaves: 15.

In the 1850 Calhoun County, Alabama Census, House Number 576, Aaron Perry, Male, 84, White, North Carolina; Mary Perry, Female, 50, Tennessee; Alexander Anderson, Male, 20, Tennessee; Monroe Anderson, Male, 17, Tennessee; Margaret Anderson, Female, 8, Alabama; Charles Anderson, Male, 7, Alabama; N. J. Cross, Female, 10, Alabama.

Aaron Perry Jr.

About 1810, Aaron Perry, Jr. was born in Mecklenburg County, North Carolina. He was the son of Aaron Perry, Sr. and Mary Kerr Perry from Greensboro, North Carolina.

On August 3, 1832, Aaron Perry Jr. married Susan E. Fowler in Morgan County, Alabama. Susan was born about 1808; she was the daughter of John Fowler (1770-1850) and Martha Olivia Vaughn (1761-1840) from South Carolina. According to the 1850 Morgan County, Alabama Census, John Fowler owned eight Black slaves.

Susan and Aaron Perry Jr. had six children-four daughters and two sons:
1. Sarah Olivia Perry (1833-1883)
2. Hyporia Perry (1837-unknown)
3. William M. Perry (1839-unknown)
4. Luisa M. Perry (1841-unknown)
5. Marcus Lamar Perry (1843-1914)
6. Emma Zuni Perry (1845-unknown)

In 1844, Aaron Perry Jr. was elected as a Democrat to the Alabama state legislature and served for two years. Aaron was a political figure in both Alabama and Texas.

Susan E. Fowler Perry died about 1846 in Morgan County, Alabama. After the death of his wife, Aaron Perry Jr. moved his family and slaves to Springfield in Limestone County, Texas.

The 1850 Limestone County, Texas Census listed Aaron Perry Jr. with five of his children still in the household.

In 1859, Aaron was elected as a House representative for Limestone, Freestone, and Falls Counties to the Eighth Texas Legislature, where he served on the Agricultural Affairs, Finance, and Public Buildings committees. He was also elected to the House of the Ninth Texas Legislature and chaired the Contingent Expenses Committee.

In the 1860 Limestone County, Texas Census, Aaron Perry Jr. was a widower and listed as a farmer in Springfield, Texas. Apparently, he never remarried. In June 1874, Aaron Perry Jr. died and was buried in Limestone County, Texas.

Griffin "Griff" Fowler - Black Slave

John Fowler gave his daughter Susan Fowler Perry and her husband Aaron Perry Jr. one of his slaves named Griffin "Griff" Fowler. Griff was born into slavery in Georgia about 1810.

In a signed last will and testimony in Morgan County, Alabama, the ownership of Griff was transferred from John Fowler to Susan and Aaron Perry Jr. In January 1843, Griff and Amie Perry had a daughter Jemima Perry who was born in Morgan County, Alabama, as slave of Aaron Perry, Jr.

In 1846 along with their baby daughter Jemima Perry, Griff Fowler and Amie Perry moved with their master Aaron Perry Jr. and his family from Morgan County, Alabama, to Limestone County, Texas. In Texas, Jemima married Jerry Henry, a free man who was brought to Texas from Tennessee.

In 1890, Griff Fowler died and was buried in Woodland Cemetery at Mexia in Limestone County, Texas (Find A Grave Memorial Number 106800666). In 1892, Amie Perry Fowler died and was buried in Woodland Cemetery at Mexia in Limestone County, Texas (Find A Grave Memorial Number 106800789).

On April 10, 1915, Jemima Perry Henry died of pneumonia. Jemima was buried next to her husband a few miles from the John R. Henry Plantation in Woodland Cemetery at Mexia in Limestone County, Texas (Find A Grave Memorial Number 97096399). Jemima Perry Henry was buried in the same cemetery where her parents were buried.

Peyton, Thomas

According to the 1830 Morgan County census records, Thomas Peyton was born between 1760 and 1770. Other records indicate that Thomas was born in 1764 in Prince William County, Virginia; he was the son of Colonel Henry and Margaret Peyton.

In 1778, Thomas Peyton married Rachel Rogers in Granville, North Carolina. Thomas and Rachel had two daughters, Martha and Sarah Peyton, who are mentioned in the will of Thomas.

From 1790 through 1820, Thomas Peyton appeared on the census in Cumberland County, North Carolina. He was also in land deed records in Wake County and Moore County, North Carolina.

In 1820, Thomas Peyton moved to Morgan County, Alabama. On October 22, 1822, Thomas Peyton married Nancy Griffin in Morgan County, Alabama. It appears that Thomas and Nancy Peyton had one son and four daughters.

On March 8, 1823, Thomas and Nancy had their only son John Randolph Peyton Sr. who was born in Morgan County, Alabama. John R. Peyton died on July 17, 1921, in Robertson County, Texas; he was buried in the Henry-Peyton Cemetery at Benchley in Robertson County, Texas (Find A Grave Memorial Number 153546623). John married Sarah Henry, the daughter of William Henry (1810-1849) and Mary Fullerton (1815-1872).

According to the 1830 Morgan County, Alabama Census, the household of Thomas Peyton had the following: White Males 0-5: 1 (John Randolph Peyton), 60-70: 1 (Thomas Peyton); White Females 0-5: 2, 5-10: , 30-40: 1 (Nancy Peyton); Slaves: Males 15, Females 8, Total Slaves: 23.

In 1833, Thomas Peyton died in Alabama. He was probably buried in Morgan County, Alabama. Based on census records, Thomas and Nancy appear to have one son and four young daughters at the time of his death.

In the 1840 Morgan County, Alabama Census, Nancy Peyton was listed as head of the house with the following: White Males: 10-15: 1; White Females: 5-10: 1, 10-15: 2, 15-20: 1, 40-50: 1; Slaves: Males 2, Females 2, Total Slaves: 4.

Rather, Captain John Taylor

On March 14, 1792, John Taylor Rather was born in Prince Edward County, Virginia. John Taylor Rather first married Barbara Walker McClellan who was born on March 13, 1800. Barbara was the daughter of Colonel John M. and Mary Wallace McClellan. Barbara was a sister to General W. B. McClellan of Talladega.

From July 8, 1818, through April 12, 1838, John Taylor Rather entered some 1,160 acres in Morgan County, Alabama (Cowart, 1981). About 1820, John Taylor Rather, an early lawyer in Somerville, Alabama, built his plantation home near the town.

John Taylor Rather

On October 26, 1826, Barbara Walker McClellan Rather died in Morgan County, Alabama. She was buried in Somerville Cemetery in Morgan County, Alabama.

On October 29, 1830, John Taylor Rather married his second wife Susan H. Roberts of Somerville, Alabama. Susan was the daughter of Philagaetius and Margaret Roberts of Culpepper County, Virginia.

On September 23, 1854, at age 49, Susan H. Roberts Rather died at Somerville in Morgan County, Alabama. She was buried in the Somerville

Cemetery at Somerville in Morgan County (Find A Grave Memorial Number 33008563).

On October 5, 1854, the obituary of Susan H. Roberts Rather appeared in the Southern Advocate as follows: "Departed this life in Somerville, Alabama, at the residence of John F. Barker, 23rd September, Mrs. Susan H. Rather, wife of Captain John T. Rather, of Decatur, in her 49th year. She was the daughter of Philagaetius and Margaret Roberts of Culpepper County, Virginia. She came to Alabama with her brother-in-law, Mr. (John) Banks, in 1826. She was united in marriage to her surviving husband, October 29, 1830. She joined M. E. Church in 1829."

On January 3, 1881, John Taylor Rather died at the home of his son John Daniel Rather at Tuscumbia in Colbert County, Alabama. He was buried between his two wives in Somerville Cemetery in Morgan County, Alabama (Find A Grave Memorial Number 33008528).

In January 1881, the following article was written and published by L.H. Grubbs, editor of the Decatur News. "Captain John Taylor Rather died at the residence of his son, General John D. Rather in Tuscumbia, on Monday the 3rd day of January 1881. He was a native of Prince Edward County, Virginia, and was born on the 14th of March 1792, and was consequently nearly eighty-nine years of age. More than sixty-three years ago, when in the vigor of young manhood, the deceased moved to the Territory of Alabama, and settled in what was then known as Cotaco County, immediately where the county site of Morgan now stands; with his own hands he built the first house that was ever erected in Somerville, and for a long number of years was a resident of that place. He was so prominent and intimately connected with every public interest of this County, that his life forms a part of the history of the same.

John Taylor Rather House
Somerville, Alabama

In 1820, he was chosen to represent it in the Lower House of the General Assembly, the Second Legislature of the then New State and while the Capitol was at Cahaba. His public service in this capacity gave such general satisfaction that he was nine times re-elected to the same responsible position and in 1835 was chosen a member of the Senate. After this, he was trusted with various important interests in the county and took an active part in all that tended to promote the interest and welfare of the people.

In 1865 when the Dark Days of the War had ended and the gloom of devastation and chaos was hanging in thick folds over the South, his ripe experience and wise counsel were again needed, and the people who had hitherto honored and trusted him, commissioned him to represent Morgan County in the Reconstruction Convention. A year or two after, he moved to Tuscumbia and resided with his only child, General Rather, until his death. His long residence and useful life here created reciprocity of good feeling between him and the citizens of the County and this was naturally followed by mutual endearment, since he made frequent visits and often spent weeks with his old friends and fond admirers. He was always a welcome guest, the easiest chair, the best meal, and the softest bed were prepared for him, and we have seen an interesting and excited street conversation calmed or silenced by his approach, such respect and veneration had all for his presence.

The last time he visited Decatur was in October, on the occasion of the reunion of himself, Colonel McElderry, Governor Chapman, General McClellan and Judge Campbell, all at one time residents of this county. The writer was present and witnessed their greeting, cordial fellowship and listened with great pleasure to the recitals of incidents of the pioneer days of the country.

Precious old men! Their next meeting will be beyond the chilling tide. Whatever may have been a leading characteristic of Captain Rather in his younger days, he was eminently sociable and full of humor in his old age. After the usual infirmities of advanced life came upon him, he was vivacious and young in spirit, always cheerful and had a word of encouragement for the depressed and despondent. He was a man of inflexible integrity and in his public and private life was governed by principle rather than policy and hence his advice was sought and his judgment much relied upon. He was a just man; exacted nothing of others that he did not accord to them. The Golden Rule was the guide of his life. He was public spirited and liberal; prompt in meeting his liabilities and unstinted in a judicious expenditure of his means. At the beginning of last year he called to pay in advance, the subscription price of this paper, and remarked, 'I never want my paper and my preaching on credit.'

Better than all our venerable and reverend friend was a Christian. For more than half a century, he was an exemplary member of the Methodist Church and during the greater part of his time filled the office of Steward. The honors of official station and the duties of public life did not cause him to reject nor neglect his place and duties in the church. In the prime of life when his intellect was strong, and his limbs active, he accepted the claim of the Christian religion and when old age and infirmities came on he enjoyed the comforts of the same, and being emancipated from the cares and affections of life was entered upon the full fruition of that 'Hope which is anchor to the Soul.'

Soon after moving to Somerville, Captain Rather was married to Miss Barbara Walker McClellan, sister of General W.B. McClellan of Talladega. By this wife was born one child, General John D. Rather, President of the present Alabama Senate. Subsequently he was again married to Miss Susan H. Roberts of Somerville, sister to Mrs. John Banks. The graves of both of these are in the cemetery at Somerville. When the last wife was buried a space between her grave and that of the former was left for his own sepulture, and there he was interred last Tuesday.

In May of last year (1880) he visited the sacred spot and looked upon the green turf that grew over the dust of forms so dear, and while the pearly tear coursed its way down his furrowed face, he said, 'soon this old body will be sleeping between them.'

We spoke of the probability of his living several years longer, but he said at last overcome by his feelings, 'the next time I am here it will be for burial.' True to his words it was so. The wheels of nature, worn by weary years, had ceased to move. The old body was dead, but the beautiful regions of the redeemed, the house of clay is basking in the sunlight presence of Him who says to the good earth, 'Come ye blessed of my Father, inherit the kingdom prepared for you.' May his kindred and friends overtake him up there."

Rather, General John D.

On January 7, 1823, John Daniel Rather was born at Somerville in Morgan County, Alabama. His parents were Captain John Taylor Rather and Barbara Walker McClellan Rather.

In appearance, John Daniel Rather was stout and robust with black hair, dark complexion, and dark eyes. He was well educated and studied under Judge Daniel Coleman at Athens in Limestone County, Alabama.

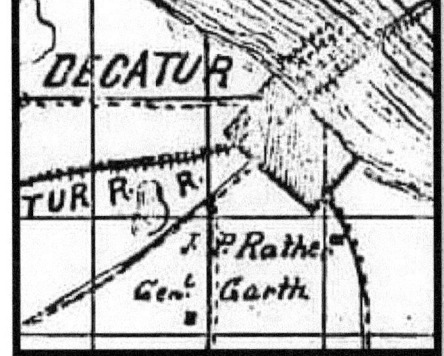

John first located at Somerville in Morgan County, Alabama, before moving to Decatur where he was very successful in his law practice. The home of John D. Rather was just north of General Jesse W. Garth.

In the early 1840's, John Daniel Rather first married Jane Charlotte Keyes. Jane C. Keyes was born in Limestone County, Alabama, on November 16, 1827;

she was the daughter of George and Ellen Keyes. Based on birth records, it appears that they had three children:
1. George Taylor Rather was born on January 5, 1844, at Somerville in Morgan County, Alabama. On September 29, 1909, he died at his home in Columbus, Mississippi, and was buried in the Oakwood Cemetery at Tuscumbia in Colbert County, Alabama (Find A Grave Memorial Number 96203767).
2. Silas P. Rather was born on February 18, 1846; he died in Decatur on March 16, 1901, and he was buried at Oakwood Cemetery in Tuscumbia (Find A Grave Memorial Number 39990080).
3. Eldon Rutledge Rather was born on November 23, 1847; he died on December 19, 1881, and he was buried at Oakwood Cemetery in Tuscumbia (Find A Grave Memorial Number 39989986).

In 1849, John Daniel Rather was elected to the Alabama State Legislature representing Morgan County, Alabama. John was subsequently re-elected to the Alabama Legislature in 1851, and he was chosen as Speaker of the House of Representatives.

In the 1850 Morgan County, Alabama Census, John Daniel Rather owned 15 slaves. In 1850, his father, John Taylor Rather, was listed with 11 slaves.

General John Daniel Rather

On March 26, 1853, Jane Charlotte Keyes died at age 25, in New Orleans, Orleans Parish, Louisiana. There were no details available on the death and burial of Jane C. Keyes Rather, first wife of John Daniel Rather.

Around 1855 after the death of his first wife, John Daniel Rather married Sarah Letitia Pearsall; she was born on June 1, 1834, in Franklin County, Alabama. Letitia was the daughter of Edward Pearsall (11/16/1785-6/3/1853) and Parthenia Shearon (3/12/1800-12/12/1892). Edward Pearsall was a cotton planter with 1,100 acres of land, and owner of 62 slaves in present-day Colbert County, Alabama.

Sarah Letitia Pearsall Rather

The children of John Daniel Rather and Sarah Letitia Pearsall Rather were the following:
1. Henry Chambers Rather January 12, 1857, at Decatur in Morgan County, Alabama. On August 4, 1912, he died and was buried at Roselawn Memorial Park at Little Rock in Pulaski County, Arkansas (Find A Grave Memorial Number 198664608).
2. Ella Pearsall Rather Kirk was born in Morgan County on September 6, 1859; she married James Thomas Kirk (1858-1938). Ella died on May 14, 1944, and was buried at Oakwood Cemetery in Tuscumbia (Find A Grave Memorial Number 117877002).
3. John Taylor Rather was born on February 25, 1863; he died on September 10, 1868 at age five. John was buried in the Pearsall Cemetery in Colbert County, Alabama (Find A Grave Memorial Number 44906737).

4. Annie "Tante" Eve Rather Weakley was born on February 18, 1865, at Somerville in Morgan County, Alabama. She died on October 14, 1965, at age 100. Annie was buried in Elmwood Cemetery at Birmingham in Jefferson County, Alabama (Find A Grave Memorial Number 202973063).
5. Charles Courtenay Rather was born on September 19, 1866; he died on December 1, 1910, and was buried in the Oakwood Cemetery at Tuscumbia in Colbert County, Alabama (Find A Grave Memorial Number 39989958).
6. Persall Rather was born on December 16, 1869; he died on April 15, 1894, and was buried in the Oakwood Cemetery at Tuscumbia in Colbert County, Alabama (Find A Grave Memorial Number 3999010).
7. Infant Daughter Rather was born on July 5, 1872; she died on August 30, 1878, and was buried in the Pearsall Cemetery in Colbert County, Alabama (Find A Grave Memorial Number 44906757).
8. John Daniel Rather Jr. was born on March 30, 1876; he died on May 20, 1959, and was buried in the Oakwood Cemetery at Tuscumbia in Colbert County, Alabama (Find A Grave Memorial Number 39976199).
9. Mary Wallace Rather was born on March 30, 1876; she died on June 24, 1881, and was buried in the Oakwood Cemetery at Tuscumbia in Colbert County, Alabama (Find A Grave Memorial Number 39989800).

From 1857 through 1861, John Daniel Rather served in the Alabama Senate from Morgan County, Alabama. He served as President of the Senate his last two years. At the end of the Civil War, John Daniel Rather moved to

Tuscumbia and lived at Locust Hill. He opened a law office and remained a resident of Tuscumbia until his death.

According to the 1860 Morgan County, Alabama, Agricultural Census, one of the wealthiest cotton planters based on their real estate value was General John Daniel Rather who had 1,100 acres worth $20,000.00. In 1860, John D. Rather owned 52 Black slaves.

In 1865 shortly after the end of the war, Locust Hill was purchased by Captain John Taylor Rather, father of General John Daniel Rather. In 1823, Locust Hill Plantation Mansion was built for William H. Winter and his wife Catherine who came to Tuscumbia from Prince William County, Virginia. During the Civil War, the home was the headquarters of Union General Florence N. Cornyn.

The 1880 Tuscumbia, Colbert County, Alabama Census had the following: John D. Rather, Letitia Rather, Annie Rather, Pearsall Rather, Courtney Rather, John Rather, Mary Wallace Rather, Ella Rather.

On November 1, 1893, at age 59, Sarah Letitia Pearsall Rather died in Colbert County, Alabama. She was buried in the Oakwood Cemetery at Tuscumbia in Colbert County, Alabama (Find A Grave Memorial Number 39976327).

On March 4, 1910, at 87 years of age, General John Daniel Rather died at his Locust Hill House at Tuscumbia in Colbert County,

GEN. JOHN D. RATHER

Distinguished Citizen of Alabama Passed Away

Tuscumbia, Ala., March 4.—Gen. John D. Rather, one of the most prominent citizens of this city, and a man of state wide reputation, died at his home in Tuscumbia this afternoon after an illness of four weeks, aged eighty-seven years. Gen. Rather had resided in this city for a long number of years, and was the oldest resident of Tuscumbia He was born near Somerville, Morgan county, Ala., and represented the county in the legislature several terms before the Civil War, being speaker of the house of representatives while a member of that body.

He moved to Colbert county in 1867, where he practiced law for several years.

He was elected to the senate from Colbert and Lawrence counties, serving from 1878 to 1880 and was made president of that body during his term. He was a member of the constitution convention of 1875, and was prominently mentioned for governor in 1882, when Gen. E. A. O'Neal, of Florence, was elected.

Gen. Rather was also president of the Memphis & Charleston Railroad company in 1873.

There were few more prominent Alabamians politically than Gen. Rather from 1867 to 1882.

He is survived by three sons, H. C. Rather of Little Rock, John D. Rather, Jr., a prominent young lawyer of this city, and C. C. Rather, and two daughters, Mrs. James T. Kirk of this city and Mrs. John B. Weakley of Birmingham.

Alabama. General Rather was buried in the Oakwood Cemetery at Tuscumbia in Colbert County, Alabama (Find A Grave Memorial Number 39976306).

The following is the obituary of General John Daniel Rather: "General John D. Rather, distinguished citizen of Alabama, passed away Tuscumbia, Alabama, March 4. General John D. Rather, one of the most prominent citizens of this city and a man of state-wide reputation, died at his home in Tuscumbia this afternoon after an illness of four weeks, aged 87 years. General Rather had resided in this city for a long number of years and was the oldest resident of Tuscumbia. He was born near Somerville, Morgan County, Alabama, and represented the county to the legislature several times before the Civil War, being speaker of the House of Representatives while a member of that body.

He moved to Colbert County in 1867, where he practiced law for several years. He was elected to the senate from Colbert and Lawrence Counties, serving from 1878 to 1880 and was made president of that body during his term. He was a member of the constitutional convention of 1875, and was prominently mentioned for governor in 1882, when General E. A. O'Neal of Florence was elected.

General Rather was also president of the Memphis and Charleston Railroad Company in 1873. There were few more prominent Alabamians politically than General Rather from 1867 to 1882. He is survived by three sons H.D. Rather of Little Rock; John D. Rather, Jr., a prominent young lawyer of this city; C.C. Rather, and two daughters, Mrs. James T. Kirk of this city; and Mrs. John B. Wesley of Birmingham."

Until 1978, the Locust Hill Plantation Mansion was the home of Mary Wallace Rather Kirk became known as the John Daniel Rather House. Mary W. R. Kirk was the daughter John Daniel Rather and Sarah Letitia Pearsall Rather.

In 1978, Locust Hill was listed on the Alabama Register of Landmarks and Heritage. In 1982, the Locust Hill or the John Daniel Rather House was placed on the National Register of Historic Places.

The television news correspondent Dan Rather was a descendant of the Rather Family. Dan served many years on the national news scene.

General John Daniel Rather House
Tuscumbia, Alabama

Reed, William

By 1818, William Reed was a land owner in Morgan County, Alabama. According to Morgan County, Alabama Census records, William Reed was born between 1770 and 1780.

On July 9, 1818, William Reed entered 79.81 acres of land in the West½ of the Southwest¼ of Section 15 in Township 6 South and Range 2 West in Morgan County, Alabama (Cowart, 1981).

According to the 1830 Morgan County, Alabama Census, the household of William Reed had the following: White Males 5-10: 2, 10-15: 1, 50-60: 1 (William Reed); White Females 10-15: 1, 15-20: 1, 20-30: 1; Total Slaves: 50.

On July 17, 1830, William Reed entered 79.81 acres of land in the Southeast ¼ of Section 22 in Township 6 South and Range 2 West in Morgan County, Alabama (Cowart, 1981).

On February 27, 1831, William Reed married Nancy Harwood in Morgan County, Alabama.

On June 24, 1831, William Reed entered 160.34 acres of land in the East ½ of the Southwest ¼ of Section 15 in Township 6 South and Range 2 West in Morgan County, Alabama (Cowart, 1981).

In the 1840 Morgan County, Alabama Census, the William Reed household had five White males with the oldest being 50-60 years old, five White females with the oldest being 40-50, and 14 slaves.

Russell, Captain William Jr.

In 1787, William Russell Jr. was born in Rutherford County, North Carolina. He was the son of Major William Russell (1762-February 16, 1825) and Agness H. McCullough Russell (1754-1840).

Major William Russell had the following children:
1. Mary "Polly" Agnes Russell Little (1780-1857) married Martin Little. She died in Lawrence County and was buried in Denton Hollow in Franklin County, Alabama.
2. Jessie Russell (1780-June 13, 1843) married Mary Farrar; he died in Clay County, Arkansas.
3. John A. Russell was born about 1782 at Boones Creek in the Watauga Settlement; he married Rutha Spencer on November 18, 1830, in Franklin County, Alabama; he died on September 8, 1846, in Tishomingo County, Mississippi.

4. Dicey Ann Russell Abney Wagner was born in 1783 in the Watauga Settlement, and she married Solomon Wagner (1776-1840); Dicey died in 1860.
5. Absolom Russell was born about 1785-1786; he died on November 23, 1813.
6. Captain William Russell (1787-1860) married Lydia Agnes Bean (1791-1860) in 1809.
7. Lemuel Smith Russell was born about 1788; he married Nancy Myatt. Lemuel died in 1853 in Dickson, Tennessee.
8. Lewis R. Russell was born about 1790; on November 25, 1850, he applied for bounty land and received 160 acres in Franklin County, Tennessee.
9. Edmund Russell (1792-1873) married Henrietta "Ritta" Kitty Sargent (1797-1876) in 1820. Edmund and Henrietta were buried in the Plansburg Cemetery in Merced County, California.
10. George Daniel Russell (1794-October 17, 1831) married in Franklin County, Alabama, to Leah Jackson Hudson (1805-1887) in December 28, 1820.
11. Thomas Jefferson Russell was born on July 27, 1800, in Wilkes County, Georgia; he died on November 17, 1885, at Athens in McMinn County, Tennessee.
12. Samuel Russell was born about 1804 in Wilkes County, Georgia.

William Russell Jr. may have been the William Russell listed in the Morgan County, Alabama, census records in 1840. He may also have been the William Russell listed as entering land in Morgan County, Alabama, from 1847 through 1852.

In 1818, William Russell Jr. entered land in Franklin County, Alabama, near his brother George. According to the Franklin County land records, William Jr. was listed as being from Madison County, Alabama (Cowart, 1986).

On December 9, 1819, William Russell of Lawrence County entered 80.04 acres in Section 2 of Township 7 South and Range 9 West in Lawrence County, Alabama, and again on October 3, 1836, William entered 79.79 acres in Section 17 of Township 6 South and Range 9 West in Lawrence County, Alabama (Cowart, 1991). In the 1820 Lawrence County, Alabama Census, William

Russell was listed with one white male over 21, one white female over 21, and two white females under 21.

Based on land and census records, William Russell Jr. was documented as being in Madison, Franklin, Lawrence Counties, and probably Morgan County, Alabama. But there could have been other men by the name of William Russell; however, William Bean entered land in Morgan County, Alabama, on September 24, 1818; the wife of William Jr. was a Bean, and members of the Bean family lived in Morgan County. Therefore, William Russell Jr. probably lived in Morgan County, Alabama, during the 1840s.

In 1809, William Russell Jr. married Lydia Agnes Bean. Lydia was born on February 15, 1791, in Washington County, Tennessee, to Jessie Bean.

William Russell Jr. and Lydia Agnes Bean Russell had the following children:
1. Polly Ann Russell was born in Tennessee on December 23, 1823; she married Mark Harrison Wagner (1816-1898) in 1845. Polly died in 1905 at age 81-82 in Arkansas; she was buried in the Dougan Cemetery at Mulberry in Crawford County, Arkansas (Find A Grave Memorial Number 6249274).
2. Lydia Bean Russell was probably born in Morgan County, Alabama, on November 23, 1837. Lydia married Solomon William Wagner (1836-1911) who was the nephew of Mark Harrison Wagner, husband of her sister. On January 11, 1903, at age 65, Lydia died in Texas; she was buried in the Oswald Cemetery at Clifton in Bosque County, Texas (Find A Grave Memorial Number 31019222).

Solomon Wagner (1776-1840) married Dicey Russell (1783-1860) who was the sister of Captain William Russell. Solomon was the father of Mark Harrison Wagner and the grandfather of Solomon William Wagner whose father was William Wagner. William Wagner and Mark Harrison Wagner were brothers; therefore, Polly and Lydia married their kinfolks.

According to the 1840 Morgan County, Alabama Census, the household of William Russell had the following: White Males 10-15: 1, 15-20: 1, 50-60: 1 (William Russell); White Females 0-5: 1, 10-15: 2, 30-40: 1; Slaves: Males 10, Females 10, Total Slaves: 20.

From November 20, 1847, through March 1, 1852, William Russell entered some 240 of land in township 6 South and Range 5 West in Morgan County, Alabama (Cowart, 1981).

On May 3, 1860, Captain William Russell Jr. died at age 72-73 at Mulberry in Crawford County, Arkansas (Find A Grave Memorial Number 153590587). Lydia Agnes Bean Russell died in 1860 at Mulberry in Crawford County, Arkansas (Find A Grave Memorial Number 153590829).

Smith, James L.

James L. Smith was born on January 8, 1793. He was married to Catherine McDonnell Smith. Catherine was born on January 14, 1804.

On July 13, 1818, James L. Smith entered 159.9 acres of land in the Southwest ¼ of Section 8 in Township 6 South and Range 4 West in Morgan County, Alabama (Cowart, 1981). On the same day, James entered 158.94 acres of land in the Northwest ¼ of Section 17 in Township 6 South and Range 4 West in Morgan County, Alabama (Cowart, 1981). His property was adjacent to Samuel Livingston in Section 18.

On October 17, 1826, James L. Smith was conveyed by deed a tract of property in Morgan County by Samuel and Pheobe Livingston who were living

Morgan County. On October 16, 1818, Samuel and Pheobe were in Madison County when they acknowledged the deed to Perry Flint.

In the 1830 Morgan County, Alabama Census, James L. Smith had the following in his household: White Males 30-40: 1; White Females 0-5: 1, 20-30: 1; Slaves: Males 7, Females 9, Total Slaves: 16.

According to the 1840 Morgan County, Alabama Census, the household of James L. Smith had the following: White Males 15-20: 1, 40-50: 1; White Females 0-5: 1, 15-20: 1, 20-30: 1, 30-40: 1; Slaves: Males 16, Females 20, Total Slaves: 36.

On September 15, 1847, James L. Smith died at age 54 years, 8 months, and 7 days. He was buried in the Spring Hill Cemetery at Decatur in Morgan County, Alabama (Find A Grave Memorial Number 47255210). Spring Hill Cemetery is located near the old Spring Hill Baptist Church on the Old Trinity Road in the western portion of Decatur in Morgan County, Alabama.

In the 1850 Morgan County, Alabama Census, Catherine Smith was reported with 20 slaves. In 1860, Catherine owned 23 slaves in Morgan County, Alabama. She probably kept the cotton plantation going until the Civil War.

In the 1860 Morgan County, Alabama, Agricultural Census, Catherine Smith owned 450 acres of improved land and 500 acres of unimproved land worth $7,000.00. She also had $200.00 worth of farm equipment and $2,500.00 worth of livestock.

On November 9, 1886, at the age of 82, Catherine McDonnell Smith died in Morgan County, Alabama. She was buried in the Spring Hill Cemetery at Decatur in Morgan County, Alabama (Find A Grave Memorial Number 47255539).

Stanback, Dixon

In 1820, Dixon Stanback was a candidate for the Alabama House of Representatives for Cotaco County, Alabama. The original home state of Dixon Stanback was not known.

According to the 1830 Morgan County, Alabama Census, the Dixon Stanback household had the following: White Males: 5-10: 2, 10-15: 2, 20-30: 1, 40-50: 1; White Females: 10-15: 2, 15-20: 1, 30-40: 1; Slaves: Males 14, Females 12, Total Slaves: 26. Also, in the 1830 Morgan County census, David Stanback owned 26 slaves; David and Dixon maybe the same.

On May 26, 1831, Dixon Stanback entered $160.52^{3/4}$ acres of land in the Northeast ¼ of Section 14 in Township 5 South and Range 5 West in Morgan County, Alabama (Cowart, 1981)

On November 7, 1835, Martha Stanback, Edward B. Stanback, Benjamin D. Stanback, and James L. Stanback entered 40.07 acres of land in the Southheast ¼ of the Northeast ¼ of Section 35 in Township 6 South and Range 3 West in Morgan County, Alabama (Cowart, 1981). These folks were probably the family of Dixon Stanback.

According to the 1840 Morgan County, Alabama Census, Edward B. Stanback owned 10 black slaves. Dixon Stanback was probably the father of Edward B. Stanback who was born between 1815 and 1825. Edward married Lucretia Nash Dickson between 1840 and 1850. Lucretia Nash Dickson was born in 1823 in Madison County, Alabama; her parents were James Dickson and Keziah Wood Dickson.

Possibly another son of Dixon Stanback was Sterling Stanback who married Maria Owen in 1831. They were married in the same vicinity that the Dixon Stanback family were living.

On March 22, 1873, Lucretia Nash Dickson Stanback died in Macon County, Mississippi. Based on death records, part of the Stanback family migrated from Morgan County, Alabama, to Mississippi.

Stephenson, Arthur

On October 25, 1792, Arthur Stephenson was born in Orange County, North Carolina. He was the son of Josiah Stephenson and Sarah Rebecca Stephenson.

Josiah Stephenson was born in North Hampton County, North Carolina, on December 15, 1770; he died on December 12, 1847. Rebecca Stephenson was born in Orange County, North Carolina on June 20, 1777; she died on August 29, 1843. Josiah and Rebecca Stephenson were buried in the Burleson-Stephenson Cemetery.

Arthur Stephenson married Elizabeth R. Garrett; she was born about 1802 according to the 1850 census records which show her age as 48. Elizabeth was the daughter of William and Ann Garrett. Ann Garrett born about 1754; she died in July 1842, and was buried in Burleson-Stephenson Cemetery in Decatur, Alabama.

Arthur Stephenson and Elizabeth Rebecca Garrett Stephenson had the following children, and all were buried in the Burleson-Stephenson Cemetery:
1. Minerva Ann Stephenson was born on January 20, 1822; she married Jonathan Burleson. Minerva Ann Stephenson Burleson died on October 22, 1907.
2. Martha Frances Stephenson (11/3/1823 6/17/1899).
3. Captain James M. Stephenson (5/24/1829-3/3/1863).
4. John Wesley Stephenson (8/31/1831-8/13/1841).
5. Elizabeth Jane Stephenson (1834-1835).

On July 15, 1818, Arthur Stephenson entered 160 acres of land in Section 36 of Township 5 South and Range 5 West in Morgan County, Alabama. From December 3, 1836, through October 28, 1854, Arthur Stephenson entered an additional 520 acres in Morgan County (Cowart, 1981).

According to the 1830 Morgan County, Alabama Census, the Arthur Stephenson household had the following: White Males 0-5: 1, 5-10: 1, 30-40: 1 (Arthur Stephenson); White Females 0-5: 1, 5-10: 2, 15-20: 1; Slaves: Males 7, Females 6, Total Slaves: 13.

In the 1840 Morgan County, Alabama Census, the household of Arthur Stephenson had the following: White Males 0-5: 1, 5-10: 1, 10-15: 2, 40-50: 1 (Arthur Stephenson); White Females 0-5: 1, 10-15: 1, 15-20: 1, 30-40: 1; Slaves: Males 14, Females 11, Total Slaves: 25.

In the 1850 Morgan County, Alabama Census, Arthur Stephenson was a 58 year old male farmer born in North Carolina. He had an estate value of $12,000.00. In addition, the following was in his household in 1850: Elizabeth R. Stephenson, 48, Female, Virginia; Martha, 25, Female, Alabama; William, 23, Male, Alabama; Caroline, 21, Female, Alabama; James, 20, Male, Alabama; Wilkens, 13, Male, Alabama; Sally, 10, Female, Alabama. In the 1850 Morgan County, Alabama Slave Census, Arthur Stephenson owned 41 slaves.

On April 28, 1858, Arthur Stephenson died at 66 years of age, and he was buried in the Burleson-Stephenson Cemetery at Decatur in Morgan County, Alabama (Find A Grave Memorial Number 24081374).

In the 1860 Morgan County, Alabama Census, Elizabeth R. Stephenson was a 55 year old female farmer born in Virginia. Her real estate value was $7,000.00, and her personal estate value was $14,000.00. Also in her household was Martha Stephenson a 35 year old female born in Alabama; she was a seamstress. Her personal estate value was $12,000.00. In the 1860 Morgan County, Alabama, Slave Census, Elizabeth Stephenson owned nine slaves.

In the 1860 Morgan County, Alabama, Agricultural Census, Elizabeth R. Garrett Stephenson owned 600 acres of improved land and 450 acres of unimproved land worth $11,000.00. She also had $350.00 worth of farm equipment and $1,500.00 worth of livestock.

Elizabeth R. Garrett Stephenson, wife of Arthur Stephenson, died after 1860. She was buried in the Burleson-Stephenson Cemetery at Decatur in Morgan County, Alabama (Find A Grave Memorial Number 24081402).

According to the 1860 Morgan County, Alabama Census, William Stephenson owned 19 Black slaves. William was the son of Arthur Stephenson and Elizabeth R. Garrett Stephenson.

Burleson-Stephenson Cemetery

The Burleson-Stephenson Cemetery was established by the Stephenson Family in the early 1800s. It was known as the Burleson Cemetery during most of the 20th century. The cemetery has approximately 36 graves with the earliest graves opened in the 1830's and the latest burials were in the 1920's. The first recorded interment was 1835 and the last was in the 1920s. The cemetery is located north of the intersection of Modaus and Danville Roads on the east side of Danville Road.

Stovall, Drury

On March 28, 1752, Drury Stovall, Sr. was born in Granville County, North Carolina; he was the son of John Stovall Sr. and wife Dorcas Abigail Stovall. John and Dorcas Stovall had the following children:
1. Drury Stovall Sr.
2. Delilah Stovall Pinson
3. Bartholomew Stovall
4. Elizabeth Stovall Poole
5. William Poole Stovall
6. Thomas Hugh Stovall
7. John Stovall, Jr.
8. George Stovall
9. Anne Stovall Griffin
10. Benjamin Stovall

11. Henry Stovall
12. Josiah Stovall was the son John and another wife.

Drury Stovall Sr. was the husband of Ann Stone; she was the daughter of John and Mildred Stone of Granville County, North Carolina. Drury Stovall, Sr. and Ann Stone Stovall had the following children:
1. Peter G .Stovall was born on July 8, 1779, in Granville County, North Carolina; he died on April 6, 1857, in Morgan County, Alabama.
2. Mildred "Malinda" Stovall was born on March 28, 1782, in Granville County, North Carolina; she died in 1862 in Morgan County, Alabama.
3. Betsy Stovall was born on February 6, 1784, in Granville County, North Carolina and died young.
4. Benjamin Stovall, b. March 04, 1786, Granville County, North Carolina, d. 1838, Morgan County, Alabama.
5. Drury Stovall, Jr. was born on December 30, 1789, in Wilkes County, Georgia. Drury married Margaret Orr; he died in July 1871, in Morgan County, Alabama.
6. Ann Dorcas Stovall was born on January 2, 1792, in Wilkes County, Georgia.
7. Thomas Stovall was born on January 24, 1794; he died before 1850.
8. Ancell Stovall was born on November 24, 1799, in Wilkes County, Georgia.

On May 12, 1826, Drury Stovall, Sr. died at Flint City in Morgan County, Alabama. He was buried in the Wise Cemetery at Decatur in Morgan County, Alabama (Find A Grave Memorial Number 33284235).

Drury Stovall, Jr.

On February 21, 1809, Drury Stovall Jr. married Margaret Orr; she was born on December 26, 1791. Margaret was the daughter of Christopher Orr and Martha Watkins. Margaret died on May 19, 1841, and Drury died in July 1864.

According to the 1830 Morgan County, Alabama Census, the Drury Stovall Jr. household had the following: White Males 0-5: 1, 5-10: 2, 40-50: 1;

White Females 0-5: 1, 10-15: 2, 15-20: 1, 30-40: ; Slaves: Males 5, Females 3, Total Slaves: 8.

In the 1840 Morgan County Alabama Census, the household of Drury Stovall Jr. had the following: White Males 10-15: 1, 15-20: 2, 50-60: 1; White Females 5-10: 1, 10-15: 1, 40-50: 1; Slaves: Males 9, Females 11, Total Slaves: 20.

Major Peter G. Stovall

On July 8, 1779, Peter G. Stovall was born in Granville County, North Carolina. Peter was the son of Drury Stovall Sr. and Anne Stone Stovall.

During the War of 1812, Peter G .Stovall served in the Fourth Division of the Georgia Militia. Peter reached the military rank of Major.

On December 8, 1812, Peter G .Stovall married Lucy Wynn (1782-January 1, 1814) in Wilkes County, Georgia. Major Peter G. Stovall and Lucy Wynn had two children:
1. Marcella Stovall Wood Wise was born on September 10, 1811. The second marriage of Marcella was to Edward Wise (1809-1868); Edward owned 31 slaves in 1850 and 28 in 1860. Marcella Stovall Wood Wise died on October 22, 1878; she was buried in the Wise Cemetery at Decatur in Morgan County, Alabama.
2. Sarah Ann Stovall (1814-1900) married Aaron Wood (1809-1878).

On July 13, 1818, Peter G. Stovall entered 79.95 acres of land in the West ½ of Northwest ¼ in Section 8 of Township 6 South and Range 4 West in Morgan County, Alabama (Cowart, 1981). Peter G. Stovall entered a total of approximately 1,283 acres of land in Morgan County, Alabama.

According to the 1830 Morgan County, Alabama Census, the household of Peter Stovall had the following: White Males 15-20: 1, 20-30: 2, 50-60: 1; White Females 15-20: 1; Slaves: Males 17, Females 11, Total Slaves: 26.

In 1840 Morgan County, Alabama Census, Peter Stovall was a White male between 60 and 70 years old. He was the owner of four male slaves and one female slave. In the 1850 Morgan County, Alabama Slave Census, Peter Stovall owned 6 slaves.

On April 6, 1857, Major Peter G. Stovall died at the age of 77 years old in Morgan County, Alabama. He was buried in box tomb in the Wise Cemetery at Decatur in Morgan County, Alabama (Find A Grave Memorial Number 33284331).

Morgan County Orphans Court Records-Peter Stovall

On September 29, 1827, Peter G. Stovall was appointed guardian of two minor boys over the age of 14 years-William H. Tabor and John H. Tabor by Morgan County, Alabama, Orphans Court. Peter Stovall was the brother to the mother of the boys-Dorcas Stovall Tabor.

On January 25, 1830, Peter Stovall reported to Morgan County Orphans Court as guardian of William H. Tabor and John H. Tabor as follows: "I received of their four negroes, Buck, Easter, Daniel and Almedy, two feather beds and furniture and the sum of $811.71. The above received January 1, 1828, for the hire of Buck and Easter for two years due the first $180. Benjamin Stovall note due January 1, 1831. Thomas Stovall note due January 1 next for $134.81. Drury Stovall note due this January 19, 1830, for $75.18. James Evans note for hire of Buck due January 1, 1831, for $18.62 and $70.

Captain HEP note for the hire of Easter due January 1, 1831, for $30.11 bringing the total forward as $1,320.32 1/2. They have and interest of 1/5 part of two notes on Johnson Hendon due Dec 25, 1825, for $25 each which are sued for but doubtful as to the collection. Daniel and Lameda are hired to Henry Stovall for the board of William H. Tabor and John H. Tabor the year 1830." The above inventory sworn to before me January 25, 1830, Ch. W. PETERS.

In 1832, Peter Stovall guardian of John H. Tabor and made report of all the effects of his wards since his last report, and by said report, it appearing to the satisfaction of the court that said guardian has settled in full with his ward which more fully will appear by said wards receipt of the 20th January 20 last for the Negros belonging to him one feather bed and furniture, also the sum of $1,242.14 & 3/4th cents. It is therefore ordered by the court that the said guardian be released from any further liability as guardian aforesaid and that said report be entered of record.

April 18, 1832-Morgan County, Alabama Orphans Court, book 6, page 14, Final report for John Tabor. His note due the 25th for the hire of Easter with her two ? $200.

On December 30, 1831, William Tabor was paid $125.00 cash by order of court. His part of the fees were $4.18 and $2.50 paid by cash to the court. The payment was a correct return for the hire of slaves of John Tabor. The amount was paid out by Peter Stovall, guardian.

According to the Morgan County, Alabama Orphans Court, book 4, page 219-220, "This day came Peter Stovall Guardian of William H. Tabor and John H. Tabor and made a return of a division of the property belonging to his said wards agreeable to the report of the commissioners heretofore appointed to McKinney Holderness, Jonathon Burleson, and Benjamin Johnson purporting that the lot of negroes designed to William H. Tabor amounted to $800 and the lot to John H. Tabor $1,050. It is therefore ordered by the court that the Guardian pay William H. Tabor the sum of $125 which will make the division of his said ward, William H. Tabor equal in value to that of John H. Tabor and that said report entered of record."

Sykes, Benjamin Sr.

The Englishman Benjamin Sykes Sr. married Alice Wren in Greenville County, Virginia; they were the ancestors of the Sykes Family of North Alabama and Mississippi. Two of their sons were Benjamin Sykes Jr. and Dr. William Sykes. The families of these two Sykes men moved to North Alabama and Mississippi.

Ten members of the Sykes Family moved from Greenville County, Virginia, and settled in Morgan and Lawrence Counties of North Alabama. Before several of the Sykes moved on west to Mississippi, they settled around Decatur and Courtland. Several cousins of the Sykes family intermarried in Alabama and Mississippi.

Benjamin Sykes, Jr.

Benjamin Sykes Jr. was born in Greenville County, Virginia; he was the son of Benjamin Sykes Sr. and Alice Wren. Benjamin Sykes Jr. married Mary Rives; they had the following sons:

1. Richard Sykes had Augustus James Sykes who married Georgiana A. Sykes, the daughter of Dr. George Augustus Sykes of Aberdeen, Mississippi. According to the 1860 Lowndes County, Mississippi, Slave Schedules, Richard J. Sykes owned 95 slaves.
2. William Sykes moved from Lawrence County, Alabama, to Columbus, Mississippi.
3. James William Sykes Sr., born about 1810 in Virginia, married Martha W. Lanier, the daughter of Robert and Elizabeth Lanier, of Greenville County, Virginia. They moved from Lawrence County, Alabama, to Columbus, Mississippi. Their son, James William Sykes Jr., married his cousin, Marcella Sykes, daughter of Dr. William A. Sykes, of Aberdeen, Mississippi. According to the 1860 Lowndes County, Mississippi, Slave Schedules, James W. Sykes Sr. owned 76 slaves; James W. Sykes Jr. owned 44 slaves;
4. John Sykes never married, and he died at 26 years old. According to the 1860 Lowndes County, Mississippi, Slave Schedules, John H. Sykes owned 42 slaves.

Dr. William Sykes

In 1745, Dr. William Sykes was born in Greenville County, Virginia; he was the son of Benjamin Sykes Sr. and Alice Wren. Dr. William Sykes married Burchett Lundy Turner; they had the following children:

1. Colonel James Turner Sykes was discussed with his wife Sarah "Sallie" Winfield Dancy Sykes of the Dancy Family.
2. Joseph Sykes married Louisa W. Dancy.
3. Dr. William Augustus Sykes (ca. 1798-1873)
4. Benjamin Sykes

5. Reverend Simon Turner Sykes had a daughter Indiana who married Judge Rogers. Simon had a son, Captain Turner Sykes who married Mary Bynum, of Courtland, Alabama, and they had son, Lawson Sykes who married a daughter of Harvey Gilchrist
6. Mary Ann Sykes
7. Dr. George Augustus Sykes
8. L. B. Sykes

The sons of William Sykes and Burchett Lundy Turner Sykes were slave owners and cotton planters in Morgan County. Many of the Sykes family moved to Mississippi around 1845.

Colonel James Turner Sykes

Colonel James Turner Sykes was discussed with Sarah "Sallie" Winfield Dancy Sykes of the Francis Dancy Sr. family. The information on Colonel J. T. Sykes was located with the Dancy Family near the beginning of the family profiles in this book.

Joseph Sykes

Joseph Sykes was the son of Dr. William Sykes and Burchett Lundy Turner; Joseph was born in Virginia around 1796. Joseph Sykes married Louisa W. Dancy; she was the daughter of Captain William Dancy and Priscilla Turner.

Captain William Dancy was the son Francis Dancy Sr. and Mary Winfield Mason Dancy. Priscilla Turner was born to Simon Turner and Elizabeth Person on March 18, 1784. Her sister was Burchett Lundy Turner who married Dr. William Sykes.

Joseph Sykes and Louisa Winfield Dancy Sykes had the following children:
1. Major William Joseph Sykes (1818-1898)
2. Elizabeth Lundy Sykes(1828-1856)
3. Cornelia W. Sykes(1833–)
4. Alberta Sykes(1839–1935)
5. Mollie Eleanor Sykes(March 4, 1840–1903)

From July 15, 1818, Joseph Sykes entered some 1,206 acres of land in Sections 16, 21, 22, 23, and 24 in Township 5 South and Range 5 West in Morgan County, Alabama (Cowart, 1981). Based on land and census records, it appears that Joseph arrived in Morgan County, Alabama, around 1818 and left for Mississippi after 1840.

According to the 1830 Morgan County, Alabama Census, the Joseph Sykes household had the following: White Males 5-10: 1, 20-30: 1; White Females 0-5: 1, 5-10: 2, 10-15: 1, 20-30: 1; Slaves: Males 16, Females 21, Total Slaves: 37.

In the 1840 Morgan County, Alabama Census, the household of Joseph Sykes had the following: White Males 40-50: 1 (Joseph Sykes); White Females 0-5: 1, 5-10: 1, 10-15: 1, 15-20: 2, 30-40: 1; Slaves: Males 21, Females 24, Total Slaves: 45.

After 1840, Joseph Sykes and his family moved from Morgan County, Alabama, to Columbus in Lowndes County, Mississippi. By the 1850 Lowndes County, Mississippi Census, Joseph was living in ward three at Columbus. In 1870, he was also listed as a resident of Township 17 in Lowndes County, Mississippi.

On October 29, 1873, Joseph Sykes died in Lowndes County, Mississippi. He was buried in the Friendship Cemetery at Columbus in Lowndes County, Mississippi (Find A Grave Memorial Number 12914832).

On March 31, 1887, Louisa W. Dancy Sykes died at 71 years of age. She was buried in the Friendship Cemetery at Columbus in Lowndes County, Mississippi (Find A Grave Memorial Number 13259893).

Dr. William A. Sykes

Dr. William A. Sykes was born on January 27, 1798, in Greenville, County, Virginia; he was the son of Dr. William Sykes and Burchett L. Turner. Based on land records, William A. Sykes appears to have been in North Alabama by 1818.

In 1819, Dr. William A. Sykes (1798-1873) married Rebecca Jane Barrett (1801-1851); they had the following children:

Dr. William A. Sykes
1798-1873

1. Susan Turner Sykes was born on September 20, 1828; she married Judge John B. Sale in 1843; John became a judge in Monroe County, Mississippi. Their son, Dr. Eugene Paul Sale, was born January 15, 1845, at Courtland, Alabama; he married Mary "Mollie" Edmunds Sykes, daughter of Dr. George Augustus Sykes. On February 27, 1848, at age 19, Susan Turner Sykes Sale died at Aberdeen in Monroe County, Mississippi, and was buried at Odd Fellows Rest Cemetery (Find A Grave Memorial Number 112775249).

2. Marcella Jane Sykes was born on September 8, 1830; in 1851, she married James William Sykes Jr. (1830-1861). Marcella died on May 24, 1868; she was buried in the Friendship Cemetery at Columbus in Lowndes County, Mississippi (Find A Grave Memorial Number 12916005).
3. Josephine Sykes married Dr. Evans.
4. Captain Thomas Barrett Sykes was born in Morgan County, Alabama, on May 24, 1834; he married Maria Hortense Jones (1843-1938). Thomas moved with his family to Aberdeen, Mississippi; he was a captain in the Civil War. Thomas died on June 19, 1894, at age 60; he was buried Odd Fellows Rest Cemetery in Monroe County, Mississippi (Find A Grave Memorial Number 112778246).
5. Captain Eugene Sykes married a daughter of Judge Rogers. Eugene moved to Aberdeen, Mississippi, with his family; he was a captain in the Civil War.
6. Dr. Augustus Sykes had two sons-Dr. Richard Sykes and E. T. Sykes who lived in the City of Columbus, Mississippi.
7. Dr. Lucien Melville Sykes was born on May 4, 1838, in Morgan County, Alabama; in 1868, he married Louisa A. Walker. Louisa was the daughter of John Allen Walker (1789-1871) and Mary Boone Grimes (1815-1858). Lucien died on July 16, 1879, at 41 years old; he

Marcella Jane Sykes

Captain Thomas Barrett Sykes

was buried in the Odd Fellows Rest Cemetery (Find A Grave Memorial Number 112780193).
8. Pauline Sykes was born in 1841 in Morgan County, Alabama; in 1859, she married Jeremiah Early Cunningham (1841-1878). Pauline died on February 13, 1914, at Aberdeen, Mississippi; she was buried in the Odd Fellows Rest Cemetery in Monroe County, Mississippi (Find A Grave Memorial Number 116467055).
9. Dr. William Granville Sykes was born on August 23, 1845; in 1872, he married Eliza Brandon Clopton (1854-1886). Granville served with the Confederate State of America during the Civil War. On January 18, 1931, at 85 years old, William Granville Sykes died and was buried in the Odd Fellows Rest Cemetery (Find A Grave Memorial Number 11279714).

On July 13, 1818, William A. Sykes entered 159.12 acres of land in the Northwest ¼ in Section 22 of Township 6 South and Range 4 West in Morgan County, Alabama (Cowart, 1981). From July 13, 1818, through April 12, 1838, Dr. William A. Sykes entered some 1,360 acres of land in Range 4 West in Morgan County, Alabama (Cowart, 1981).

According to the 1840 Morgan County, Alabama Census, the house hold of William A. Sykes had the following: White Males 0-5: 1, 5-10: 2, 30-40: 1; White Females 0-5: 1, 5-10: 1, 10-15: 1, 30-40: 1; Slaves: Males 36, Females 31, Total Slaves: 67.

Between 1840 and 1850, Dr. William Augustus Sykes moved from Morgan County, Alabama, with family members to Mississippi. He and his family settled near Aberdeen in Monroe County, Mississippi, where he was enumerated in the 1850 census.

In the 1850 Monroe County, Mississippi Slave Census, William A. Sykes owned 122 slaves; a few of these were Mulattos. He was among the largest slave holders and cotton planters in Monroe County, Mississippi.

On January 12, 1873, at age 74, Dr. William A. Sykes died at Aberdeen, Mississippi; he was buried Odd Fellows Rest Cemetery in Monroe County, Mississippi (Find A Grave Memorial Number 112775732).

Benjamin Sykes

Benjamin Sykes was the son of Dr. William Sykes and Burchett Lundy Turner. On July 11, 1818, Benjamin Sykes entered some 320.76 acres of land in Sections 29 and 33 of Township 5 South and Range 4 West in Morgan County, Alabama (Cowart, 1981). On August 1, 1818, Benjamin Sykes entered 91.20½ acres of land in the East ½ of the Northwest ¼ in Section 12 of Township 4 South and Range 3 West in Limestone County, Alabama (Cowart, 1984).

According to the 1830 Limestone County, Alabama Census, Benjamin Sykes owned 23 Black slaves. From April 31, 1831, through August 16, 1845, Benjamin Sykes entered some 320 acres of land in Sections 28, 29 and 34 of Township 5 South and Range 4 West in Morgan County, Alabama (Cowart, 1981).

After 1845 based on land records of Morgan County, Benjamin Sykes moved from Alabama to Columbus, Mississippi. Some of his descendants still reside in Mississippi.

Dr. George Augustus Sykes

On July 29, 1805, Dr. George Augustus Sykes was born to Dr. William Sykes, and his wife, Burchett Lundy Turner Sykes in Greenville County, Virginia. Dr. George Augustus Sykes married Mary Edmunds Sykes; she was born May 8, 1811, in Northampton County, North Carolina.

Dr. George Augustus Sykes and Mary Edmunds Sykes had the following children:

1. Colonel Columbus Sykes was born on February 23, 1832, in Virginia. He married Emma Pauline Moore Barbour (1839-1922) on November 24, 1875, in Lowndes County, Mississippi. On January 7, 1865, at age 32, he died during the Civil War when a tree fell on the bivouac where he was sleeping. Colonel Sykes was buried in the Odd Fellows Rest Cemetery at Aberdeen in Monroe County, Mississippi (Find A Grave Memorial Number 86135601).

Colonel Columbus Sykes

2. Dr. William Edwin Sykes was born on January 28, 1835. At age 29 during the Civil War, Dr. William E. Sykes was killed on October 27, 1864, in a battle near Decatur, Alabama. He was buried in the Friendship Cemetery at Columbus in Lowndes County, Mississippi (Find A Grave Memorial Number 12915034).

3. Georgiana A. Sykes married Major Augustus James Sykes; Georgia and Augustus were the grandchildren of Benjamin and Alice Wren Sykes. Major Augustus James Sykes was born on September 1, 1824, in Virginia; he was the oldest of ten children. Augustus and Georgia had: Augustus

James Sykes Jr. (10/26/1865-10/9/1884); Columbus Sykes; Richard Sykes was born February 1867; Clifton Sykes was born about 1868; Ada Sykes was born May 18, 1869; and others. Augustus James Sykes Sr. died September 11, 1882, at age 58, at Aberdeen in Monroe County, Mississippi (Find A Grave Memorial Number 86135102).
4. Orville Summerfield Sykes was born July 21, 1845; he died May 20, 1855 (Find A Grave Memorial Number 8613521).
5. Mary "Mollie" Edmunds Sykes was born on January 3, 1849, in Alabama; in 1871, she married Dr. Eugene Paul Sale. He was the son of Susan Turner Sykes Sale and Judge John Burrus Sale. Paul was born January 15, 1845, at Courtland in Lawrence County, Alabama; he died on June 8, 1901 (Find A Grave Memorial Number 112773505). Mollie and Paul were the grandchildren of Dr. William Augustus Sykes and Rebecca Barrett Sykes. On January 23, 1940, Mollie died at age 91 at Aberdeen. She was buried in Odd Fellows Rest Cemetery in Monroe County, Mississippi (Find A Grave Memorial Number 112749786).

From June 28, 1932, through April 12, 1838, George Augustus Sykes entered some 278 acres in Morgan County, Alabama (Cowart, 1981). Prior 1850, George and his family moved with several other members of the Sykes family to Aberdeen in Monroe County, Mississippi.

According to the 1850 Monroe County, Mississippi Census, Family number 135, the George A. Sykes had the following: George A. Sykes, 45; Mary E. Sykes, 36; Columbus Sykes, 18: William E. Sykes, 15; Georgiana A. Sykes, 12; Orvel J. Sykes, 5, Mary A. Sykes, 1.

On September 5, 1861, Mary Edmunds Sykes, wife of Dr. George Augustus Sykes, died at age 50. She was buried in the Odd Fellows Rest Cemetery at Aberdeen in Monroe County, Mississippi (Find A Grave Memorial Number 86135796).

On September 13, 1874, at age 69, Dr. George Augustus Sykes died in Mississippi. He was buried in the Odd Fellows Rest Cemetery at Aberdeen in Monroe County, Mississippi (Find A Grave Memorial Number 8613574).

Sykes, L. B.

L. B. Sykes was probably born between 1800 and 1810. More than likely, L. B. was the child of Dr. William Sykes and his wife, Burchett Lundy Turner.

On April 12, 1838, L. B. Sykes entered 19 acres of land in the Southwest¼ of Section 20 in Township 6 South and Range 1 West in Morgan County, Alabama (Cowart, 1981). L. B. Sykes entered the land on the same day that Dr. William Augustus Sykes entered two tracts of land. Also on April 12, 1838, George Augustus Sykes entered land in Section 8 of Township 6 South and Range 1 West in Morgan County, Alabama, which was the same Township and Range of L. B. Sykes; Section 8 is just a mile north of Section 20; therefore, L. B. and George had land within about one mile of each other.

According to the 1840 Morgan County, Alabama Census, the household of L. B. Sykes had the following: White Males: 0-5: 2, 5-10: 1, 20-30: 1, 30-40: 1; White Females: 5-10: 1, 30-40: 2; Slaves: Males 33, Females 31, Total Slaves: 64.

Sykes, James P.

James P. Sykes is buried in Morgan County, Alabama. He is probably buried in the Sykes Cemetery in Decatur, Alabama.

According to the 1830 Morgan County, Alabama Census, the household of James P. Sykes had the following: White Males: 0-5: 1, 5-10: 1, 10-15: 1, 30-40: 1 (James P. Sykes); White Females: 0-5: , 10-15: 1, 15-20: 1, 30-40: 1; Slaves: Males 26, Females 19, Total Slaves: 45.

Terry, William Price

On Sept 25, 1809, William Price Terry was born in Roane County, Tennessee. The parents of William were Jesse Terry and Hannah Price McNair Terry; who were married on April 8, 1798. The parents of Jesse Terry were James Terry and Martha Price McNair.

On November 12, 1835, William P. Terry married Mary Louise Turner. William P. Terry and Mary Louise Turner Terry had the following children:
1. John Turner Terry: Born 1836
2. William Terry: Born 1838
3. Martha A. Terry: Born ca 1840
4. Mary A. Terry: Born: ca 1842
5. Harriet Terry: Born: 1844
6. Henry Terry: Born: 1848
7. Daughter Terry: Born: 1847
8. Winston Terry: Born 1854.

By 1840, William P. Terry and Mary Louise Turner Terry were living in Somerville, Alabama. According to the 1840 Morgan County, Alabama Census, the William P. Terry household had the following: White Males 0-5: 2, 30-40: 1; White Females 0-5: 1, 20-30: 1, 50-60: 1; Slaves: Males 12, Females 11, Total Slaves: 23.

The 1850 Somerville, Morgan County, Alabama, United States Census, House Number 445 had the following: William P. Terry, Male, White, Virginia; Nancy Turner, Female, 75, Virginia; Mary Louise Terry, Female, 32, Virginia; John T. Terry, Male, 14 Alabama; William Terry, Male, 12, Alabama; Martha A.

Terry, Female, 10, Alabama; Mary A. Terry, Female, 8, Alabama; Henry Terry, Male, Alabama.

In the 1850 Morgan County, Alabama Slave Census, Nancy Turner (mother-in-law of William P. Terry) owned 10 slaves. In 1850, William, Mary, and their family were living with Mary's mother, Nancy Turner (born 1775) near of Somerville.

On May 13, 1858 William Price Terry died in Morgan County, Alabama. His burial site is not known, but probably in the Somerville area.

Thomas, Joseph G.

Joseph G. Thomas was born about 1810 in Tennessee. The father of Joseph was Henry A. Thomas who was born about 1775 and died in Morgan County, Alabama, on July 27, 1836.

Henry and his family were in Morgan County by 1818. On July 6, 1818, Henry Thomas entered 158.89 acres of land in the Southwest¼ of Section 15 of Township 6 South and Range 1 West in Morgan County, Alabama (Cowart, 1981).

On May 3, 1828, Joseph G. Thomas married Sarah "Sally" Shaver/Shafer in Limestone County, Alabama. Based on census records, they had the following children:
1. Elizabeth was born about 1832;
2. Eliza was born about 1835;
3. Sarah was born about 1838;
4. James was born about 1840;
5. Henry was born about 1842;
6. Lucinda was born about 1844;
7. Emaline was born about 1846; and
8. Andrew was born about 1848.

According to the 1840 Morgan County, Alabama Census, the household of Joseph G. Thomas had the following: White Males 0-5: 1, 10-15: 1, 20-30: 1

(Joseph G. Thomas); White Females 0-5: 2, 5-10: 1, 10-15: 1, 20-30: 1; Slaves: Males 16, Females 21, Total Slaves: 37.

In the 1850 Somerville, Morgan County, Alabama, United States Census, House Number 426 had the following: J.G. Thomas, Male, 40, White; Sarah Thomas, Female, 38; Elizabeth Thomas, Female, 18, Alabama; Eliza Thomas, Female, 15, Alabama; Sarah Thomas, Female, 12, Alabama; James Thomas, Male, 10, Alabama; Henry Thomas, Male, 8, Alabama; Lucinda Thomas, Female, 6, Alabama; Emaline Thomas, Female, 4, Alabama; Andrew Thomas, Male, 1, Alabama.

In the 1860 Morgan County, Alabama, Agricultural Census, James Thomas, the son of Joseph G. Thomas, owned 190 acres of improved land and 680 acres of unimproved land worth $1,200.00. He also had $125.00 worth of farm equipment and $920.00 worth of livestock.

On January 17, 1890, Joseph G. Thomas died in Morgan County, Alabama. He was probably buried near Somerville in Morgan County, Alabama.

Thompson, Edward and Margaret

On April 20, 1772, Edward Thompson was born in North Carolina. Margaret Thompson, the wife of Edward, was born in 1786 in the Old Pendleton District of South Carolina.

Edward and Margaret Thompson had the following children:
1. Jane Thompson Pulliam Poteet
2. Mary Thompson Vance (1811-1882)
3. Edward Newton Thompson
4. William James Thompson (1818-1868)
5. Margaret Thompson McKleskey
6. Alice Thompson Dawson
7. Nancy E. B. Thompson
8. John A. Thompson

In 1818, Edward and Margaret Thompson settled southeast of Fennel's Turnout near present-day Trinity in Morgan County Alabama. Edward Thompson entered the following tracts of land in Morgan County, Alabama, (Cowart, 1981).

1. July 15, 1818, 160.74 acres, Southwest ¼ of Section 34, Township 5 South and Range 5 West.
2. July 16, 1818, 79.97$^{3/4}$ acres, East ½ of the Northwest ¼ of Section 2 in Township 6 South and Range 5 West.
3. May 23, 1828, 161.12 acres, North ½ of Section 22 in Township 6 South and Range 5 West.
4. September 21, 1829, 80.34 acres, East ½ of the Northeast ¼ of Section 33 in Township 5 South and Range 5 West.
5. June 20, 1831, 159.58 acres, Northwest ¼ of Section 3 in Township 6 South and Range 5 West.
6. September 8, 1831, 79.97$^{3/8}$ acres, West ½ of the Northwest¼ of Section 23 in Township 6 South and Range 5 West.
7. October 31, 1831, 80.50¼ acres, West ½ of the Southwest ¼ of Section 14 in Township 6 South and Range 5 West.
8. October 31, 1831, 80.54 acres, East½ of the Southeast¼ of Section 15 in Township 6 South and Range 5 West.
9. June 18, 1832, 40.28¼ acres, Southwest¼ of the Southwest¼ of Section 22 in Township 6 South and Range 5 West.
10. June 18, 1832, 40.02$^{13/16}$ acres, Southeast ¼ of the Southeast ¼ of Section 21 in Township 6 South and Range 5 West.
11. September 25, 1832, 79.70$^{3/8}$ acres, West½ of the Southeast¼ of Section 4 in Township 6 South and Range 5 West.
12. September 25, 1832, 80.50¼ acres, East ½ of theSouthwest¼ of Section 14 in Township 6 South and Range 5 West.
13. October 6, 1832, 39.85$^{3/4}$ acres, Northeast ¼ of the Northeast¼ of Section 4 in Township 6 South and Range 5 West.

According to the 1830 Morgan County, Alabama Census, the household of Edward Thompson had the following: White Males 0-5: 1, 10-15: 1, 15-20: 1, 20-30: 1, 30-40: 2, 50-60: 1 (Edward Thompson); White Females 0-5: 1, 5-10: 1, 10-15: 1, 15-20: 1, 40-50: 1; Slaves: Males 15, Females 15, Total Slaves: 30.

On September 1, 1834, at 62 years old, Edward Thompson died in Morgan County. He was buried in the Spring Hill Cemetery at Decatur in Morgan County, Alabama (Find A Grave Memorial Number 47255247). After the death of Edward, his wife Margaret took over the cotton plantation.

The 1840 Morgan County, Alabama Census had the following for the household of Margaret Thompson (Widow of Edward): White Males: 10-15: 1, 20-30: 1; White Females: 15-20: 2, 50-60: 1; Slaves: Males 9, Females: 12 Total Slaves: 21.

In the 1850 Morgan County, Alabama Slave Census, Margaret Thompson owned 37 slaves. She continued to increase the value of the cotton plantation after the death of her husband.

According to the 1860 North West Division, Morgan County, Alabama, United States Census, Margret Thompson was a 74 year old White female who was born in South Carolina. Her real estate value was $25,000.00, and her personal estate value was $60,000.00. In 1860, she owned 52 slaves.

According to the 1860 Morgan County, Alabama, Agricultural Census, Edward Newton Thompson, son of Edward and Margaret Thompson, owned 700 acres of improved land and 1,000 acres of unimproved land worth $15,000.00. He also had $400.00 worth of farm equipment and $2,000.00 worth of livestock.

In the 1860 Morgan County, Alabama, Agricultural Census, Margaret Thompson, wife of Edward, owned 700 acres of improved land and 800 acres of unimproved land worth $20,000.00. She also had $400.00 worth of farm equipment and $1,200.00 worth of livestock.

By the 1870 Morgan County, Alabama, United States Census, Margaret Thompson had a real estate value of only $4,800.00 with a personal estate value $500.00. The aftermath of the Civil War was devastating to economic value of cotton plantations including that of Margaret Thompson.

Margaret Thompson added to the cotton plantation estate until the early 1860s. Then after the Civil War, the values of her estate took a drastic plunge. She died in her 90's left with little after all her diligent work.

Margaret Thompson died in 1878 in Morgan County. She was buried in Spring Hill Cemetery at Decatur in Morgan County, Alabama (Find A Grave Memorial Number 67078889).

Thompson, William

By 1809, William and Henrietta Williams Thompson had moved from their cotton plantation in Elbert County, Georgia, to Huntsville in Madison County of Mississippi Territory. William Thompson had married his cousin Henrietta Williams.

From August 12, 1809, through February 2, 1818, William Thompson entered some 1,043 acres of land in Madison County of Mississippi Territory. Some of his Madison County land became the property of his sons Elbert Hartwell Thompson and Robert Asa Thompson.

According to the 1830 Morgan County, Alabama Census, the household of William Thompson had the following: White Males 20-30: 1, 60-70: 1 (William Thompson); White Females 15-20: 1, 50-60: 1; Slaves: Males 16, Females 10, Total Slaves: 26.

William Thompson and Henrietta Williams Thompson had the following children:
1. John H. Thompson was born in Elbert County, Georgia, in 1787; he died in 1843 in Mississippi.
2. William Thompson was born Elbert County, Georgia.

3. Nancy Thompson was born in Elbert County, Georgia; she married Dr. Frederick Weeden of Huntsville, Alabama; they moved to Florida.
4. Robert Asa Thompson was born in Elbert County, Georgia; he married Mary J. Williams.
5. Caroline Thompson was born in Elbert County, Georgia; she married William Rogers.
6. Elizabeth Thompson was born in Elbert County, Georgia; she married Walter Troup of Georgia.
7. Elbert Hartwell Thompson was born in Elbert County, Georgia; he married Martha Scott the daughter of Francis and Nancy Wyatt Scott from Lawrence County, Alabama. Elbert Hartwell Thompson died in Columbus, Mississippi.
8. Prudence Thompson married Reverend Williams.

Elbert Hartwell Thompson

In 1790, Elbert Hartwell Thompson was born in Elbert County, Georgia. His parents were William Thompson (1765-???) and Henrietta Williams Thompson (1768-August 3, 1827). William and Henrietta moved to Morgan County, Alabama, where they died.

On August 7, 1817, Elbert Hartwell Thompson married Martha Scott in Huntsville, Alabama. Martha Scott was born on September 9, 1794, in Charlotte County, Virginia; she was the daughter Major Francis and Nancy Wyatt Scott.

Elbert Hartwell Thompson and Martha Scott Thompson had the following children:
1. Francis Scott Thompson was born on June 29, 1818.
2. Julia Thompson
3. De Witt Thompson
4. Sarah Thompson
5. Elbert Thompson was born on June 26, 1834.
6. Dandridge Thompson.

From 1818 through 1837, Elbert Hartwell Thompson entered the following tracts of land in Morgan County, Alabama, (Cowart, 1981).

1. July 13, 1818, 159.28 acres, Southwest ¼ of Section 24, Township 6 South and Range 4 West.
2. July 13, 1818, 159.28 acres, Southeast ¼ of Section 24, Township 6 South and Range 4 West.
3. July 13, 1818, 160.48 acres, Northeast ¼ of Section 25, Township 6 South and Range 4 West
4. May 23, 1828, 161.12 acres, North ½ of Section 22 in Township 6 South and Range 5 West.
5. November 24, 1830, 79 acres, Southwest ¼ of Section 15, Township 6 South and Range 3 West.
6. April 29, 1837, 39 acres, East ½ of the Southeast ¼ of Section 20 in Township 6 South and Range 3 West.

According to the 1830 Morgan County, Alabama Census, the Elbert H. Thompson household had the following: White Males 0-5: 1, 10-15: 1, 30-40: 1; White Females 5-10: 1, 30-40: 1; Slaves: Males 16, Females 15, Total Slaves: 31.

Since Elbert H. Thompson is not listed in 1840 Morgan County, Alabama, Census, he had probably moved to Lowndes County, Mississippi, after 1837. Several slave owners from North Alabama continued their migration west and many settled out and died in Mississippi.

In 1843, Bridget Carroll Heard Thompson, wife of Elbert Hartwell Thompson, died at Columbus in Lowndes County, Mississippi. Sometimes after the 1830s, Elbert Hartwell Thompson married Bridget Carroll Heard.

According to the 1850 Lowndes County, Mississippi Slave Census, Elbert H. Thompson owned 36 slaves; he continued his cotton farming in Mississippi. The 1850 census had the following for House Number 414: Elbert H Thompson, Male, 60, White, Georgia; Saul W. Jones, Male, 50, Georgia. The property value of Elbert H. Thompson in 1850 was $5,000.00.

In the 1860 City of Columbus, Lowndes County, Mississippi, United States Census, it appears that Elbert H Thompson was living with his daughter, Julia Thompson O'Neal. The following was noted in the 1860 census: Milton O'Neal, Male, 47, North Carolina; Julia O'Neal, Female, 35, Alabama; Harry P.

O'Neal, Male, 9, Mississippi; Elbert H. Thompson, Male, 69, Georgia; Jane O. Cox, Female, 18, Missouri.

On June 1, 1869, at age 78, Elbert Hartwell Thompson died at Columbus in Lowndes County, Mississippi. His grave site was not found.

Thompson, Robert Asa

On November 30, 1801, Robert Asa Thompson was born in Elbert County, Georgia. He was the son of William Thompson (1765-???) and Henrietta Williams Thompson (1768-August 3, 1827).

On February 2, 1818, Robert Asa Thompson was the assignee of 160.32 acres of land in the Southwest¼ of Section 30 in Township 4 South and Range 1 West in Madison County, Alabama. The tract of property was originally assigned to William Thompson. On the same date, Asa Thompson entered the adjacent 160.51 acres in the Northeast¼ of Section 31 in Township 4 South and Range 1 West in Madison County, Alabama. Also, Elbert Hartwell Thompson entered the 160.32 acres adjacent to Robert in the Southeast¼ of Section 30 in Township 4 South and Range 1 West in Madison County, Alabama (Cowart, 1979). It appears that Asa and Robert Asa Thompson was the same person.

On September 27, 1836, Robert Asa Thompson married Mary J. Williams. Mary was born on August 20, 1816, born in Christian County, Kentucky.

Robert Asa Thompson and Mary J. Williams Thompson had the following children:
1. Henrietta E. P. Thompson Stephenson (1837-1856)
2. James Thompson (1839-1839)
3. Caroline Frances Thompson Roberts (1842-1888)
4. Mary J. Thompson Rountree (3/25/1843-8/23/1865) married Dr. Scott LaFavre Rountree.
5. Caledonia S. Thompson (1845-1853)
6. Georgia Anna Thompson Rountree (1847-1910) married Dr. Scott LaFavre Rountree.
7. Martha O. Thompson (1850-1905).

In 1840, Robert A. Thompson was listed on page 34, regiment 39 in the Morgan County, Alabama Census. According to the 1840 Morgan County Census, Robert A. Thompson owned 26 Black slaves.

The 1850 Morgan County, Alabama Census listed the following for the Thompson household: Robert A. Thompson, 49, Male, farmer, 10,000, Georgia; Mary J., 33, Female, Kentucky; Henrietta, 13, Female, Alabama; Caroline, 9, Female, Alabama; Josphine, 7, Female, Alabama; Caladonia, 5, Female, Alabama; Georgianna, 3, Female, Alabama; Malvina Hamerly, 22, Female, Alabama; Luvina Key, 17, Female, Alabama. According to the 1850 Morgan County, Alabama, Slave Schedule, Robert A. Thompson owned 48 slaves-30 slaves were Black and 18 were Mulatto.

According to the 1860 Somerville, Morgan County, Alabama Census, Robert A. Thompson was a 58 year old male farmer born in Georgia with a real estate value of $10,000.00 and a personal value of $60,000.00. Also in his household was Mary J., 43, Female, Housewife, Kentucky; Josephine, 17, Female, Alabama; S. Georgianna, 13, Female, Alabama; S. Martha, 10, Female, Alabama; Idella, 7, Female, Alabama.

In 1860, Robert A. Thompson owned 58 slaves. Of those slaves, 45 were Black and 13 Mulatto with 30 males and 28 females.

In the 1860 Morgan County, Alabama, Agricultural Census, Robert A. Thompson owned 550 acres of improved land and 1,600 acres of unimproved land worth $10,000.00. He also had $700.00 worth of farm equipment and $2,000.00 worth of livestock.

On December 29, 1862, Robert Asa Thompson died in Morgan County, Alabama. He was buried in the Rountree Cemetery in Morgan County, Alabama (Find A Grave Memorial# 32969434).

On January 13, 1896, Mary J. Williams Thompson died in Morgan County, Alabama. She was the wife of Robert Asa Thompson, and daughter of John Williams. The following inscription stated: "Blessed are the dead who die in the Lord." Mary was buried in the Rountree Cemetery in Morgan County, Alabama (Find A Grave Memorial Number 32969421).

On January 16, 1896, The Alabama Enquirer reported the following: "Mrs. Mary J. Thompson died January 13th, 1896, at the residence of Dr. S. L. Rountree near Hartselle, with pneumonia and dropsy.

She was born in Christian County, Kentucky, August 20, 1816. In early life she embraced religion and joined the M. E. Church South, and was devoted to the church whose doctrines and policy she always firmly believed and loved, but was not a sectarian or religious bigot.

She as united in marriage to Robert Asa Thompson on September 27th, 1836, and moved with him to Morgan County, Alabama, and settled near Priceville where she lived for fifty nine years. She belonged to a wealthy and influential family and occupied a prominent place in the social circles of the country where she lived. Her husband and his family were loved and respected by all who knew them. She had eight children, but only three of them survive her.

She brought her church letter with her from Kentucky and joined the church at Twelve Corners. From there she moved her membership to Rascom's Chapel and from there to Walnut Grove. She lived and died a consistent member of that church and from there moved her membership to the general assembly and church of the first born in Heaven. She was a true Christian; at home, in the family circle, in social life and at church. She was always consistent and correct in all her words and actions, and her daily walk was in harmony with the teachings of Christ. She was a prayerful Christian. We learn from those who knew her best that three times daily in one spot sacred to her, she knelt and made her wants and wishes known to her Heavenly Father and poured out her soul in praise and petition to Him who always hears His children's cry. She possessed an affectionate and kindly nature and a disposition as genial as the sunshine. She always had a kind word and pleasant look for all she met and this without the least guile or hypocrisy. She deeply sympathized with those who were in sorrow or suffering and none were turned away without such aid as she could afford.

As a mother she was affectionate and indulgent, but firm enough in her discipline. She had 23 grandchildren, all of whom will rise up and call her blessed. As a neighbor she was obliging and had many friends. She had a warm place in her heart for every true child of God. Her home was open to the ministers of the Gospel, especially those of her own church. For fourscore years, she lived with us here amid the sorrows and joys, the sunshine and shadows of life, but her life's work is done, her record is made and her works do follow her. When the last hours came, she was ready, and was anxious to go and after many hours of suffering, she died in peace."

Thompson, James

James Thompson of Morgan County, Alabama, was born between 1780 and 1790. According to the 1830 Morgan County, Alabama Census, the household of James Thompson had the following: White Males 10-15: 1, 40-50: 1 (James Thompson); White Females 0-5: 1, 5-10: 2, 10-15: 1, 30-40: 1; Slaves: Males 10, Females 8, Total Slaves: 18.

On February 17, 1831, James Thompson married Sarah B. Thompson in Morgan County, Alabama. In the 1840 Morgan County, Alabama Census, the following was listed for the household of James Thompson: White Males 5-10: 2, 15-20: 2, 20-30: 1, 40-50: 1, 50-60: 1 (James Thompson); White Females 0-5: 2, 10-15: 2, 15-20: 2, 40-50: 1; Slaves: Males 6, Females 11; Total Slaves: 17.

Thurmon, John

John Thurman was born between 1750 and 1760. John came to Morgan County, Alabama, from Elbert County, Georgia. John became the father-in-law of Charles McClaran when Charles married his daughter Eliza Ann Thurman.

On July 11, 1818, John Thurmon starting entering land in Morgan County, Alabama. The following were the tracts of land he entered:
1. July 11, 1818, 80.2 acres, E ½ of SE ¼, Section 32, T5S, R4W;
2. July 13, 1818, 80.24 acres, W ½ of NW ¼, Section 4, T6S, R4W;
3. October 20, 1818, 159.44 acres, NE ¼, Section 9, T6S, R4W;
4. November 30, 1818, 160.48 acres, SW ¼, Section 4, T6S, R4W;
5. December 9, 1818, 80.42½ acres, E ½ of NE ¼, Section 13, T6S, R5W;

6. July 26, 1830, 80.2 acres, W ½ of SE ¼, Section 32, T5S, R4W;
7. July 26, 1830, 160.48 acres, NE ¼, Section 4, T6S, R4W;
8. May 26, 1831, 80.2 acres, W ½ of NE ¼, Section 32, T5S, R4W.

According to the 1830 Morgan County, Alabama Census, John Thurmon had the following in his household: White Males 70-80: 1; White Females 15-20: 2, 30-40: 1, 70-80: 1. In 1830, John Thurman owned 27 male slaves and 28 female slaves.

In the 1840 Morgan County, Alabama Census, Regiment 39, John Thurman had the following: White Males 80-90: 1; White Females: 40-50: 1. In 1840, John owned seven male slaves and ten female slaves.

On November 21, 1840, John Thurman died in Morgan County, Alabama. He was buried in the Blackwell Cemetery at Decatur in Morgan County, Alabama (Find A Grave Memorial Number 57060739). The Blackwell Cemetery is located on Country Club Lane in Decatur, Alabama.

Eliza Ann Thurman

On December 12, 1832, Eliza Ann Thurman, the daughter of John Thurman, married Charles McLaren. Charles was 25 years old at the time he married Eliza. They were married in Morgan County, Alabama.

On November 3, 1812, Eliza Ann Thurman was born, in Elbert County, Georgia. In 1807, Charles McLaren, husband of Eliza, was born in Baltimore, Maryland. Around 1828 the age of 21, Charles left home to go to Birmingham, Alabama, where he went into business for himself. After inheriting a small fortune, he moved to Morgan County, Alabama, and became a slave owner. Charles engaged extensively in cotton planting for many years.

According to the 1840 Morgan County, Alabama Census, Charles McLaren had the following in his household: White Males 10-15: 1, 15-20: 1, 30-40: 1; White Females 10-15: 1, 20-30: 1. In 1840, Charles McLaren owned 48 slaves which included 21 male slaves and 27 female slaves.

In the mid-1840s, Charles and Eliza moved to their in Columbus, Mississippi. Charles became one of the largest land owners in Lowndes County, Mississippi.

In 1847, their Riverview Plantation Mansion was completed, and they moved into their beautiful home. Charles was one of the founders of what later became the First National Bank of Columbus, Mississippi, and later became its first president. He occupied a position of great prominence in the state and was frequently urged by his friends to run for governor, but he declined. While in Mississippi, he became a member of the Masonic order in Columbus and attained the Royal Arch degree.

Charles McLaran House, also known as **Riverview** and as **Burris House**, at 512 Second Street South in Columbus, MS. The house was built in 1847 for Charles McLaran, a native of Alabama who was then one of the county's largest landowners. McLaran only lived in the house until 1856, when he moved to St. Louis, Missouri

The strip of ground between the Baptist and old Methodist church on 2nd Ave North was owned by Col Charles McLaren, a Baptist and wealthy citizen of his day (1847 - 1856). He made an division of the land, giving half to the Baptists and half to the Methodists which was his wife's church. Eliza Ann Thurman McLaren.

On July 27, 1851, Eliza Thurman McLaren died at Columbus, Mississippi. She was buried in the Friendship Cemetery at Columbus in Lowndes County, Mississippi (Find A Grave Memorial Number 12915819).

Around 1853, Charles remarried to Ann Marie "Anna or Annie" Jennings. She was born on October 31, 1831, in Cumberland County, Virginia. In 1856, Charles and Anna moved to St. Louis, Missouri. He became actively in public affairs and worked with the leading citizens in bettering the municipal government. Among other things, he was made a member of the first board of police commissioners and helped to organize the metropolitan police system of St. Louis.

About 1867, Charles McClaran embarked in the wholesale hardware business with his nephew under the firm name of McLaren & Williams. The warehouse became one of the largest of its kind in St. Louis and the west. After continuing at the head of this firm for eight years, he retired from active mercantile pursuits and busied himself with the care of his estate until his death.

On December 12, 1891, Charles McLaren died at age 83-84 in St. Louis, Missouri. He was buried in the Bellefontaine Cemetery in St. Louis (Find A Grave Memorial Number 121190709). Ann Marie McLaren, second wife of Charles, died on April 11, 1919, in St. Louis, Missouri.

Troup, John

On September 8, 1808, Colonel John Troup of Morgan County, Alabama, was born. He was the son of John Troup Sr. who was born between 1760-1770.

According to the 1830 Morgan County, Alabama Census, John Troup had the following in his household: White Males 15-20: 1, 20-30: 1, 60-70: 1; White Females 10-15: 1, 20-30: 1. In 1830, John Troup owned 14 slaves which included eight male slaves and six female slaves.

On July 28, 1831, John Troup Sr. entered 156.07 acres in the southwest ¼ of Section 7, Township 6 South, and Range 2 West which he entered. On April

30, 1832, John Sr. also entered 156.59 ¾ acres in the northwest ¼ of Section 18, Township 6 South, and Range 2 West which he entered (Cowart, 1981).

From December 1835 to December 1838, John maintained a partial list of customers who bought goods from his store; the store was known as Troup's General Store. His business was located at Somerville in Morgan County, Alabama. His customers were in the area of Somerville during the time he kept the list of names. In January 1836, John and his son John Jr. are listed as making purchases at the store.

On September 26, 1837, Waller Troup entered 79.61 acres in Section 10 and 94.2 acres in Section 3 of Township 6 South and Range 3 West (Cowart, 1981). Waller Troup was probably related to John Troup.

In the 1840 Morgan County, Alabama Census, John Troup Sr. had the following living in his household: White Males 5-10: 1, 20-30: 1, 30-40: 1, 70-80: 1 (John Troup Sr.); White Females 5-10: 2, 20-30: 1, 30-40: 2. In 1840, John Sr. owned 39 slaves which included 20 male slaves and 19 female slaves.

Colonel John Troup

On August 22, 1842, Colonel John Troup was married Sarah Elizabeth Orr by D. M. Dancy in Morgan County, Alabama. On October 24, 1822, Sarah was born to Watkins Orr (1793-1849) and Cynthia Reeves Orr (1803-1863). In the 1840 Morgan County, Alabama Census, Watkins Orr owned 27 black slaves.

On June 10, 1843, Colonel John Troup and Sarah E. Orr had one child John Watkins Troup who was named after his paternal father and maternal grandfather. At nine years of age, their son died on June 16, 1852.

On February 6, 1844, Sarah Orr Troup died in Morgan County. She was buried in the Hopewell Baptist Church Cemetery at Danville in Morgan County, Alabama (Find A Grave Memorial Number 51778424).

On September 8, 1847, Colonel John Troup married Elizabeth "Lizzie" J. S. Fennell (1813-1889). John and Elizabeth Fennell Troup had two children:
1. Mary Temperance Troup (October 28, 1852-June 30, 1855)

2. John Wesley Troup (May 4, 1854-December 7, 1870).

According to the 1850 Morgan County, Alabama Slave Census, John Troup Jr. owned 37 Black slaves. John Troup Jr. was a cotton farmer as was his father; he probably inherited his slaves from his father John Troup Sr.

On May 3, 1851, Colonel John Troup entered 39.75 ½ acres in the northeast ¼ of the southeast ¼ of Section 11, Township 6 South, and Range 3 West which he entered. John owned five other parcels in Township 6 South and Range 3 West as follows: Section 23 containing 238.5 acres and Section 26 containing 39.88 acres. John entered a 39.75 parcel in Section 23 on April 6, 1853, with the other four parcels entered October 25, 1854.

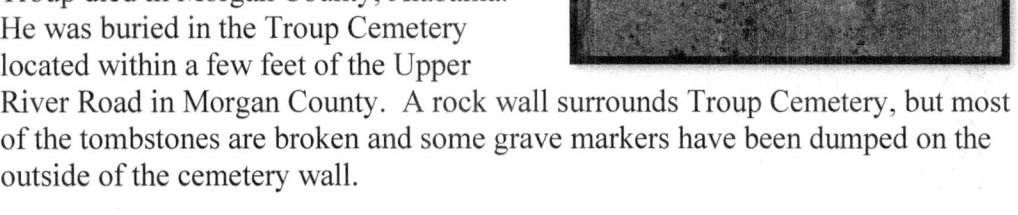

On August 4, 1855, Colonel John Troup died in Morgan County, Alabama. He was buried in the Troup Cemetery located within a few feet of the Upper River Road in Morgan County. A rock wall surrounds Troup Cemetery, but most of the tombstones are broken and some grave markers have been dumped on the outside of the cemetery wall.

Colonel John Troup has a four sided tomb stone with inscriptions which say: "In Memory of Col. John Troup, born Sep. 8, 1808, Died Aug. 4, 1855, Aged 46 ys. 10 mo. 26 d." Another inscription says: "John W. Troup and Mary T. Troup." John and Mary were the small children of Colonel John Troup (Find A Grave Memorial Number 33153201).

On August 15, 1855, the Southern Advocate posted the following: "Died on 4th in this county at the residence of Isham J. Fennell, Esq. Colonel John Troup of Morgan County aged about 47 years."

On July 1, 1889, at age 75-76, Elizabeth "Lizzie" J. S. Fennell Troup died. She was buried in the Troup Cemetery in Morgan County, Alabama (Find A Grave Memorial Number 33153326)

Wiggins, James

On October 5, 1773, James Wiggins was born in Johnston County, what was Dobbs County, North Carolina. He was the son of Gersham Wiggins and Sarah Herring Wiggins.

James married Susannah Lassiter: she was born on December 31, 1785, in North Carolina. Susannah was the daughter of Stephen Lassiter (1761-1820) and Nancy Uzzell (1767 1838).

From February 3, 1818, through July 2, 1831, James Wiggins entered approximately 950 acres of land in Madison County, Alabama. The land he entered was in Township 4, 5 South and Range 2 West in Madison County (Cowart, 1979).

From December 4, 1819, through June 28, 1831, James Wiggins entered 635.65 acres of land in Morgan County, Alabama. James Wiggins entered the following tracts of land in Morgan County as follows:
1. 156.94 acres in Section 31 of Township 7 South and Range 4 West on March 28, 1825;
2. 78.47 acres in Section 31 of Township 7 South and Range 4 West on March 28, 1825;
3. 160.28 acres in Section 6 of Township 8 South and Range 4 West on December 4, 1819;
4. 159.42 acres in Section 36 of Township 7 South and Range 5 West on June 28, 1831;
5. 80.54 acres in Section 12 of Township 8 South and Range 5 West on March 28, 1825 (Cowart, 1981).

Based on land records, James Wiggins and his family probably moved to Morgan County, Alabama, in 1819. The land he entered in Section 6 of Township 8 South and Range 4 West was adjacent to Jonathan Orr and Francis Dancy owned the rest of the land in section (Cowart, 1981).

According to the 1830 Morgan County, Alabama Census, a total of eight White males and five White females were living in James Wiggins household. James was listed as being 50-60 years old and the oldest female was 40-50 years old. No slaves were mentioned in the 1830 census.

According to the 1840 Morgan County, Alabama Census, the household of James Wiggins had one White male between 10-15, one White male between 15-20, one White male between 60-70, one White females between 10-15, two White females between 15-20, and one White female between 50-60. By the time of the 1840 census, James Wiggins owned a total of 29 Black slaves with 13 being male and 16 females.

According to the History of Morgan County, Alabama, James Wiggins settled in Cedar Plains and became a Postmaster. His home was built with square hewn cedar logs plastered inside and out. The Wiggins house was two stories and contained eight rooms and a log hall. All the rooms had fourteen foot ceilings. The kitchen was detached behind the main house, and it was fourteen feet square.

James Wiggins and Susannah Lassiter Wiggins had ten children:
1. Anna Wiggins Herring (1805-1877);
2. Lucy Jane Wiggins McDonald (1810-1886);
3. James Wiggins (1812-1854);
4. George Wiggins (1815-1856);
5. Jacob Lassiter Wiggins (1818-1868);
6. Susan Wiggins Harris (1821-1890);
7. Jesse Wiggins (1822-1878);
8. Harriett Wiggins Key (1824-1875);
9. John Robert Wiggins (1826-1904);
10. Mary Elizabeth Wiggins Aycock (1828-1856).

On June 29, 1849, James Wiggins died at his home at Cedar Plains of heart disease (Find A Grave Memorial Number 15527818). James was buried in Herring Cemetery at Hartselle in Morgan County, Alabama

On October 30, 1861, Susannah Lassiter Wiggins, wife of James Wiggins, died (Find A Grave Memorial Number 15527814). Susannah buried in Herring Cemetery at Hartselle in Morgan County, Alabama. Susannah Lassiter Wiggins had one brother Jesse Lassiter (1800-1866).

Wilson, Greenberry Sr.

Greenberry Wilson Sr. was born in 1755. During Revolutionary War which lasted from April 19, 1775, through September 3, 1783, Greenberry Wilson, Sr. served in the colonial army against the British. In 1797, Greenberry Sr. was one of the first settlers to build a house in Sequatchie Valley, Tennessee.

Greenberry Wilson Sr. married Temperance "Tempie" Bradshaw (1770-1840). Greenberry Wilson Sr. and Temperance "Tempie" Bradshaw Wilson had eight children; some of those children are listed below:
1. Sarah Wilson Oxsheer (1780-1837)
2. William Bradshaw Wilson was born on December 24, 1782, in North Carolina. On April 6, 1846, he died in Milam County, Texas, and was buried in the Wilson Cemetery (Find A Grave Memorial Number 94044089).
3. Elizabeth A. "Betsy" (1784)
4. Nancy Ann Wilson Talett/Tollett (1786-1842)
5. Greenberry Wilson Jr. (1790-1864) was born in Burke City, North Carolina.

In 1805, Greenberry Wilson Sr. was on the tax list in Roane County, Tennessee with identification number TNS1a3538835. Between 1790 when his youngest child was born and 1805, the Greenberry Wilson family left North Carolina and moved to Roane County, Tennessee.

In 1807, Greenberry Wilson Sr. received 150 acres of bounty land as part of the Hugh Dunlap grant. In 1808, Greenberry Wilson Sr. received a land grant in Bledsoe County, Tennessee. The land grant was signed by Willie Blount, then Governor of Tennessee. In 1809, he added 36 additional acres to his farm.

On August 29, 1812, Greenberry Wilson Sr. died in Bledsoe County, Tennessee. He was buried in the Wilson Cemetery in Cumberland County, Tennessee (Find A Grave Memorial Number 59508866).

After his death, his son, Charles Bradshaw Wilson, became the second owner of the farm Greenberry Wilson Sr. Today, the farm is owned by Greenberry Wilson's great great grandchildren and great great great grandchildren. The Greenberry Wilson House is listed on the National Register of Historical Places and the Greenberry Wilson Farm was honored as a Century Farm.

By 1818, two sons of Greenberry Wilson Sr. moved to Morgan County, Alabama. Based on land records, it appears that William Bradshaw Wilson and his brother Greenberry Wilson Jr. moved from Bledsoe County, Tennessee, to

Morgan County, Alabama. On July 10, 1818, William entered land in Morgan County about two months prior to Greenberry Jr. entering his first tract of land in Morgan County on September 18, 1818.

William Bradshaw Wilson

William Bradshaw Wilson was born on December 24, 1782, in North Carolina. He was the son of Greenberry Wilson Sr. (1755-1812) and Temperance "Tempie" Bradshaw Wilson (1770-1840). When he was a young boy, his family moved to Tennessee.

In Bledsoe County, Tennessee, William Bradshaw Wilson married Margaret Tollett (1793-1873) who was a native of Virginia. William Bradshaw Wilson and Margaret Tollett Wilson had the following children:
1. William Sewell Wilson (1819-1896),
2. Temperance Wilson Eichelberger (1822-1884),
3. Greenberry J. Wilson (1826-1887),
4. Clara A. Wilson McLennan (1829-1866),
5. John T. Wilson (1830-1865),
6. Thomas H. B. Wilson (1834-1858),
7. Nancy L. Wilson Ackerman (1835-1879). .

All the children of William Bradshaw Wilson and Margaret Tollett Wilson were born in Morgan County except Nancy who was born on February 5, 1835, in Lowndes County, Mississippi. They were probably on their way to Texas when Nancy L. Wilson was born.

On July 10, 1818, William B. Wilson first entered 160 acres in the northwest ¼ of Section 14 of Township 7 South and Range 3 West in Morgan County, Alabama. Again on May 31, 1831, William entered another 160 acres in the Southwest ¼ of Section 14 of Township 7 South and Range 3 West in Morgan County, Alabama (Cowart, 1981). At that time, William and his brother Greenberry Jr. owned all 640 acres in Section 14.

It was known that William B. Wilson owned slaves while he was living in Morgan County, Alabama, because it was reported that he took his slaves to Texas from Alabama. In the spring of 1833, William B. Wilson made a trip to Texas to seek out new farm lands for him and his family. He stayed three years before returning to his family in Morgan County, Alabama. In December 1839, William Bradshaw Wilson returned to Texas with his family, flocks, herds, and Black slaves. They settled near Wheelock in Robertson County, Texas.

On April 6, 1846, William B. Wilson died in Milam County, Texas. William was buried in the Wilson Cemetery (Find A Grave Memorial Number 94044089). His wife died in 1873.

Greenberry Wilson Jr

On October 22, 1790, Greenberry Wilson Jr. was born in Burke City, North Carolina. He was the son of Greenberry Wilson Sr. (1755-1812) and Temperance "Tempie" Bradshaw Wilson (1770-1840).

In 1810, Greenberry Wilson Jr. was listed on the Roane County, Tennessee Census with identification number TNS1a3538833. In 1813, Greenberry Wilson, Jr. received a land grant in Bledsoe County, Tennessee, that was signed by Governor Willie Blount. Then in 1818, he received another land grant in Bledsoe County, Tennessee, which was signed by Governor Joseph McMinn.

By 1818, Greenberry Wilson Jr. came to Morgan County, Alabama, from Roane County, Tennessee. Starting on September 18, 1818, Greenberry Wilson Jr. entered the following tracts of land in Morgan County, Alabama. He owned a total of some 1,450 acres listed by date, Township, Range, Section, and acreage (Cowart, 1981):

1. 9/18/1818, T7S, R3W, S14, 80.03 acres
2. 4/21/1819, T7S, R1W, S14, 80.01 acres, with Thomas Briscoe
3. 6/30/1831, T6S, R2W, S14, 159.64 acres, with Reuben Chapman
4. 7/4/1831, T7S, R3W, S12, 160.3 acres
5. 9/16/1831, T7S, R3W, S1, 80.00 acres
6. 9/23/1831, T7S, R3W, S14, 80.03 acres
7. 2/27/1832, T7S, R3W, S14, 80.03 acres
8. 4/12/1838, T7S, R3W, S14, 80.03 acres
9. 4/12/1838, T7S, R3W, S15, 80.13 acres
10. 10/8/1839, T7S, R3W, S15, 80.13 acres
11. 11/10/1847, T7S, R3W, S10, 39.96 acres
12. 9/16/1831, T7S, R3W, S1, 80.00 acres
13. 9/29/1851, T7S, R3W, S19 39.84 acres
14. 9/29/1851, T7S, R3W, S19 39.84 acres
15. 10/9/1852, T7S, R3W, S19 39.84 acres
16. 10/9/1852, T7S, R3W, S19 39.84 acres
17. 11/23/1852, T7S, R3W, S30 39.93 acres
18. 11/28/1854, T7S, R3W, S20 40.16 acres
19. 12/12/1854, T7S, R3W, S10 79.92 acres
20. 12/12/1854, T7S, R3W, S10 79.92 acres

Two records of marriage exists for Greenberry Wilson and Mary Bradshaw.

1. On March 9, 1820, Greenberry Wilson Jr. married Mary Bradshaw; she was born on December 30, 1803. They were married in Adair City, Kentucky.
2. According to the 1822 Alabama Marriage Records, Greenberry Wilson Jr. married Mary Bradshaw.

Greenberry Wilson Jr. and Mary Bradshaw Wilson had the following children:

1. Elizabeth Wilson was born about 1827.

2. George W. Wilson was born on April 1, 1830. He died on October 19, 1894, at age 64. George was buried in the Brindley Cemetery at Hartselle in Morgan County, Alabama (Find A Grave Memorial Number 33395076)
3. Mildred Ann "Millie" Wilson was born in 1832, and she died in 1907.
4. Isaac Wilson was born about 1833.
5. Joel B. Wilson was born about 1835.
6. Mary Sylvester Wilson was born about 1837
7. Peachy Ann Wilson Brindley was born on March 9, 1841. In 1857, she married Asa Benton (1835-1893). On October 26, 1924, Peachy died and was buried in the Brindley Cemetery at Hartselle, in Morgan County, Alabama (Find A Grave Memorial Number 33395225).
8. Sarah C. Wilson was born about 1842.
9. Tusia A.
10. John
11. Crockett
12. Bradshaw

In the 1830 Morgan County, Alabama Census, Greenbury Wilson was listed with the following: White Males 0-5: 1, 5-10: 1, 30-40: 1; White Females 0-5: 1, 5-10: 1, 20-30: 1. In the 1830 census, Greenberry was listed with 10 slaves including three male slaves and seven female slaves.

In the 1840 Morgan County, Alabama Census, Greenberry Wilson had the following in his household: White Males 5-10: 2, 10-15: 1, 15-20: 1, 40-50: 1; White Females 0-5: 1, 10-15: 1, 15-20: 1, 30-40: 1. According to the 1840 census, Greenberry Wilson Jr. owned 20 slaves with nine male slaves and eleven female slaves.

In 1842, Greenberry Wilson Jr. had a bill of sale for a slave named Alfred. Greenberry was buying and selling slaves in Morgan County, Alabama.

In 1850 Morgan County, Alabama Slave Census, Greenberry Wilson Jr. owned 24 Black slaves. At that time in 1850, he was living at Somerville in Morgan County.

According to the 1850 Morgan County, Alabama, United States Census, House Number 362, Greenberry Wilson was a 59 year old White male born in North Carolina. Also living in his household was the following: Mary Wilson, Female, 45, North Carolina; George W. Wilson, Male, 19, Alabama; Isaac Wilson, Male, 17, Alabama; Joel B. Wilson, Male, 15, Alabama; Mary Wilson, Female, 13, Alabama; Peach A. Wilson, Female, 11, Alabama; Sarah Wilson, Female, 8, Alabama; Elizabeth Wilson, Female, 23, Alabama; and James Simmons, Male, 24.

According to the 1860 Morgan County, Alabama Census, page 373, Greenberry Wilson Jr. was living in Somerville. In 1860, Greenberry Wilson Jr. owned 25 black slaves.

In the 1860 Morgan County, Alabama, Agricultural Census, Greenberry Wilson Jr. owned 300 acres of improved land and 1,700 acres of unimproved land worth $1,500.00. He also had $100.00 worth of farm equipment and $3,000.00 worth of livestock.

On August 24, 1864, Greenberry Wilson Jr. died in Morgan City, Alabama. He was buried in the Wilson-Brindley Cemetery at Hartselle in Morgan County, Alabama (Find A Grave Memorial Number 33372645). Wilson Mountain in Morgan County is named for Greenberry Wilson Jr.

On October 31, 1864, Mary Bradshaw Wilson died in Morgan City, Alabama. She was buried in the Wilson-Brindley Cemetery in Morgan City, Alabama.

Wood, Aaron

On March 8, 1831, Aaron Wood entered 40 acres of land in Section 26 of Township 5 South and Range 1 West in Morgan County, Alabama (Cowart, 1981).

According to the 1840 Morgan County, Alabama Census, Aaron Wood had the following in his household: White Males 0-4: 1, 5-10: 1, 20-30: 1; White Females 5-10: 1, 20-30: 1. In the 1840 census, Aaron owned 17 male slaves and 17 female slaves for a total of 34 slaves.

References

1830 Morgan County, Alabama, United States Census

1840 Morgan County, Alabama, United States Census

1850 Morgan County, Alabama, Agricultural Census

1850 Morgan County, Alabama, United States Census

1860 Morgan County, Alabama, Agricultural Census

1860 Morgan County, Alabama, United States Census

1870 Morgan County, Alabama, United States Census

Burleson, David A., The "Orr" Family: Early Settlers in Morgan County, Alabama and Lawrence County, Alabama, December 2020.

Cosby, Gary Jr., Uncirculated Confederate Cash found in Courthouse, Decatur Daily, Associated Press, June 23, 2009.

Cowart, Margaret Matthews, "Old Land Records of Colbert County, Alabama," 7801 Tea Garden Road Southeast, Huntsville, Alabama, 1985.

Cowart, Margaret Matthews, "Old Land Records of Franklin County, Alabama," 7801 Tea Garden Road Southeast, Huntsville, Alabama, 1986.

Cowart, Margaret Matthews, "Old Land Records of Lauderdale County, Alabama," 7801 Tea Garden Road Southeast, Huntsville, Alabama, 1996.

Cowart, Margaret Matthews, "Old Land Records of Lawrence County, Alabama," 7801 Tea Garden Road Southeast, Huntsville, Alabama, 1991.

Cowart, Margaret Matthews, Old Land Records of Limestone County, Alabama," 7801 Tea Garden Road Southeast, Huntsville, Alabama, 1984.

Cowart, Margaret Matthews, "Old Land Records of Madison County, Alabama, 7801 Tea Garden Road Southeast, Huntsville, Alabama, 1979.

Cowart, Margaret Matthews, "Old Land Records of Morgan County, Alabama," 7801 Tea Garden Road Southeast, Huntsville, Alabama, 1981.

Elliott, Carl, "Winston: An Antebellum and Civil War History of a Hill County of North Alabama," by Donald B. Dodd and Wynelle S. Dodd, Oxmoor Press, Birmingham, Alabama, 1972.

Find a Grave, www.findagrave.com

Fulenwider, Dan, "Historic Westview: A Walk Back In Time," The Cullman Tribune, Thursday, October 22, 1998, Vol. 125, No. 40.

Foreman, Grant, "Indian Removal," University of Oklahoma Press. Norman, 1932.

Gentry, Dorothy, "Life and Legends of Lawrence County, Alabama," Nottingham-SWS, Inc. Tuscaloosa, Alabama, 1962.

Royall, Anne, Letters from Alabama 1817-1822, University of Alabama Press, 1969.

Saunders, James Edmund, "Early Settlers of Alabama," Southern Historical Press, 1977, Reprint edition of 1899.

Index

Adkins, Joseph, 125
Allen, John Franklin, 133
Allen, Margaret Fennel, 133
Allison, America M., 193, 195
Anderson, Charles, 24, 153, 219
Appalachia, 5
Barnett, Elizabeth, 196, 197
Bean, Benjamin F., 148
Bean, Lydia Agnes, 235, 236, 237
Bean, Mary Ann Garner, 148
Bean, Nancy Susan E., 149
Bean, Temperance, 214
Bean, William, 24, 236
Berlin, 5
Betts, Catherine, 130
Bibb, John Dandridge, 64, 65, 66, 67, 147
Bibb, Martha Dandridge, 146, 147
Bibb, Mary Xenia Oliver, 64, 67
Bibb, William Crawford, 65, 67, 147
Bibb, William Wyatt, 64, 146
Black Fox, 4, 5, 7, 19
Blacks Ferry, 17, 33
Blackwell, Augustine S., 70, 71, 72
Blackwell, Elizabeth Tyler, 67, 73
Blackwell, Samuel, 67, 68, 69, 70, 71, 73, 74
Blackwell, William Henry, 67, 68, 70, 73, 74, 75, 102
Blackwell, William Richard, 69, 70, 71
Blount County, 22, 129, 178
Bouldin, Epharaim, 77
Bouldin, Green, 75, 76, 77, 78, 79, 81, 132
Bouldin, James Massey, 76, 79, 80

Bouldin, Richard, 79, 132
Bouldin, Richard M., 132, 133
Bouldin, Richard Moseley, 132
Bouldin, Thomas, 75, 101, 103, 104
Boyd, Rachel, 172, 173, 174
Bradshaw, Temperance "Tempie", 277, 278, 279
Brindley, Peachy Ann Wilson, 281
Brooks, Milton, 82
Brown, Catherine, 30
Brown, John, 16, 24, 30
Brown's Ferry, 3, 4, 46
Brown's Ferry Road, 3, 4
Bryant, Cornelius, 82, 83, 84
Bryant, Daniel, 82, 84
Burleson Ferry, 9, 33
Burleson Mountain, 91, 95, 97, 98
Burleson Trace, 9, 11, 12
Burleson, Aaron, 8, 85, 86, 97
Burleson, Aaron Adair, 86, 94
Burleson, Ann Roby Humphreys, 163
Burleson, Dabney Adair, 88, 94, 212
Burleson, David and Anne, 96, 97, 98
Burleson, James, 6, 7, 8, 9, 85, 86, 89
Burleson, John, 6, 7, 9, 84, 85, 86, 89, 90
Burleson, Jonathan, 20, 24, 84, 85, 86, 88, 89, 90, 91, 93, 94, 95, 96, 97, 98, 163, 240
Burleson, Joseph, 6, 7, 9, 10, 11, 12, 13, 20, 85, 89
Burleson, Minerva Ann Stephenson, 240
Burleson, Roby, 163
Burleson, Roby A., 93
Burleson's Ferry, 89, 90

Burnett, Bolling Clark, 100
Burnett, Daniel, 100
Burnett, Greenville, 24, 98, 99, 100
Burt, Delia, 180
Burt, Delia Lane, 181, 182, 183
Burt, John, 24, 52, 181, 182, 183, 203
Byler Road, 11, 12
Bynum, Mary, 248
Byrd, Elizabeth Caroline, 86
Cain Landing, 33
Campbell, Harriet A., 162, 163
Cedar Plains, 276
Celtic, 5
Cherokee, 5
Chickasaw Island, 39
Coffee, John, 4, 21, 22, 24, 27, 38, 101
Colbert, Rhoda, 24, 100, 101
Collier, Bouldin Carter, 102, 104, 105, 106, 107
Collier, Charles, 74
Collier, Charles Ephraim, 104, 105
Collier, Eliza Wyatt, 73, 75, 102
Collier, Henry Watkins, 103
Collier, James Bouldin, 69, 70, 102
Collier, James E., 101, 102, 104, 105, 106, 107
Collier, Martha W., 69, 70, 71, 105
Collier, Martha Watkins, 102, 105, 106, 107
Collier, Thomas B., 103
Collier, William Edward, 102, 106
Coosa Path, 30
Cotaco, 1, 19, 20, 21, 22, 23, 24, 27, 28, 29, 35, 48, 152, 179, 224, 239
Cotaco Ferry, 34
Cotton Gardens, 159
Cow Ford Landing, 6, 9, 11
Crabb Ferry, 32

Crabb, Thomas D., 24, 32
Creek Path, 30
Crockett, Elijah, 107, 109, 110
Crockett, John, 83, 107, 108, 109, 110, 111
Crockett, Mary Davie, 108, 110
Crockett, Robert, 109, 110
Crockett, Robert Karr, 108
Cypress Land Company, 27
Dallas, Dennis, 111, 112, 113
Dancy, Charles Fenton Mercer, 154
Dancy, Charles Francis Mason, 114
Dancy, Francis, 113, 115, 116, 117, 118, 119, 120, 121, 124, 125, 248, 275
Dancy, John Winfield Scott, 114
Dancy, Louisa T., 114
Dancy, Louisa W., 247, 248, 249
Dancy, Louisa Winfield, 248
Dancy, Martha Mason, 113, 124, 125, 127
Dancy, Sarah "Sallie" Winfield, 113, 121, 123, 124, 247, 248
Dancy, William, 24, 113, 114, 115, 116, 117, 125, 248
Dancy-Polk House, 119
Dandridge, Nathaniel West, 153, 154, 156
Dandridge, Unity Spotswood, 154, 159
Dandridge, Unity Spottswood, 153, 154
Davies, Mary Haynes, 110, 111
Davis, Absalom Leonidas, 136, 140, 141, 142, 143
Davis, Francis "Frank" Mark, 136, 139, 140
Davis, John Summerfield, 136
Davis, Riley S., 128
Decatur Land Company, 39, 40, 124, 153, 156, 184

Decatur, Stephen, 38
Delony, Edward, 143
Delony, Rebecca, 136
Delony, Sarah J., 143, 144
Dent, Mary, 103
Dent, Sarah M., 68, 70, 71
Dickey, John C., 113
Dinsmore, James, 24, 215
Ditto Ferry, 33
Ditto, James, 33
Ditto's Landing, 17
Doublehead, 2, 3, 4, 85
Dougan, Agnes, 112, 113
Draper Ferry, 34
Elk River Shoals, 6
Emory, Susannah, 13, 14, 18
Evans, Elizabeth J., 175
Evans, Joseph Morgan, 130
Evans, Nathaniel, 25, 129, 130, 131
Fearn, Maria Eliza, 160, 161
Fennel, Ann, 133, 136, 140, 141, 142, 143
Fennel, Celia, 10, 132, 136, 139, 140, 141
Fennel, Celia Bonner, 132
Fennel, Henry "Harry" W., 133
Fennel, Henry W., 143, 144, 145
Fennel, James, 10, 117, 132, 134, 135, 136, 137, 138, 139, 140, 141
Fennel, James C., 136
Fennel, Nelson, 133
Fennel, Susan, 136
Fennel, Wiley, 131, 132, 134, 135, 143
Fennel's Turnout, 134, 260
Fields Ferry, 17, 31, 33
Fields, George, 14, 15, 16
Fields, Richard, 13, 14, 16, 17, 18, 19, 25

Flint Creek, 1, 18, 20, 39, 48, 89, 92, 95
Ford, Jonathan, 149
Forest Home, 140, 141, 143
Foster, George W., 121
Fowler, Amie Perry, 221
Fowler, Griffin "Griff", 221
Fowler, John, 220, 221
Fowler, Susan E., 220
Fox, Margaret, 143
Fox, Sarah "Sally", 131, 132, 135
Fox's Creek, 1, 3, 4, 6, 10, 19, 48, 88, 134, 182, 203
Freeman, Ailsie, 211
Freeman, Eleanor, 211
Freeman, Elsey, 208, 209, 210
Freeman, Fleming, 145, 146, 147, 148
Freeman, Nancy, 147
Freeman, Zenas Frederic, 150
Garner, Celia Jane, 149
Garner, Hezekiah Franklin, 149
Garner, Kate E., 150
Garner, Lawson, 148, 149, 150, 151
Garner, Sarah F., 150
Garner, Sidney F., 150
Garner, Thomas Daniel, 149
Garner, Zerelda Jane, 149
Garrett, Elizabeth R., 240, 242
Garth, Jesse Winston, 25, 39, 121, 124, 151, 152, 153, 154, 155, 156, 157, 158, 159, 160
Garth, Mary "Mollie" Frances, 154
Garth, Sarah Dandridge, 114, 154
Garth, Susan Elizabeth, 121, 154
Garth, William Willis, 154, 159, 160, 161
Gibbs, Thomas, 50
Gibson, John, 208
Gibson, Sylvanus, 208, 211

Gilchrist, Malcolm, 23, 25
Gill, William Gardner, 174, 175
Glenn, Sarah Allen, 208, 211, 214
Grant, Ludovic, 13
Graves, Mary "Polly", 76, 77
Gregg, General John, 154, 155
Gunter's Landing, 5, 17, 20, 30, 31, 44, 45
Harrison, Ann, 190, 191
Harwood, Nancy, 234
Henry, Jemima Perry, 221
Henry, Jerry, 221
Henry, Sarah, 222
Hewlett, Augustin, 219
Hickory Hills, 27
Hodges, Margaret, 214
Holderness, McKinney, 25, 39, 124, 153, 246
Horsehoe Bend, 111
Hubbard, David, 23, 25
Humphreys, Ann Roby, 93, 163
Humphreys, Carlisle, 162, 163
Humphreys, David Campbell, 162, 163, 164, 165
Humphreys, John, 162
Hunter, Isaac, 178, 181, 184
Hunter, Pherebee, 178, 180, 183
Indian, 5, 6
Johnson Landing, 34
Johnson, Benjamin, 25, 165, 166, 246
Johnson, Robert Malone, 209
Keyes, Jane Charlotte, 227, 229
Kimbell, Edmond, 25, 166, 167, 168, 170, 203
Kimbell, Edmund, 37, 166, 167
Kimbell, James, 166, 167, 168
Kimbell, Mary C., 191
Kimbell, Mary "Polly", 203
King, Mary Curtis, 135, 136, 139, 140, 141
Kolb, David G., 172, 175, 176
Kolb, James, 171, 172, 174, 175
Kolb, Joseph, 172, 173, 175, 176
Kolb, Rachel Catherine, 172, 174, 175
Lacey Springs, 14
Lacy, John William, 176, 177
Lacy, Theophilius "Thomas", 176
Lacy, Thomas Henderson, 177
LaGrange, 114, 139, 140, 142, 206
Lane, Delilah, 178
Lane, Isaac, 25, 39, 117, 124, 125, 153, 178, 180, 182, 183, 184, 185, 186, 203
Lane, Jesse, 179
Lane, Jesse A., 133, 179, 182
Lane, Joseph, 25, 178, 179, 180, 181, 184
Langham, Jane, 148, 150
Lanier, Martha W., 247
Lassiter, Susannah, 274, 276
Lauderdale County, 3
Leman Ferry, 34
Lewis Ferry, 32
Lewis, Arthur Meriwether, 186, 187, 190
Lewis, Harding P., 188, 190
Lewis, Nicholas, 32, 186, 187, 188, 189
Lile, John A., 50, 194, 195
Lile, John Allison, 193, 195, 196
Lile, Peyton Harrison, 191, 192
Lile, Samuel, 190, 191
Lile, Thomas, 50, 191, 193, 194, 195
Lockhart, Charles, 21, 25
Locust Hill, 231, 232
Looney, John, 4, 5
Looney, William (Bill) Bauck, 5

Lundy, Sarah "Sallie" Ethelred, 121
Lundy, William M., 50
Malone, Samuel Booth, 64, 121
Manning, Virginia, 155
Mason, Elizabeth, 116
Mason, Mary Winfield, 113, 116, 121, 124, 248
McCellan, Mary Elizabeth, 178
McClanahan, Alexander, 196, 197
McClanahan, John, 196, 197, 198
McClanahan, Sarah Moore, 196, 197
McClaran, Charles, 268, 271
McClellan, Barbara Walker, 223, 226, 227
McClellan, General W.B., 226
McCroskey, John E., 173, 174
McDaniel, Elizabeth Jane, 212
McDowell, James, 176
McKee Ferry, 34
McKenzie, John, 108, 109, 111
McLaren, Charles, 269, 270, 271
McLeod, Margaret, 163
McMahan Ferry, 34
McNair, Hannah Price, 257
Meigs, Return Jonathan, 14, 18, 20
Melton, John, 3
Melton's Bluff, 3
Menefee, John, 25, 198
Menefee, Thomas, 198, 199
Military Road, 10, 11
Monroe, James, 22, 38
Morgan, Daniel, 28
Morris, Sarah A. Fennel Lane, 133
Morris, Sarah Fennel Lane, 50, 133
Moseley, Drury V., 50, 203
Moseley, Edward, 75, 199
Moseley, Elizabeth, 75, 79, 132
Moseley, John P., 202
Moseley, Martha Matilda, 75
Moseley, Thomas T., 199
Moseley, William, 50, 75, 199, 200, 201, 202, 203
Mouse Town, 3, 4, 6, 7, 8, 9, 10, 11, 88, 89
Moye, Wyatt, 119, 120
Murphey, George, 203, 204, 205, 207
Murphey, Mary Kimbell, 204, 205
Murphey, Smith, 203, 207
Murphey, William E., 204, 205, 206
Murphy, William E., 50, 205
Myrtle Grove, 69, 105, 107
Orr, Ann Nancy, 208
Orr, Christopher, 207, 209, 211, 214, 243
Orr, Daniel Jonathan, 212
Orr, Frances Elizabeth, 209, 210
Orr, Jacob, 26, 208
Orr, John, 208, 209, 210
Orr, Jonathan, 26, 208, 211, 213, 275
Orr, Jonathan Gibson, 88, 212
Orr, Margaret, 208, 243
Orr, Martha, 209, 212
Orr, Martha "Patty" Watkins, 211
Orr, Mary "Polly", 208
Orr, Philip Lewis, 212
Orr, Sallie Ann V., 88
Orr, Sarah Ann "Sallie" Glenn, 212
Orr, Sarah Elizabeth, 214, 272
Orr, Simeon Watkins, 210
Orr, Watkins, 209, 210, 211, 212, 214, 215, 272
Orr, Willis F., 214
Patterson, Andrew McDonald, 216
Patterson, Andrew McDonald "Andy", 215, 218
Patterson, Malcolm, 26, 215

Patterson, Sarah Louisa Robinson, 218
Pearsall, Edward, 229
Pearsall, Sarah Letitia, 229, 231, 232
Peck, George, 10, 26, 39, 40, 124, 132, 134, 153
Peck, John W., 50, 132
Peck's Landing, 10
Perry, Aaron, 219, 220, 221
Peyton, John Randolph, 222
Peyton, Thomas, 222
Philpot, Horatio, 26, 153, 155
Pikeville, 10, 11, 12
Polk, Thomas Gilchrist, 118, 119
Price, Charles W., 50
Pride, Edward, 183, 184
Pride, Jane, 129, 130
Pride, Mary "Polly" Hunter, 183
Purden, Richard, 23, 26
Puryear, Virginia, 134
Rather, John D., 50, 224, 226, 231, 232
Rather, John Daniel, 224, 227, 228, 229, 230, 231, 232
Rather, John T., 26, 155, 224
Rather, John Taylor, 153, 223, 224, 227, 228, 229, 231
Reed, William, 233, 234
Reeves, Cynthia, 209, 214, 215, 272
Reeves, Jane, 149
Rhodes Ferry, 32, 37, 38
Rhodes, Frances, 198
Rhodes, Henry W., 26, 32, 37, 39, 114, 117, 123, 124, 125, 126, 127, 153, 203
Rice, Mary Ann, 82, 83, 84
Rising Sun Masonic Lodge, 115, 117, 156
River Road, 4, 30, 38, 39, 134, 167, 204, 273

Riverview, 138, 270
Roberts, Susan H., 223, 224, 226
Robertson, Berry, 22, 26
Robinson, James Henry, 150
Robinson, Madison B., 150
Roby, Ann, 93, 163
Roby, William W., 210
Rogers, Rachel, 222
Rolfe, Oscar A., 50
Rountree, Georgia Anna Thompson, 265
Rountree, Mary J. Thompson, 265
Rountree, Scott LaFavre, 265
Russell, William, 13, 234, 235, 236, 237
Sale, Eugene Paul, 250, 255
Sale, Judge John B., 250
Sale, Judge John Burrus, 255
Scots Irish, 5
Scott, Martha, 263
Sharp, Thomas, 20
Shaver, Sarah "Sally", 258
Sherrod, Benjamin, 40, 41
Sims Settlement, 85, 104, 105
Skidmore, Mary A., 82
Slaughter Landing, 34
Slaughter, Francis, 70
Slaughter, James, 104
Slaughter, John, 104, 105
Slaughter, Sarah, 105
Slaughter, William, 105
Slaughter, William Alexander, 102, 105
Smith, Catherine, 238
Smith, Catherine McDonnell, 237, 239
Smith, James L., 26, 237, 238
Soldier's Wife, 5
Somerville, 20, 29, 30, 31, 32, 35, 36, 40, 93, 111, 128, 130, 148, 149, 150, 151, 173, 174, 187, 223, 224, 226,

227, 228, 230, 232, 257, 258, 259, 266, 272, 281, 282
St. Mary's Parish, 118, 119, 120
Stanback, David, 239
Stanback, Dixon, 239, 240
Stephenson, Arthur, 26, 240, 241, 242
Stephenson, Elizabeth R., 241
Stephenson, Elizabeth R. Garrett, 241
Stephenson, Josiah, 240
Stone, Ann, 243
Stovall, Drury, 26, 208, 242, 243, 244, 245
Stovall, Peter G., 244, 245
Stringfield Ferry, 34
Summerville, Robert M., 29
Swoope, Emma, 122
Swoope, John, 122
Sykes, Andrew Jackson, 160
Sykes, Andrew Jackson "Jack", 122
Sykes, Augustus, 251
Sykes, Augustus James, 247, 254, 255
Sykes, Benjamin, 26, 246, 247, 253
Sykes, Columbus, 254, 255, 256
Sykes, Eugene, 251
Sykes, Francis "Frank" Winfield, 121
Sykes, Francis Winfield, 154
Sykes, George Augustus, 247, 248, 250, 253, 254, 255, 256
Sykes, Georgiana A., 247, 254, 256
Sykes, James P., 256, 257
Sykes, James T., 26, 117, 121, 122, 123, 124, 125, 135, 154, 155
Sykes, James Turner, 121, 123, 124, 247, 248
Sykes, James William, 247
Sykes, John, 247
Sykes, Joseph, 26, 114, 247, 248, 249
Sykes, L. B., 248, 256

Sykes, Lawson, 248
Sykes, Lucien Melville, 251
Sykes, Marcella Jane, 251
Sykes, Mary "Mollie" Edmunds, 250, 255
Sykes, Pauline, 252
Sykes, Rebecca Barrett, 255
Sykes, Richard, 247, 251, 255
Sykes, Simon Turner, 248
Sykes, Susan Turner, 250, 255
Sykes, Thomas Barrett, 251
Sykes, William, 26, 114, 121, 246, 247, 248, 250, 251, 253, 256
Sykes, William A., 247, 250, 252
Sykes, William Augustus, 247, 252, 255, 256
Sykes, William Edwin, 254
Sykes, William Granville, 252
Tabor, Dorcas Stovall, 245
Tabor, John H., 245, 246
Tabor, William H., 245, 246
Terry, Jesse, 257
Terry, William Price, 257, 258
The Oaks, 102
Thomas, Henry A., 258
Thomas, Joseph G., 258, 259
Thompson, Edward, 26, 259, 260, 261
Thompson, Edward Newton, 259, 261
Thompson, Elbert Hartwell, 262, 263, 264, 265
Thompson, Henrietta Williams, 262, 263, 265
Thompson, James, 26, 259, 265, 268
Thompson, Margaret, 50, 259, 260, 261, 262
Thompson, Mary J. Williams, 265, 266
Thompson, Robert Asa, 262, 263, 265, 266, 267

Thompson, William, 26, 189, 262, 263, 265
Thurman, Eliza Ann, 268, 269, 270
Thurman, John, 26, 268, 269
Tollett, Margaret, 278
Tripoli, 5
Troup, John, 214, 271, 272, 273, 274
Troup, Sarah Orr, 272
Tucker, Sarah "Sallie" Adaline, 144
Tunstall, Elizabeth M., 167, 169
Turner, Burchett Lundy, 114, 121, 247, 248, 253, 256
Turner, Mary Louise, 257
Turner, Nancy, 257, 258
Turner, Priscilla, 113, 114, 115, 154, 248
Turney, Jane, 216, 217
Turney, Joseph, 26, 216
Tuscumbia Landing, 30, 39, 41, 42, 44
Tuscumbia Road, 37, 134, 167
Valhermoso Springs, 30, 34, 188
Vaughn, Temperance, 199, 200, 201
Wagner, Solomon, 235, 237
Wagner, Solomon William, 236, 237
Walker, Janet Jane, 102
Walker, John Allen, 251
Walker, Louisa A., 251
Walker, Rickey Butch, 5
Walker, William (Bill), 5
Wallis, James Williamson, 108, 109
Wallis, John McK. A., 23
Wallis, John McKnitt Alexander, 108, 109, 110
Wallis, Joseph, 26, 108, 109, 110
Wallis, Joseph Edmund, 109, 110
Walnut Grove, 10, 135, 139, 140, 141, 267
Warrior Mountains, 5, 6
Westview, 86, 91, 92, 93, 95, 96, 97, 98, 285
Whitaker, William, 203
Wiggins, James, 274, 275, 276
Wiggins, Sarah Lane, 212
Wiggins, Susannah Lassiter, 276
Williams, John, 266
Wilson, George W., 281, 282
Wilson, Greenberry, 20, 26, 276, 277, 278, 279, 280, 281, 282
Wilson, Margaret Tollett, 279
Wilson, Mary Bradshaw, 280, 282
Wilson, William Bradshaw, 277, 278, 279
Winston, Louis, 7
Wise, Edward, 244
Wise, Elizabeth, 208
Wise, Marcella Stovall Wood, 244
Witt, Jeremiah, 149
Wood, Aaron, 244, 283
Wren, Alice, 246, 247, 254

www.ingramcontent.com/pod-product-compliance
Lightning Source LLC
Chambersburg PA
CBHW060231240426
43671CB00016B/2904